Reclaiming YOU

ENDORSEMENTS

In its core, the Enneagram provides a path to living in presence, developing our capacity to truly show up in our lives and relationships. Yet, in my many years of teaching, I have seen how often unresolved trauma can thwart the sincere efforts of students to inhabit their lives more fully.

In *Reclaiming You*, Sharon Ball and Renée Siegel have written an engaging and clear map of both the different forms of trauma and the ways in which the nine Enneagram points can express trauma. More importantly, they offer pathways of healing for the nine types, with lucid explanations and rich and inspiring real-life examples.

This is a very important contribution to the Enneagram field as well as to the field of trauma work. Everyone is sure to find some healing in these pages.

Russ Hudson
Author of *The Enneagram: Nine Gateways to Presence*
Coauthor of *The Wisdom of the Enneagram*

Sharon Kay Ball and Renée Siegel have written a book that is both prudent and generous for those of us who intuitively know that the experience of trauma is inextricably connected to the wisdom of the Enneagram. If trauma has touched your life in any way, whether personal or professional, I wholeheartedly, and without reservation, recommend that you read this book. *Reclaiming You* is a compilation of knowledge you can trust.

Suzanne Stabile
Author of *The Journey Toward Wholeness*
Host of *The Enneagram Journey* Podcast

Sharon and Renée use real stories and experiences from trauma victims, allowing readers to connect with the different ways trauma is experienced and the tools necessary to heal.

Their detailed explanation of the Enneagram makes this book equal parts information and toolbox.

I will be going back to this book often as my own healing process continues. It is full of great reminders and exercises designed to keep the healing process moving forward while providing a better understanding of your personality's response to trauma.

Storme Warren
Country Music Radio Host of the *Storme Warren Morning Show*
on SiriusXM: The Highway

We are all built a little differently, so of course we respond in our own ways to life's challenges. The Enneagram is perhaps the most elegant model to understand these differences.

In *Reclaiming You*, you'll draw upon the authors' deep understanding of the Enneagram to create a truly fresh approach to recovery from trauma and a unique path back to resilience. This book could hardly be timelier.

Henry Emmons, MD
Author of *The Chemistry of Joy* and *The Chemistry of Calm*

This brilliant book breaks new ground. It's easy to read, it's practical, and it brings new insights into one of the most important issues of our time—healing trauma.

The authors provide insight into how each Enneagram type demonstrates both vulnerability and resilience with different forms of trauma, including family violence, addiction, sexual abuse, racism, disasters, and others. They also describe an approach to recovery using personal stories, specific practices, and examples of intervention based on the Three Ms™ of Resilience: movement, meaningful connections, and mindfulness.

This book will be hugely valuable to Enneagram practitioners and students, trauma therapists and clients, and anyone who wants to understand the impact of trauma and how we can heal it.

Peter O'Hanrahan
Enneagram Teacher Since 1981
Faculty Member of the Narrative Enneagram School

Renée Siegel and Sharon Kay Ball have written a book for trauma therapists who are not familiar with the Enneagram and their types, and Enneagram students who are not familiar with traumas and their treatments.

Using case studies, in successive chapters they introduce each Enneagram type vis a vis a particular trauma they endured. The authors then talk about this kind of trauma, how each of the Enneagram types might characteristically respond to the trauma, and they offer a tailored therapeutic intervention to manage the trauma.

This approach is a practical summary of Enneagram and trauma theory and brings the two together in a way that supplements both domains.

Jerome Wagner, PhD

Trauma care, like therapy, should never be a one size fits all approach. Each person has their own true north. The authors of this book provide another pathway to healing. Thank you for adding to the conversation!

Rebecca Bailey, PhD

Psychologist, Equestrian, Author, and Founder of
Polyvagal Equine Institute

Wow! This is a brilliant gateway to open critical conversations toward the healing of our individual and collective trauma. Seize this opportunity to explore this rich and deep work of two extraordinary practitioners!

Anne Geary

Founder and CEO of The Enneagram Approach™
Author and International Enneagram Association Accredited Professional

This groundbreaking work weaves the invaluable wisdom of the Enneagram into the field of healing trauma. Enneagram-informed™ trauma work is a gamechanger in the way individuals or trained professionals can support themselves or their clients to move beyond the devasting impact of various forms of trauma, many of which are clearly delineated in this book.

The work comes alive with stories of clients and suggestions for how each of the nine types may move from vulnerability to resilience in working with their trauma. Full of resources for both individuals and professionals, this timely and significant book will help change the course of trauma therapy for years to come.

Terry Saracino

Founding President and Core Faculty: The Narrative Enneagram

Can we understand trauma and resilience without looking at the deeper structure where environment and personality type interact? This book will convince you that personality type, seen through the rich structure of the Enneagram, is an essential ingredient in understanding, healing, and growth.

There is an impressive amount of information and practical tools, along with powerful illustrations that enlighten and inspire. I highly recommend this book for both general readers and those in the helping professions who want new insight.

Judith Sugg, PhD

The authors have found a unique and powerful way to bring the Enneagram to light when it comes to trauma. As I took in the information, the trauma response made more sense in connection to types.

This is a must read for therapists and anyone who wants to understand the Enneagram and trauma on a soul-searching level.

Gigi Veasey, LCSW, LISAC, CCBT

What a wonderful resource Renée and Sharon offer us in their book on trauma and the Enneagram.

For therapists and other mental health practitioners, they offer perspectives and practices for healing trauma, tailer-made to their client's Enneagram Type.

For coaches and spiritual guides, they offer encouragement to include mindfulness practices in their work in order to help their clients or students develop and strengthen resilience.

For Enneagram teachers and students, they suggest that our life-force energy is always working on our behalf, that we can cooperate with our life-force energy, especially through mindfulness practices related to our type.

For all of us, really, they point to an opportunity to strengthen our resilience now as a way to provide the capacity to weather the storms of stress in the future without leaving a trail of trauma.

Carole Whittaker
Spiritual Director and Enneagram Teacher

Reclaiming

YOU

Using the Enneagram to
Move from Trauma to Resilience

SHARON KAY BALL, LPC-MHSP
RENÉE SIEGEL, LISAC, ACC

NEW YORK

LONDON • NASHVILLE • MELBOURNE • VANCOUVER

Reclaiming **YOU**

Using the Enneagram to Move from Trauma to Resilience

Published in New York, New York, by Morgan James Publishing. Morgan James is a trademark of Morgan James, LLC. www.MorganJamesPublishing.com

Proudly distributed by Ingram Publisher Services.

ISBN 9781631958625 paperback
ISBN 9781631958632 ebook
Library of Congress Control Number:
2021953354

Cover Design by:
Christopher Kirk
www.GFSstudio.com

Interior Design by:
Chris Treccani
www.3dogcreative.net

Morgan James is a proud partner of Habitat for Humanity Peninsula and Greater Williamsburg. Partners in building since 2006.

Get involved today! Visit MorganJamesPublishing.com/giving-back

To those who have suffered or are suffering
and to those who try to alleviate suffering.
May courage rise from within you,
compassion flow from you,
and knowledge empower you.
For we are only human but once—
connecting us to each other
~Sharon

To the innate brilliance of our bodies, minds, and spirits
calling us to discover the resilience within
~Renée

TABLE OF CONTENTS

Foreword   xvii
Introduction   xix

Part One   **Trauma and the Enneagram**   1
Chapter 1   *Trauma: A Universal Reality*   3
                  What Is Trauma?   5
                  Is Stress the Same as Trauma?   11
                  The Role Trauma Bonding Plays   18
                  How Does Trauma Affect Your Body?   19
                  How Your Brain Communicates with Your Body   23
                  Why This Lesson on Neuroscience?   26
                  How Does Trauma Affect Your Emotions?   32
                  What Happens During a Trauma Feedback Loop?   33
                  Can Unresolved Trauma Be Dangerous?   36
                  How Do You Resolve Trauma?   36
Chapter 2   *We All Handle Trauma Differently*   38
                  Determining Your Type   39
                  Trauma Intervention and the Enneagram   41
                  What is Enneagram-Informed Trauma Resolution?   42
                  The Three Centers of Intelligence   44
                  The Three Centers and the Three-M Triad™ of Resilience   49
                  Anchoring in Safety   52
Chapter 3   *The Nine Personality Types*   54
                  Descriptions of the Nine Types   56
                  Center of Intelligence: The Body   57
                  Center of Intelligence: The Heart   61
                  Center of Intelligence: The Head   64
Chapter 4   *Resilience and Recovery: Interrupting the Trauma Response* 69
                  What Is Resilience?   70
                  Interrupting the Trauma Feedback Loop   71
                  Learning to be Resilient   72
                  The Power of Resilience   73
                  Skills Needed to be Resilient   73

Part Two	**Moving from Trauma to Resilience**	77
Chapter 5	*Thomas's Story of Classic Post-Traumatic Stress Disorder*	*79*
	Resilience in the Face of PTSD	81
	The Nine Types and PTSD	84
	A Movement Intervention	89
	Facts About PTSD	89
	Signs/Symptoms of PTSD	90
Chapter 6	*Amy's Story of Dealing with Family Violence*	*91*
	Resilience in the Face of Family Violence	93
	The Nine Types and Family Violence	94
	A Movement Intervention	99
	Facts About Family Violence	99
	Signs/Symptoms of Domestic Violence	101
Chapter 7	*Saman's Story of Dealing with a Natural Disaster*	*102*
	Resilience in the Face of a Natural Disaster	105
	The Nine Types and Natural Disasters	106
	A Movement Intervention	110
	Facts About Natural Disasters	111
	Signs/Symptoms of Victims of Natural Disasters	112
Chapter 8	*Remy's Story of Complicated Grief*	*113*
	Resilience in the Face of Complicated Grief	116
	The Nine Types and Complicated Grief	117
	A Movement Intervention	121
	Facts About Complicated Grief	122
	Signs/Symptoms of Complicated Grief	122
Chapter 9	*Clint's Story of Growing up in Poverty*	*124*
	Resilience in the Face of Poverty	125
	The Nine Types and Poverty	127
	A Movement Intervention	131
	Facts About Poverty	132
	Signs/Symptoms of Poverty	133
Chapter 10	*Georgette's Introduction to Racism*	*134*
	Resilience in the Face of Racism	136
	The Nine Types and Racism	138
	A Mindfulness Intervention	143
	Facts About Racism	143
	Signs/Symptoms of Racism	147

Chapter 11   *Carter's Story of Complications from Addictions*   *148*
               Resilience in the Face of Addiction   150
               The Nine Types and Addiction   152
               A Mindfulness Intervention   157
               Facts About Addiction   157
               Signs/Symptoms of Substance Use and Process Addictions 159
Chapter 12   *Brie's Story of Verbal, Emotional, and Spiritual Abuse*   *160*
               Resilience in the Face of Abuse   162
               The Nine Types and Verbal, Emotional, and
               Spiritual Abuse   164
               A Mindfulness Intervention   169
               Facts About Abuse   169
               Signs/Symptoms of Verbal, Emotional, and
               Spiritual Abuse   170
Chapter 13   *Avery's Story of Sexual Assault*   *171*
               Resilience in the Face of Sexual Abuse   173
               The Nine Types and Sexual Abuse   174
               An Intervention of the Integration of Movement and
               Mindfulness   179
               Facts About Sexual Abuse   179
               Signs/Symptoms of Sexual Abuse   180
Chapter 14   *Mina's Story of Historical and Intergenerational Trauma*   *181*
               Resilience in the Face of Intergenerational and
               Historical Trauma   183
               The Nine Types and Historical and Intergenerational
               Trauma   184
               Interventions for Historical and Intergenerational Trauma 189
               Facts About Historical and Intergenerational Trauma   190
               Signs/Symptoms of Historical and Intergenerational
               Trauma   192
Chapter 15   *Renée and Sharon's Stories of Experiencing a*
               Global Pandemic   *193*
               Renée's Experience   193
               Sharon's Experience   196
               The Pandemic: A Collective Trauma   201
               The Nine Types and a Pandemic   204

An Intervention of the Integration of Mindfulness and
Meaningful Connection   209
An Intervention of the Integration of Movement,
Mindfulness, and Meaningful Connections   209
Facts About the COVID-19 Pandemic   210

Part Three   **Practice Interventions**   **211**
Chapter 16   *The Groundwork for Success*   *213*
                  Coping Mechanisms and the Enneagram   215
                  Moving from Reactivity to Receptivity   216
Chapter 17   *The Practices*   *218*
                  Interventions Associated with Movement   218
                  Interventions Associated with Meaningful Connections 219
                  Interventions Associated Mindfulness   219
                  Practices to Access Your Resilience   220
                  Twenty Ways to Improve Your Vagal Tone   240
Chapter 18   Now What?   242

Postscript   *245*
Acknowledgments   *246*
About the Authors   *249*
Appendix   *251*

FOREWORD

Go to any bookstore or library, and you will find countless books on trauma and a slew of books on the Enneagram. In a deeply insightful and easily understandable manner, Sharon Ball and Renée Siegel fused these two fields to provide us with practical insights on how to approach trauma recovery in light of your Enneagram type.

As an Enneagram teacher focused on the field of business, I have been hoping for a long time that someone would write a book like this. I have known both authors for decades and have been Sharon's mentor for several years, so when she asked what I thought about her writing a book on trauma and the Enneagram, I didn't hesitate. I told her, "Absolutely! You are the perfect person to do this. Just make sure it's a great book, not just a good one."

I can think of no one better to have written what you are holding in your hands than Sharon and Renée. Not only have they themselves walked the path of recovery; they have worked with trauma clients for decades and have a deep understanding of the Enneagram.

Whether you have experienced trauma yourself, are a counselor or therapist who works with clients who have had trauma, or have a family member, friend, or colleague whose background includes trauma, this book is for you. It is impressive how Sharon and Renée fit so much important content into one book that reads as easily as it does.

Reclaiming You will increase your understanding of trauma as well as of the Enneagram. It will provide you with skills that are easy to apply and resources that are easy to understand. It will also increase your level of compassion toward yourself and those around you who have experienced traumatic events.

Through stories of real people from all nine Enneagram types, you will discover how different types move through trauma to recover their inner resilience. Despite the stories being filled with real struggles and pain, they are not hard to read. Instead, these stories are fascinating and inspiring, taking the reader into spaces we may or may not have experienced ourselves: PTSD, family violence, natural disasters, complicated grief, poverty, racism, sexual assault, historical and intergenerational trauma, and a pandemic.

While every story is told through the lens of one type, Sharon and Renée provide insights on how each of the nine types might handle the particular kind of trauma.

Are you curious about the difference between stress and trauma, and what the difference is between big-T Trauma and little-t trauma? Sharon and Renée explain it all. They also provide the reader with practices that you can try on your own or in your journey with others, whether in a personal or professional context.

As an Enneagram teacher and author, I am also a trained Gestalt therapist. I work with the Enneagram in my professional certification programs and constantly meet people who have experienced varying forms of trauma and who are at varying stages of recovery. I have seen over and over how my clients also have different degrees of accessing their inner resilience. I could have recommended this book to people hundreds of times, and without a doubt, I will do so now that it is available.

On a personal level, big-T Trauma and little-t trauma have been part of my story since I was five years old through physical violence, incest, physical abuse, family violence, neglect, and parental mental illness. My first husband, who eventually would become a prominent psychiatrist, was a wife beater and a sex addict. Plus, I was sexually harassed in the workplace in the 1980s in a case that was very public.

Through it all, I have learned and grown; I have healed and am still healing. Along the way, someone I respect but who had no knowledge of my background once told me, "You have the 'peculiar kindness' of the afflicted." I felt seen.

My hope is that this book allows you to feel seen, and that it will give you the courage to face and resolve past trauma so you can move forward and reclaim *you* by using the Enneagram to discover your resilience.

Thank you, Sharon and Renée. You are worthy guides on this path to healing and for showing us how to use the Enneagram with trauma recovery. You are the real deal, and *Reclaiming You* is daunting in such a good way. It is clear, substantive, and beautifully written. I believe it will contribute to the healing of many and will be a classic in the field of trauma healing and the Enneagram.

Ginger Lapid-Bogda, PhD
Enneagram Teacher, Business Consultant, and Author
of Eight Enneagram Books, Including the Best-selling
Bringing Out the Best in Yourself at Work and *The Art of Typing*

INTRODUCTION

"Trauma is hell on earth. Trauma resolved is a gift from the gods."
~ PETER A. LEVINE

Trauma, for many people, is an unspoken word. It is often felt in isolation or simply unrecognized, thereby preventing treatment, recovery, and healing.

Until the pandemic, some might say they have never experienced trauma. But even then, for some, the pandemic was simply a stressor. For others, it turned into a full-blown traumatic experience. For all, the pandemic moved trauma out of the shadows and into plain sight, so much so that experts predict a tsunami of behavioral health challenges.

The pandemic forced the world to acknowledge trauma and seek ways to recover from it. And the idea that trauma affects the whole self—your mind, body, heart, and soul? It no longer was in doubt.

Not only did the pandemic create *new* trauma; it impacted preexisting trauma. Even before the world was turned upside down by the events of 2020...

- nearly a billion people lived with a mental disorder. In low-income countries, more than 75 percent of those suffering from psychological symptoms did not have access to treatment;[1]
- close to three million people died every year due to substance abuse, and 75 percent of substance users reported histories of abuse and trauma;[2]
- among the female homeless population in the United States, childhood abuse was linked to having a negative impact, making women more at risk for substance abuse and intimate-partner abuse;[3]

---

1   bit.ly/MentalDisordersFacts
2   bit.ly/SubstanceAbuseAndDeath
3   bit.ly/HomelessnessImpact

- an astounding 50 percent of women reported a history of severe domestic violence in their past, with this contributing to them ending up homeless rather than be trapped in the abuse;[4]
- suicide rates have long been shocking. Globally, a person dies by suicide every forty seconds.[5] That means that since you started reading this chapter, someone somewhere in the world ended their life.

And all of that was *before* 2020 and its multitude of traumatic events. In 2020, there was the shock of having to quarantine and practice social distancing, the burden on frontline workers, the stark reality of inequities in healthcare, not to mention the high rates of death. It all surfaced in a matter of just weeks, but then it dragged on like a bad movie where you want to get up and walk out, but you cannot.

Simultaneously, racial tension in the United States came to a point where it would no longer be ignored. The deaths of Ahmaud Arbery, Breonna Taylor, and George Floyd sparked riots in cities the world over.

Meanwhile, political tension and opinions tore families and friends apart.

Next came reminders of traumas we had suffered for years prior to the pandemic, things many of us thought we had suppressed so well. Uninvited, these symptoms showed up: emotional dysregulation, irritability, insomnia, depression, post-traumatic stress symptoms, anxiety, anger, isolation, substance use disorders and other addictions, and obsessive-compulsive patterns of behavior.

It became clear that the pandemic amplified pre-existing stressors and traumas while creating new ones.

From a mental-healthcare perspective, we noticed a silver lining, though. Trauma, chronic stress, self-care, treatment, and recovery became common topics of conversation. These topics came out from the shadows and into the light.

It is not that mental health issues only show up later in life, after you have been exposed to *more* trauma. Fifty percent of mental health disorders begin by the age of fourteen,[6] and suicide is the second leading cause of death among individuals between the ages of ten and thirty-four.[7]

In light of all the above, we have chosen to not only write this book with mental-healthcare professionals in mind, but also for the public. **It was written for someone like you—someone who may be going through trauma, who**

---

4   bit.ly/DVAndHomelessness
5   bit.ly/FactsAboutSuicide
6   bit.ly/WarningSignsOfMentalIllness
7   bit.ly/SuicideInTheUSA

may be recovering from trauma, or who may be supporting someone who has been impacted by trauma.

Our goal is for it to help you grow not only in knowledge but also in empathy with yourself and those around you.

How this Book Is Organized

In Part One, we take a closer look at what trauma is, and what resilience and recovery entails. Using the lens of the Enneagram, we consider how different personality types respond differently to trauma. Even if you are familiar with the Enneagram, it may be helpful to learn how the three centers of intelligence—the main way through which you process the world around you—intersect with trauma. We also introduce you to the Three-M Triad™ as a formula we developed to move from trauma into recovery.

In Part Two, we share real-life stories of how different personality types deal with trauma, and we provide insights into how each type can find a path to recovery and resiliency. While the stories we share are real, the names and identifiable details have been changed to protect our clients. In the stories, we refer to clients coming to "us." However, we do not have a joint practice. We have collaborated on several projects, but we live and work in Arizona and Tennessee, respectively.

In Part Three, we offer multiple practice interventions we have used extensively in our practices to help clients reclaim their resilience.

Who We Are

We are Enneagram-certified, licensed counselors specializing in trauma recovery and addictions. Combined, we have over sixty years of experience in this field, stemming from a multidisciplinary study of trauma: psychology, stress physiology, neuroscience, nutrition, biology, holistic healthcare, and specialized trauma interventions.

In our practices, we found that different personality types responded uniquely to the exact same therapeutic approach. As we navigated this terrain on our own—both personally and professionally—we noticed how our Enneagram types influenced both our *vulnerability to traumatic situations* and our *ability to recover from trauma*. Implementing these insights in our practices is something we refer to as **taking an Enneagram-informed™ approach to trauma resolution.**[8]

We also discovered in our journeys that **good trauma counseling and therapy requires being trauma informed.** Being trauma informed means we notice our reactivity, that is how we navigate our personal relationships and the rapid ebb and flow of negative and positive thoughts.

Being trauma *and* Enneagram informed has helped us in our own personal journey as well as with the journeys of those we have been able to serve. As we implemented insights based upon clients' personality types—their Enneagram number—we noticed that they tended to respond better to therapeutic interventions.

We knew that our findings on using the Enneagram in trauma recovery needed to be shared with other professionals in the field of mental healthcare, but we also realized that we could equip *all* readers with the knowledge to observe, pause, and pivot from those protective coping mechanisms so you can reclaim your resilience.

Please note that some of the ways clients refer to themselves and their experiences may not be what you consider to be politically correct. Our world is constantly changing, as is our language. **We have chosen to use our clients' language as this is their narrative, and it would not be their story if we changed it.**

To that extent, we also recognize that the field of trauma is forever growing. Nowadays, embodied practices are recognized as important. We have come to a place of acknowledging means and ways of calming the nervous system as foundational to trauma healing. Doing so brings trauma victims into a state of receptivity rather than reactivity.

How to Use this Book

We have chosen several stories to unpack what trauma looks like and to share how the person in the story responded to the traumatic event. These include post-traumatic stress disorder, family violence, natural disasters, com-

---

8   In the therapy world, we often refer to the idea of taking a trauma-informed approach to therapy and recovery. When using this approach, we recognize the role trauma has played in impacting the entire person—their reactions, emotions, thoughts, and the relationships with those they love.

     Here, we are coining a new concept, taking an Enneagram-informed™ approach to counseling or therapy and recovery. We use this phrase to refer to the fact that a person's personality type could make them more vulnerable as well as more resilient to various types of trauma.

plicated grief, poverty, substance use disorder and other addictions, a global pandemic, abuse (emotional, physical, verbal, and sexual), and intergenerational, cultural, and historical trauma.

In telling these stories, we also describe how each Enneagram type might be more susceptible and can be vulnerable—and resilient—to their specific type of trauma. Finally, we offer interventions you may use based on each of the centers of intelligence.

By sharing what we have learned, it is our intention that you will be able to integrate insights from the best practices in trauma recovery based upon your Enneagram type. In doing so, **we aim to provide you with a roadmap to reclaim *you* by discovering resilience from the impact of trauma.**

———————●———————

Give yourself plenty of time to tackle the first four chapters as they are packed with essential information to better understand trauma, resilience, and the Enneagram.

As you move through the stories of trauma, allow yourself to be fully present with each victim/survivor, accessing your ability to be compassionate.

Next, try some of the practices on your own, or work closely with a trusted and experienced trauma-informed therapist as you implement the recommended practices.

Hearing about trauma can create a trigger for unresolved trauma. Therefore, please take care of yourself. Do what you need to be kind to yourself—including taking a break or stopping when you need to.

Be prepared to journal, for your recovery might one day become a roadmap for someone else.

Finally, we encourage you to proceed with a growth mindset. There is something each of us can learn from each of the stories.

Before You Read this Book

If you are a survivor of trauma, it is important to assess whether or not you are ready to dive into a book like this. Reading about trauma—even when it is someone else's—might be a trigger for you. It could also be that it would rob you of the energy you need to focus on your basic needs in life right now: safety, food, clothing, and shelter.

We offer clients Connect Five, a trauma-informed method to determine their physical, emotional, mental, and spiritual levels of risk prior to embarking on a journey of healing. **We encourage you to do the same before implementing the practices in this book.**

If you determine the trauma you are enduring is not safe, or if by reading through the Connect Five you find that you need a counselor, we encourage you to put the book down and seek help from a professional.

The foundation upon which Connect Five is anchored is safety—physical, emotional, as well as mental safety. The five elements are interdependent; you cannot have one without the other. And though it is a non-linear approach, safety is paramount.

You can use Connect Five to determine your safety level, and then you can proceed to the practices we offer in Chapter Seventeen. Read and assess yourself in each of the five areas that follow.

1. Safety

Being safe is the foundation for understanding how trauma affects your body, heart, and mind. Without physical or emotional safety, your body, heart, and mind will create coping strategies to *pretend* it is safe.

Once safety is secured, you can move to the next step. Keep in mind, though, that throughout the process of healing, it is normal to pause and check if you are still safe.

To determine your level of safety, check the boxes that apply to you.

- ☐ I am living with someone who is physically abusing or bullying me, throws things at me, or breaks things around me.
- ☐ I am living with an abuser who has access to weapons.
- ☐ Someone has threatened to kill me.
- ☐ I have thoughts of harming myself.
- ☐ I have thoughts of harming others.
- ☐ I do not have complete access to my money.
- ☐ I am isolated from my friends and family.
- ☐ I am in a temporary shelter.
- ☐ I have been evacuated out of a natural disaster area in the last sixty days.

If you checked one of these boxes, it is important that you seek professional help and involve a trusted person to develop a safety plan for you. Your and your family's safety and wellbeing are paramount. And in situations of family violence, you will need expert advice.

2. Equitable and Collaborative Power

It is paramount your therapist and supportive relationships mirror equitable and collaborative power. When mutual influence exists in your relationships, it will contrast your traumatic experience of powerlessness.

Equal and collaborative relationships understand the historical, cultural, and ethnic challenges that arise in healing from trauma. It is within such equitable relationships that you will cultivate trust.

3. Trust

Trust vanishes when trauma enters your life. The confidence you had in yourself, others, and your surroundings ceases to exist. This affects knowing and understanding who you are. Lack of confidence is usual for anyone who has encountered a traumatic experience. It may cause confusion and hypervigilance, creating restless days and nights.

Trust is a basic instinct that validates your intuition that someone or something is safe for you to be around. It is disorienting when your trust is gone, and you will doubt your intuition. It will take patience from you and others to rebuild your trust and intuition. As trauma resolves, your confidence will return.

4. Empowerment

Empowerment is vital both in the trauma-informed and Enneagram-informed models. Through your support system, remind yourself of your strengths, of how resilient you are. As you feel more empowered, your ability to believe in yourself and your strengths will take root.

5. Trauma Education

What you do not understand, you cannot begin to change. Learning never stops—including learning about trauma. Trauma education is powerful in that it gives you compassion regarding the trauma you or others have gone through. It also gives you the knowledge you need to be empowered to move forward. And it brings clarity amid the confusion caused by trauma.

———•———

As we mentioned, Connect Five is a guide to determine your physical, mental, emotional, and spiritual safety. Although securing your physical safety is number one, it may be that you begin to reclaim your resilience starting with what you learn about trauma. From there, you might seek safety and then move to securing equitable and collaborative relationships. You will learn to trust again, and finally, you will be empowered to be fully integrated as all systems within your body are communicating the way they should.

We cannot stress enough, though, that if you are *not* safe and you do not have support in this journey, please find a therapist or someone you trust to help you figure out a plan.

———•———

There are many paths in trauma resolution, and there are giants in this field who have contributed to our foundational understanding. A few mentors of mention are Deb Dana, Dr. David Daniels, Dr. Henry Emmons, Dr. Janina Fischer, Dr. Peter Levine, Dr. Gabor Mate, Dr. Stephen Porges, Dr. Karyn Purvis, Dr. Francine Shapiro, Dr. Dan Siegel, and Dr. Bessel van der Kolk.

Building on our knowledge of this foundation, we will introduce our Enneagram-informed approach to trauma resolution by integrating the study of the Enneagram with trauma recovery.

Trauma resolution has piqued the interest of medical practitioners as well mental health practitioners. As more of each make contributions to the field, we anticipate more and better options for trauma recovery and healing.

Part One

Trauma and the Enneagram

CHAPTER ONE

Trauma: A Universal Reality

Frozen, Kim stood by her office window as winds of 140 miles per hour ripped apart the world outside. The freak storm, called a derecho, had come out of nowhere.[9]

The National Weather Bureau had issued no warnings. Tornado sirens remained silent. But for close to an hour, the wind rumbled like a freight train passing overhead.

Homes were ripped apart by the winds and ravaged by trees and debris. Corn silos, like gigantic toothpicks, were snapped in half as were miles upon miles of power lines, leaving close to 100 percent of the county without power for weeks. And for weeks, no national news outlets covered the storm.

There were bigger issues to focus on, like the murders of George Floyd and Breonna Taylor that had ignited Black Lives Matter protests not only around the United States but even around the world.

And around the world, political differences were tearing families apart.

Meanwhile, shortly before the derecho, locusts were eating their way through East Africa. The people of Beirut were reeling after massive chemical

---

9   A derecho is a storm stretching more than 240 miles producing straight-line winds of at least fifty-eight miles per hour. It is named for the Spanish word meaning straight. The derecho of August 10, 2020 carved a path of close to 800 miles through nine states and hit Cedar Rapids, Iowa the hardest. The damage was comparable to that of a category four hurricane.

explosions left hundreds dead and thousands injured. Not to mention that the COVID-19 pandemic surpassed five million cases in the United States at that time, and the global death rate was closing in on a million deaths.

The pandemic was the biggest news item globally. It had been for five months by then, and it would continue to be for—well, time will tell how much longer. **Because of the pandemic, the world was facing collective trauma worse than any time in recent history.**

Like Kim staring at the world being ripped apart outside her office window, unable to do a single thing to stop the storm, we have *all* been impacted by the events of 2020 and beyond. We have *all* experienced trauma.

There is something we can do to heal from these events, though. Which is what this book is about.

———◆———

Picking up a book on trauma can be a brave step to take. It may mean you are ready to deal with issues you may have tried to ignore for a while—maybe even your entire life. Or it could mean that you are desperate to gain some skills so you can help someone close to you.

No matter your motivation for reading this book, we applaud you.

It is time for us all to work collaboratively to better address trauma. If you are doing the work of resolving the impact trauma has had on *you*, your soul will thank you. So will your body, your emotions, your mind, and your spirit. And no doubt, so will those with whom you share space at home, at work, or around the Thanksgiving table.

We would know. We are psychotherapists specializing in trauma recovery, and we have also personally walked the road from trauma to resilience.

Despite not knowing you and your life circumstances, we have seen enough in our more than sixty years of combined professional and personal experience in this field to know that **if you do the work we describe in this book, you *will* experience breakthroughs.**

You may even offer hope to someone else who is stuck in the grip of trauma, showing the world that trauma does not need to control your life.

What Is Trauma?

Trauma is what happens in your body in response to something distressing or threatening that overwhelms your nervous system.[10] You experience trauma after an acute event such as your house burning down, being involved in a car accident, or being a victim of a violent crime. But you also experience trauma as a result of a series of stressful events or experiences, like growing up in an abusive environment or in a country marked by war.

Trauma is what happens in your body in response to something distressing or threatening that overwhelms your nervous system.

To understand trauma and reclaim your resilience, it is important to look closely at the individual differences—a person's experience with the traumatic event, their existing or past experiences with childhood trauma, their access (or lack of access) to support systems, and their personality type.

Like their fingerprints, each person's response to trauma is unique, as is their healing journey. And to heal from trauma, you must recognize that trauma affects your wellbeing: psychologically, physically, neurologically, socially, spiritually, cognitively, even intergenerationally.

Though the trauma response and healing path is unique to each person, there are also similarities. It is those similarities that guide us.

Case in Point

The 2017 Las Vegas Harvest Festival Mass Shooting

At the 2017 Harvest Festival in Las Vegas, Nevada, a deranged perpetrator fired over a thousand rounds of ammunition, killing sixty people and wounding more than 400. The panic that ensued left close to a thousand people injured.

The incident is considered the deadliest mass shooting in the history of the United States. Yet amid this life-threatening situation, people responded

---

10   The nervous system is the system that controls and regulates everything within your body. It is also the communication system of the body and the center of all mental activity. We will provide an overview later in this chapter.

very differently. Some ran to the exits, some laid frozen in time, and some ran toward the danger to help others.

People also processed the tragic event in a variety of ways. Some felt instant anger while others had delayed emotional responses. Some exhibited a fear of public places. The emotions following the events ranged from shame to confusion, numbness to agitation, shock to isolation.

Personality type, history, and individual vulnerability is significant in response to an event like this. The hotel doormen, concertgoers, artists, taxi drivers—even the children in the community who heard about the event—everyone involved experienced *some* level of trauma from that event. While everyone's experience was unique, there were also many similarities.

From working with the victims of the shooting, we know that…

- Recognizing and acknowledging your trauma is the beginning of the healing journey. It validates you are normal—it is the traumatic event that is abnormal.
- Trauma-informed education[11] is key to victims fully understanding the impact of trauma. It helps you to understand how the nervous system response traps the body in a trauma feedback loop, creating a body memory that causes you to relive the event.
- Once you begin your journey of healing, self-judgment moves toward self-compassion and understanding.
- Finding safety and support with others helps to rewire and repattern responses through co-regulation.

Regulation *happens when you bring your body to a state of balance, calming your body, emotions, and thoughts.*

Co-regulation *is the state you experience when you are in a nurturing and supportive relationship with a caregiver figure or parent. You return to a state of balance by soothing and managing difficult emotions and situations through the interaction in this relationship.*

---

11   As pointed out in the introduction, in the counseling and therapy world, we often refer to taking a trauma-informed approach to therapy and recovery. Likewise, trauma-informed education takes into consideration the role trauma has played in impacting the entire person—their reactions, emotions, thoughts, and the relationships with those they love.

In this book, we introduce the idea of taking an Enneagram-informed™ approach to therapy and recovery. We use this phrase to refer to the fact that a person's personality type could make them more vulnerable as well as more resilient to various types of trauma.

Unpacking trauma is about much more than just the four bullet points above. Just like how what people pack for a trip differs from one person to another, the same is true for how we all differ in what we pack into our "trauma suitcase."

There are similarities, differences, and intriguing nuances related to trauma, and opening your trauma suitcase will be one of the bravest actions you will ever take. Doing so will help you to better define your trauma and the effects it has had on you.

Doing the work of unpacking your trauma will help you reclaim your resilience by helping you choose your response to trauma. It will also help you identify triggers[12] that cause the trauma to resurface.

Unpacking your trauma also helps you discover what boundaries you need to put in place so you can find safety, certainty, and security. Finally, it helps you explain to those around you how they can best support you.

Although this may seem complicated, once you recognize and acknowledge trauma, your path to healing will be clearer. It is also far more hopeful than the constant confusion and disorientation of living with unresolved trauma.

It is entirely possible to ignore the impact of a traumatic event. In fact, many people do just that. They refuse to acknowledge the trauma of, say, news that a loved one has advanced-stage cancer and only has a short time to live. They carry on as if nothing happened. However, the impact is bound to be felt, sometimes years down the road when they find themselves overreacting at a checkout clerk in a supermarket, not realizing hearing a ringtone within earshot triggered the memories of the day they got the news.

Once you are ready to do the work of unpacking your trauma, it will simultaneously be the most difficult and the most courageous step you can take. And doing so will set you on a path to resilience reminding you of hope, healing, and the strength that lies within.

———●———

Trauma can feel like an ocean wave coming out of nowhere, smacking you down, filling your lungs with water while pushing you further and further from

---

12   A trigger is an evocative cue, something felt, including sounds and smells. In the section on trauma feedback loops later in this chapter, we will say more about triggers.

the shore as you frantically tread water while watching the land—your safety, community, normality, and peace—disappear.

If you are good at treading water or swimming, you might make your way back to land and focus your attention on how you survived. Or you might pretend the wave never hit you and never to talk about what happened and why it happened.

But unaddressed trauma does not like to be silenced. It will eventually show up—which is what happened during the pandemic. The myriad of traumatic events of 2020 and beyond appeared unexpectedly, adding new trauma to our lives. These events also amplified trauma from the past.

**The pandemic added new trauma to our lives. It
also amplified trauma from the past.**

The pandemic and everything that came along with it squeezed us all in ways that caused everything we had oh-so-carefully packed away to surface. The pandemic also brought attention to the complex nature of trauma and how people respond differently, whether verbally, emotionally, mentally, or behaviorally.

More than any other time, people turned to counselors to process what they were going through, which is one good outcome of the pandemic. Processing trauma sets you on a path to resolving the impact that the traumatic experiences have had on you. But talking is not the only way to process trauma. There are lots of strategies you can employ to deal with trauma.

Our experience has taught us that using an embodied approach to trauma recovery along with insights from the Enneagram is highly effective. Depending on your personality type, the strategies will differ. We will focus on those differences throughout this book.

We will also explain why it is important to approach trauma recovery in a holistic manner. (Hint: You cannot just cry it out, talk it out, or journal until it goes away.) Traumatic memories can get trapped in the body. We will offer you ways in which you can address your body, heart, and mind to release the hold those memories have.

**Embodied trauma resolution refers to working
with the body to integrate experiences from your
five senses to find safety and reason.**

Because traumatic memories are trapped in the body, events in the present can trigger those memories, making it seem as if they are happening *now*. In that way, if you had been at the Harvest Festival in 2017, hearing fireworks, for example, can still cause your heart to race years later. By using holistic trauma-healing strategies, though, you can carefully resolve the memories of the shooting event, so those memories simply describe the experience you went through in Las Vegas rather than causing you to relive the events as if they were happening in the present.

Once your body, heart, and mind work in alignment with one another, you will be able to integrate the aspects that keep you from being present when you are confronted with and relive memories from the past. The same can be true for resolving any trauma from the past.

> **Trauma integration** *occurs when you can acknowledge that you have the necessary strength within you to overcome the trauma so all the systems of your body—physical, emotional, and cognitive—function as they should.*
>
> *When trauma reoccurs, you know within your body, emotions, and your mind that you need not fight, flee, freeze, or fawn. Instead, you have the resilience to move through the traumatic event.*

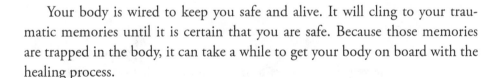

Your body is wired to keep you safe and alive. It will cling to your traumatic memories until it is certain that you are safe. Because those memories are trapped in the body, it can take a while to get your body on board with the healing process.

Case in Point

Brandon's Memories of Life in the Chicago Gangs

Some of our client Brandon's earliest memories are of when he was just three years old, living in Chicago. He remembers hearing screams for help at all hours of the night. Like many of his friends, by the time Brandon was a teenager, he joined a gang.[13] This satiated his need for money and gave him a sense of family, neither of which he had.

Brandon quickly learned he had to fight to survive. He also learned that he not only needed protection but also money. Brandon dealt drugs to meet his basic needs. He was never the typical addict himself; however, he moved into process addictions such as excess spending and gambling. He was also codependent and a thrill seeker—all to try and mask his trauma.

What led Brandon to find "family" in a gang was the insidious trauma of growing up being neglected and subjected to emotional abuse. He survived his teenage years on the streets of Chicago hearing bullets whiz past his house. He was even shot at.

Brandon eventually left the gang, but he still lived in a constant state of vigilance. It was not until years later, in his early thirties, that he realized his reactions to everyday situations were different from the responses of people around him.

The sound of sirens or gunshots would cause his body to tense up and move into fight mode. If this occurred while Brandon was at home, he would turn off the lights and draw the shades. Whether he was at home or out and about, the trigger sounds would cause his body to be so tense, his heart would race, he would clench his fists, and he would be easily startled.

Although Brandon knew he was physically safe, his body was not convinced. Every day, it was poised and ready for self-protection and resourcing any need he might have. As a result, Brandon was restless and found it difficult to fall asleep at night.

To help his body move to a place of certainty, Brandon had to process the painful events he had seen, heard, and been a part of as a young man. Today, he continues to have startle reflexes to noises; however, his reactivity to these triggers looks different.

When Brandon goes to a restaurant, to this day, he positions himself with his back against the furthest wall so he can see all the windows and exits. But he has learned to breathe with his body, talk to his body, and grant kindness to those places of hurt.

13　Chicago has a deep history of violence going back to the 1970s. It is home to the largest and most active street gangs in the United States, with around sixty gangs and 100,000 active members—most being between thirteen and nineteen years old.

———•———

The trauma response such as what Brandon was experiencing is called a **trauma feedback loop** or a **trauma loop**, in short. We will address this phenomenon more later in this chapter. For now, suffice it to say that these unresolved traumatic memories are stored improperly in your body, whether in your neck, arms, feet, stomach, head, fingers, or heart.

> The terms **trauma feedback loop** and **trauma loop** are used interchangeably. While it is easier to simply talk about a trauma loop, it is important to remember that the loop—reliving the trauma—happens as a result of the trauma providing your body with feedback messages based on a previous traumatic experience or experiences.

When triggered, the memories stored in your body activate the nervous system as if you were experiencing the trauma in real time rather than as a memory. This inhibits your ability to stay in the present moment and be grounded in your body. Instead, your body is constantly on guard, waiting for the next traumatic event.

Instead of using your energy simply to live life, the energy is used to manage the unresolved trauma memories.

That is exhausting.

Is Stress the Same as Trauma?

The short answer? No. Stress occurs daily when the balance of life is disturbed. These stressful events rarely are traumatic, though. They are not even necessarily harmful. Some stress can even be motivating and can be healthy.

When your alarm clock goes off, for example, it can cause a stress response in your body. It may startle you, and for a moment you may even feel disoriented, even frustrated. Depending on how deep of a sleep rhythm you were in, your heart may even race. But moments later, your heart rate is back to its regular pace. You know where you are, and you can get on with your day.

Whether stressful events are brief or continuous, you can move on and return to a healthy balance of life. These events do not affect your day-to-day functioning.

When stress becomes chronic, though—such as what happened when the pandemic dragged on much longer than anticipated—your body, heart, and mind might engage your nervous system's trauma response.

While you may have had no problem sleeping in the past, it may be that you now toss and turn every night, unable to get good rest. This trauma response is not momentary. It *does* affect your day-to-day functioning.

While not all stressful events are traumatic—they do not elicit a full-blown trauma response—all traumatic events are stressful in that they disturb the balance of life.

> *Stressful events do not affect your day-to-day functioning. Trauma does affect your day-do-day functioning. Not all stressful events are traumatic, but all traumatic events are stressful.*

You may try to manage trauma the way you manage stress, by simply carrying on with your day. But then you notice unusual emotions such as anger toward a colleague for no apparent reason. If you paid close attention, you might notice that his cologne—the same type that someone who had harmed you in the past used to wear—is what is causing you to want to explode. But instead, you brush it off, hitting snooze on the emotions and the tension in your body that show up time and again.

Ignoring such a response is not helpful because unlike stress, silencing trauma is almost always harmful.

Not all trauma is the same, though. Trauma comes in all different shapes and sizes. It is wrapped up in a variety of unpleasant experiences and interactions. In the world of psychotherapy, we distinguish between "little-t trauma" and "big-T Trauma."[14]

Little-t Trauma

A little-t trauma may create continuing significant stress; however, it does not threaten your physical safety or life. Little-t traumas disrupt your typical day-to-day functioning and can disorient your life course.

---

14 In the rest of the book, *trauma* will mostly be used without capitalization. It does not mean that we are referring to a little-t trauma, though. In this book, we focus predominantly on big-T Trauma.

Some examples of little-t traumas include job loss, infidelity, financial instability, divorce, career change, marriage, and legal battles. Sometimes, little-t traumas go unrecognized until symptoms of the trauma response begin to surface—emotional swings, appetite changes, an inability to concentrate, memory fog, agitation, or sadness. With support and personal resourcefulness, however, finding your resilience from little-t traumas is not out of reach.

Should the little-t trauma be chronic or happen concurrently with multiple other little-t traumas and/or stressful events (job loss along with financial instability and legal battles, for example), it can turn into a significant big-T Trauma.

Big-T Trauma

Remember the different responses victims of the Harvest Festival shooting exhibited? Each victim's nervous system either moved into fight, flight, freeze, or fawn mode, causing a chain reaction in their psychological, neurological, and physical states. That is what happens when you experience big-T Trauma.[15]

As we have explained before, your body is constantly looking for ways to keep you physically safe. But when something is too much for your nervous system to process and integrate, it reacts by triggering a fight, flight, freeze, or fawn response. Your body, heart, and mind experience a hodgepodge of sensations, emotions, and thoughts. And until you can find safety and resolution, your body holds tightly to the experience of your safety being threatened.

There are four main types of big-T Traumas: acute, chronic, insidious, and complex.[16] Each of these traumas create their own aftermath that need to be considered in recovery.

Acute Trauma

This is a one-time event such as being in a car accident, experiencing sudden loss, being a victim of sexual assault, or witnessing a crime or a natural disaster.

---

15 The fight, flight (flee), or freeze responses are the best-known responses to trauma. However, fawning is another response, causing you to give in to appease someone rather than causing conflict.
   See bit.ly/FightFlightFreezeAndFawn

16 Normally, only acute, chronic, and complex traumas are listed as big-T Traumas. From our experience, insidious trauma should also be included in this list.

The Harvest Festival shooting was considered an acute trauma; however, many who were recovering from their wounds and those who underwent surgery and therapy experienced chronic trauma as well.

Similarly, witnessing the August 2020 derecho was an acute event for some in and around Cedar Rapids, Iowa, but for those in the community who spent a year or longer trying to get their properties repaired, it became a case of chronic trauma. Other survivors of the derecho and similar natural disasters may find the internal and external resources to meet their needs and return to a state of balance. They might even move through the event so their experience becomes one of stress, not trauma. At the same time, other folks in the same community may *seem* to be coping, yet they are not.

Those who experience an event—whether a mass shooting or a natural disaster—as *traumatic* may be unable to function well for months or years to come. They may even fail to function altogether. Until the trauma has been resolved, the impact will continue to affect them. And the event will be compounded by other traumatic events, whether from before or after the acute event.

Chronic Trauma

This is trauma that is repeated and drawn out. It includes traumatic events such as neglect, family or intimate-partner violence, human trafficking, or a battle with cancer. It may also include single, acute traumas happening one right after the other.

Because the body is exposed to prolonged stressors and challenges, chronic trauma can compromise the physical and psychological wellbeing of the victim more so than acute trauma does.

Although trained and prepared for war, many soldiers experience chronic trauma. The same is true for refugees who have grown up in war-torn countries. These individuals are most at risk for developing chronic post-traumatic stress disorder (PTSD) due to long-term exposure to the elements of war such as exposure to combat and being involved in harming civilians or prisoners.[17]

Due to chronic exposure to trauma, their five senses—what they see, what they hear, what they taste, what they touch, and what they smell—embed the trauma into their bodies. And until they deal with the trauma, their bodies will be in a constant state of alert. This increases their vulnerability to developing long-term mental health challenges.

17   bit.ly/WhyOnlySomeDevelopPTSD

The same is true for someone like Brandon—who grew up in the midst of gang wars in Chicago—and first responders to the World Trade Center bombings on September 11, 2001.

Case in Point

Pete's Memories of 9/11

Pete, a New York City police officer, was one of the first to respond to the attack on the north tower of the World Trade Center. Although the events of that day were acute in nature, the prolonged search and recovery efforts moved Pete's experience into chronic trauma.

For many years, Pete found himself encountering flashbacks triggered by his five senses. Certain smells, the sounds of people yelling, the sight of smoke or fire, or the touch of certain clothing on his body would cause extreme flashbacks to the many days he heard victims screaming and the foul smell of dead bodies. Even the smell and taste of dust when he was around new construction or working on projects around the house triggered Pete.

First responders to the Surfside condominium collapse in Miami, Florida in June 2021 would be able to relate. For two weeks, they conducted round-the-clock search and rescue operations. The sounds of rubble being cleared into buckets, the smell of decay, the taste and the feel of construction dust—these are all embedded in their bodies and need to be addressed so the memories can live on in their minds, not in their bodies.

———●———

Another example of chronic trauma is poverty. Around the world, about a billion children—almost an eighth of all the people in the world—live in poverty, lacking basic nutrition and clean water.

Due to the pandemic, another 150 million children were forced into poverty. Many of these children come from stable homes. They have healthy parents and attend school. They have no history of abuse and yet the financial strain on the family due to the pandemic is placing psychological and physical strain on these children and their families.[18]

---

18 bit.ly/ImpactOfChildPoverty

The chronic financial stress that led to poverty and food insecurity creates a chronic stressor. And for the children more than for their parents, this turns into trauma.

Insidious Trauma

This type of trauma results from the psychological impact that discrimination has on a person. Discrimination can show up through microaggressions, being marginalized, dehumanized, and intimidated. Even if these dehumanizing actions are not directed *at* you but you live and work in an environment where this is the norm *around* you, you can start showing symptoms of insidious trauma.

Beyond discrimination, insidious trauma also includes being the victim of spiritual, emotional, and verbal abuse. Being beaten down in any of these manners forces a person to question their sanity or their worth. Over time, this subtle marginalization can create an impact similar to water drip-drip-dripping until it wears away a rock.

This leads to uncertainty and a lack of predictability, and it causes self-doubt and disorientation. Because insidious trauma is not easily identified, the victim keeps trying to figure out what they are doing wrong. They are unable to orient themselves to what is their responsibility and what is the responsibility of the abuser. This leads to mental and emotional fatigue.

Case in Point

Natalia's Experience in Corporate America

Single and in her midthirties, Natalia is a Black female who has been working her way up in leadership at her workplace. This has been no easy feat. For as far back as Natalia could remember, not a day has gone by where her Blackness was not attacked, whether in subtle or not-so-subtle ways.

At stoplights during her commute out of the city to the suburbs where the company was, Natalia would be called names. And during meetings, when she would voice her opinion looks of disapproval and disgust appeared on some coworkers' faces.

At one point, Natalia led an important project, directing the project from start to finish. When it came time to present, though, her supervisor decided to give the presentation. During and after the presentation, even while many accolades were given to the presenter, not once did they mention Natalia's leadership.

Natalia often fought hard to remind herself of her value despite everything in her environment telling her she had no value. Her safest place—the place where her authentic self was allowed to breathe—was found when she crossed the threshold of her home and closed the door.[19]

Complex Trauma

Complex trauma is similar to chronic trauma; however, its impact is the result of chronic exposure to adverse interpersonal experiences beginning in childhood. This type of trauma typically is perpetrated by a caregiver or a trusted person in a trusted environment. It is compounded by dysfunction across several generations.

At the intersection of acute, chronic, and interpersonal trauma—trauma perpetrated *by* people *to* people, especially in early childhood by their caregiver or from their environment—you will find a petri dish for complex trauma.

Research has shown that complex trauma causes fundamental changes to the development of the brain. It also influences your neurochemistry, and your physiological stress response. If that is not bad enough, it can cause changes in identity, behavior, and relationships due to your battle to endure, escape, or make sense of these experiences.

Acute Trauma: *A one-time traumatic event such as being in a car accident, experiencing sudden loss, being a victim of sexual assault, or witnessing a crime or a natural disaster.*

Chronic Trauma: *Trauma that is repeated and drawn out. It includes events such as neglect, family or intimate-partner violence, human trafficking, or a battle with cancer. It may also include single, acute traumas happening one right after the other.*

Insidious Trauma: *This results from the psychological impact that discrimination has on a person.*

Complex Trauma: *This type of trauma typically is perpetrated by a caregiver or a trusted person in a trusted environment. It is compounded by dysfunction across several generations. At the intersection of acute,*

---

19   Natalia's experience would come as no surprise to Black or Brown readers as in many places around the world, they are still marginalized.

chronic, and interpersonal trauma—trauma perpetrated by people to people, especially in early childhood by their caregiver or from their environment—you will find a petri dish for complex trauma.

The Role Trauma Bonding Plays

Perpetrators and abusers exploit people, and such exploitive relationships cause a trauma bond to form, where—insane as it may be—the self-doubt and disorientation caused by the trauma leads to the victim bonding with the perpetrator not *despite* the abuse, but *because* of it. This is a natural and very common reaction to trauma.[20]

The trauma victim is more likely to form a trauma bond with the perpetrator than with most other people, with the abuse of power over the victim fusing the abuser and victim and creating a life-altering love/hate relationship between the victim and the abuser in which the two replay their original trauma.[21]

The repetitive cycle of abuse reinforces a sense of powerlessness and certainty that the victim will never be able to escape. To the victim, this is a reality they have constructed for survival, tolerating the abuse as it was the abuser who made them feel cared for. This strategy may seem to work while the trauma is occurring, but in the long term it has devastating consequences to the victim.

Trauma resolution requires a return to discernment, safety, authentic support from another, truly meaningful connections, and a host of other healthy traits—none of which can exist in the trauma-bonded relationship.

Trauma bonding occurs due to surviving ongoing cycles of abuse. In general, trauma bonding occurs between abuser and victim in which the two replay their original trauma. Breaking such a bond is essential for recovery.

---

20   Dr. Patrick Carnes coined the phrase *trauma bond* to describe "the misuse of fear, excitement, sexual feelings, and sexual physiology to entangle another person." Patrick J. Carnes, PhD, *The Betrayal Bond: Breaking Free from Exploitive Relationships* (Deerfield Beach: Health Communications Inc., 2019).
21   bit.ly/TraumaBonds

Case in Point

Zoe and the Foster Care System

Zoe experienced a violent, neglectful first nine months of life before she was taken into protective custody by Child Protective Services. By the time she was nine, Zoe had lived with thirty different families. Some families were verbally violent and emotionally unsafe. Others were kind and attentive, but Zoe would soon enough be moved to another home.

At one of these homes, she had a room of her own, her own dresser full of clothes, and a closet where her backpack of the last five years could finally stay. She thought this might be her "forever home."

Zoe began to trust the caregivers a little more every day. But more than any other family, they exploited her vulnerability. Eight months into her stay—the longest she had stayed in one place by then—the foster dad started to sexually abuse Zoe. A trauma bond formed between Zoe and her foster dad who provided consistency, food, clothing, and shelter. The young Zoe disappeared into the abuse for sheer survival.

The abuse finally stopped when Zoe she was nine and was moved to another family. By that time, everything within her felt tired. On some days, Zoe would say, instead of feeling nine, she felt like she was an adult.

Whether you saw it in Zoe's physical fatigue, Natalia's ability to finally breathe once she closed her front door behind her, Pete's flashbacks from the 9/11 recovery efforts, or the sudden yet deep pain victims of the Harvest Festival shooting and the Iowa derecho experienced, big-T Trauma does far more than merely leave victims with a fleeting headache. Trauma takes up residence in your body.

How Does Trauma Affect Your Body?

As we have pointed out, your body essentially has a singular role: to protect itself so it can keep you alive. To achieve that goal, *all* of your body's systems are hardwired to respond to trauma. As a result, when trauma threatens your wellbeing, it affects your *whole* being—your body, heart, and mind.

Trauma influences why you do what you do, feel what you feel, and think what you think. And to start healing from trauma, it is important to understand how your body, heart, and mind are affected by traumatic experiences. For you to have a better understanding of how trauma affects your body, it may be helpful if we gave you a high-level overview of the nervous system.[22]

Your Nervous System

In the simplest of terms, your nervous system exists so you can *experience* the world around you and *respond* to it. This complex system has two main branches—the central nervous system, which includes the brain and spinal cord, and the peripheral nervous system, which includes the somatic nervous system and the autonomic nervous system. The autonomic nervous system is further broken down into the sympathetic and the parasympathetic nervous systems.

Each of these branches of the nervous system plays a role in experiencing trauma, and **they all work together to resolve trauma.**

Within the central nervous system, the brain engages other systems to respond to trauma.

---

22   bit.ly/TheNervousSystemFunctions

The Human Nervous System

The **peripheral nervous system** connects the brain and spinal cord to the muscles, organs, and senses in the periphery of the body.

The **somatic nervous system** voluntarily responds to external stimuli. It relays sensory and motor information to and from the **central nervous system.** Using skeletal muscles, the somatic nervous system controls body movement.

The **autonomic nervous system** involuntarily regulates internal body functions. It controls your internal organs and glands.

The **sympathetic nervous system** is involved in stress-related activities and functions. The **parasympathetic nervous system** is associated with routine, day-to-day operations of the body. These two systems control the same bodily functions, but they have opposite effects on the functions they regulate.

The **sympathetic nervous system** prepares the body for intense physical activity. The **parasympathetic nervous system** relaxes the body, a function that is sometimes described as "rest and digest."

The Brain

The brain is an incredibly complex, hardworking organ. The brain has three main parts: the cerebrum, cerebellum, and the brain stem. However, there are other regions within the brain that play an important role in how you respond to trauma.[23]

We will not go into detail on the anatomy of the brain, but since it oversees nearly all the operations within the body—including how you move, feel, and think—it is important to have a basic understanding of the parts of the brain as it relates to trauma.[24]

The Brain Stem

As a baby develops, the first part of the brain to develop is the spinal cord attached to the gastrula, which occurs during the stage of embryonic development immediately preceding the development of the baby's organs. It is often referred to as the "reptilian brain."

As a baby's senses develop, all information that is passed between the brain and the body passes through the brain stem en route to its destination.

The brain stem performs automatic functions like breathing, keeping your heart beating, sneezing, and coughing. It has no capacity to discern time.

The Diencephalon

The name for this region of the brain translates to "through brain." It is the connection between the cerebrum or cerebral cortex—the largest part of the brain—and the rest of the nervous system. This region of the brain governs sleep, arousal, appetite, movement, and posture.

The Limbic System

You can find the structures of the limbic system buried deep within the brain, underneath the cerebral cortex and above the brainstem.[25] The limbic system governs your emotional life and memory, though language is not part of the limbic system. It also plays a role in motivation.

Within the limbic system, your hypothalamus is constantly at work seeking homeostasis, a stable state of balance. For example, if a baby is hungry, the lim-

---

23   Oprah Winfrey and Bruce D. Perry MD, PhD, *What Happened to You? Conversations on Trauma, Resilience, and Healing* (New York: Flatiron Books, 2021).

24   bit.ly/TheBrain101; bit.ly/ThreePartsOfTheBrain

25   bit.ly/TheLimbicSystem

bic system will prompt it to cry so it can be fed. Or if you are cold, your body would shiver, trying to regulate so it can get back to a state of balance.

Also in the limbic system, your hippocampus converts short-term memories into long-term memories. The hippocampus is also in charge of storing those memories, allowing you to access them later.[26] However, during traumatic experiences, the hippocampus gets short-circuited and cannot properly file your memory.[27]

Another important component in the limbic system is the amygdala, a mass of neurons responsible for your perception of emotions and regulation of behavior.[28] The amygdala is most known for processing the feeling of fear and for emotional memories—where emotions are given meaning, remembered, or attached to associations of them or responses to them.[29]

Dr. Daniel Goleman coined the term "amygdala hijack" to refer to the over-reaction to a stressful experience.[30] During your reaction to stress, the amygdala disables access to your frontal lobe, and it ignites your "fight-flight-freeze-fawn" modes.

The Cortex

The cerebral cortex (or cortex, in short) includes both the cerebral and prefrontal cortex. It houses the brain's gray matter and engages conscious thought. The cortex is responsible for speech, reasoning, and learning. It also synthesizes information received from your five senses.

---

26 bit.ly/TheHippocampus; The hippocampus, located in the brain's temporal lobe, is where episodic memories are formed and indexed for later access.

27 Over time, information from certain memories that are temporarily stored in the hippocampus can be transferred to the neocortex as general knowledge—things like knowing that coffee provides a pick-me-up. Researchers think this transfer from hippocampus to neocortex happens as you sleep.

28 Although you have *two* amygdalae, we usually refer to them in the singular.

29 The amygdala, an almond-shaped structure in the brain's temporal lobe, attaches emotional significance to memories. This is particularly important because strong emotional memories (those associated with shame, joy, love or grief) are difficult to forget. The permanence of these memories suggests that interactions between the amygdala, hippocampus, and neocortex are crucial in determining the stability of a memory; in other words, how effectively it is retained over time.

There is an additional aspect to the amygdala's involvement in memory. The amygdala not only modifies the strength and emotional content of memories, it also plays a key role in forming new memories specifically related to fear. Fearful memories can be formed after only a few repetitions.

30 bit.ly/CalmingYourBrain

The prefrontal cortex, in particular, is responsible for high-level functions such as discernment, seeking social support, prioritizing, finding meaning, engaging in meaningful relationships, and differentiation. It is the last part of the brain to develop, taking almost twenty-five years to fully develop.

———•———

When you encounter trauma, the high-level brain functions are moved to the back seat since you do not necessarily need them to survive. Meanwhile, your brain stem—connected to your fight, flight, freeze, or fawn responses that are necessary for your survival—takes the driver's seat.

How Your Brain Communicates with Your Body

Throughout your nervous system, you have nerve cells. These are called neurons, and you have trillions of them. The role of neurons is to pass along signals with information. Different types of neurons have different roles.

Neurons use chemical messengers called neurotransmitters to carry the information. So, when your somatic nervous system notices a threat—whether it sees, hears, smells, feels, or tastes the threat—sensory neurons send messages to the brain neurons, and brain neurons send messages to the motor neurons.

But if your brain is overwhelmed by the message, it communicates back to the somatic nervous system, requesting backup so it can try to assimilate your traumatic experience, that is, so your brain can understand where the trauma fits in the bigger picture.

In response, the somatic nervous system calls upon all of your body's systems to respond, deciding whether you should fight, flee, freeze, or fawn. In doing so, it releases a cocktail of messengers throughout the body so everything can work together to protect you.

Due to experiences from the past, the reptilian brain and memories stored in the limbic system sometimes misinterpret the information they receive, resulting in them sometimes giving the neurotransmitters assignments that hinder instead of help.

Plus, trauma can disturb the levels of these essential messengers, causing your body to either produce too little of a particular messenger (neurotransmitter), or too much of it. Some of the most common neurotransmitters are:

Serotonin

Among other tasks, serotonin regulates your appetite, sex drive, mood, and your ability to sleep. When you have low levels of serotonin in your body, you can suffer from anxiety or depression.

Many people in the military as well as first responders, athletes, victims of domestic violence, and survivors of accidents have experienced concussions or traumatic brain injuries (TBIs). Research has shown that brain injuries can cause a decrease in serotonin, suggesting a relationship between depression and a TBI or a concussion.[31]

Dopamine

Dopamine, on the other hand, controls memory and affects your ability to concentrate. Dopamine is also essential when it comes to your ability to react and move. Trauma can do a number on your dopamine levels, though, causing difficulties paying attention at school or work, recalling information, imbalance as you move throughout your day, or simply how much effort you have to put into what you want to do.

Most people suffering from trauma will find that their motivation for life goals has simply disappeared. This could be due to an imbalance of dopamine.[32]

Endorphins

Endorphins reduce pain and stress. They play a key role in helping you get through trauma by remaining high and numbing the emotional and physical pain of the trauma. Once the trauma has ended, the endorphins will typically decrease, leading to endorphin withdrawal. This can sometimes last for days, and this period might cause emotional distress or contribute to PTSD.[33]

Cortisol

Stress and trauma also increase the level of a very powerful hormone, cortisol. This so-called stress hormone acts much the same as adrenaline in protecting you during trauma. But chronic trauma causes elevated levels of cortisol,

---

31 A TBI is a more serious form of a concussion.
    bit.ly/TBIsAndSerotonin; bit.ly/ConcussionsAndSuicide
32 bit.ly/DopamineAndMotivation
33 bit.ly/TraumaAndEndorphins

which can lead to heart disease, autoimmune disease, and more.[34] High levels of cortisol could also strengthen your memory around the traumatic experience.

Adrenaline

Epinephrine—better known as adrenaline—is typically only present during an emergency, when it causes your heart rate to increase so more oxygen can reach your muscles in order for you to act faster and think faster, and it causes your liver to release more glucose as energy. All of this is part of a fight-or-flight response.[35]

However, chronic trauma can lead to adrenal fatigue, which causes a decrease in your ability to withstand stressors, a lack of stamina, and mental fog or poor memory. Adrenal fatigue also has physical side effects such as cravings for sweet or salty, abdominal fat that is difficult to get rid of, premature aging, and recurrent infections.[36]

Norepinephrine

Norepinephrine acts in ways similar to epinephrine; however, unlike epinephrine, norepinephrine is constantly present in your body at low levels. It plays an important role in your daily moods, your memory storage, and your wakefulness.[37]

When it comes to trauma, norepinephrine increases as your levels of cortisol increase. This may explain why every detail of traumatic experiences might be burned into your memory while the positive ones fade away.[38]

GABA

Within the brain, you have two other important neurotransmitters: glutamate and GABA.[39] One communicates excitement and fear while the other suppresses it. When these two function well, you have a balanced emotional environment in your brain.

As the means to suppress excitement and fear, GABA also helps regulate your reactions to triggers. But if your body does not have a sufficient produc-

---

34 bit.ly/FunctionsOfCortisol
35 bit.ly/FunctionsOfAdrenaline
36 bit.ly/AdrenalExhaustion
37 bit.ly/Norepinephrine
38 bit.ly/StressAndMemories
39 bit.ly/GABASignaling; GABA is short for gamma-aminobutyric acid.

tion of GABA, you might find it difficult to regulate severe reactions to triggers. These triggers can include realistic flashbacks, crowded rooms, loud noises, or smells.

Alcohol stimulates GABA receptors, thereby dampening activity in the brain. This is thought to be the reason why alcohol immediate reduces anxiety, giving you the impression that your anxiety is gone while the traumatic experience has not really disappeared. This is also why an overdose of alcohol can lead to a coma.[40]

Why This Lesson on Neuroscience?

When you experience trauma, much of the communication in your body is interrupted. Your reptilian brain moves to protect you, and your body kicks into fight, flight, freeze, or fawn response. Meanwhile, your limbic system responds by storing memories of the trauma so it can again protect you in the future.

Unless you resolve the trauma, your brain stem and your limbic system—neither of which have any concept of time—will inhibit access to the cortex, the part of the brain that deals with problem solving, language, and time. And your cortex is where you access hope.

When your cortex is off-line, that is, when communication to and from the cortex is being hijacked by the rest of the nervous system, you may find yourself in Rocky Mountain National Park ducking for cover when a Harley nearby backfires. Or you could explode at a colleague for no reason, not realizing that a song was playing in the background that triggered memories of an abusive event from childhood.

Since your brain stem has no capacity to tell time, your body can be convinced you are reliving the trauma from years ago. It may take a moment for the message to finally get through to your cortex. The cortex can then help you think clearly about the situation.

Unless you understand that resolving trauma starts by addressing those memories stored in the body, you can spend years trying to talk about the events but get nowhere fast.

—————•—————

---

40   bit.ly/GABAandAlcohol; bit.ly/AlcoholAndMentalHealth

Before you jump to the part of the book where we provide you with some practices you can try, you may be curious to learn that there are other parts of the body that play key roles in resolving trauma. These are the gut and the endocrine system.

Your Gastrointestinal System

The gastrointestinal (or GI) system—also referred to as the gut—consists of the esophagus, stomach, and bowels. The main function of your GI system is to transport, digest, and absorb food nutrients.

Your gut contains 500 million neurotransmitters that are connected to your brain through nerves in your nervous system.[41] The longest nerve is one that is part of your autonomic nervous system—that is the system that involuntarily regulates your body's internal functions, including your organs and glands. This nerve is called the vagus nerve.

The vagus nerve is one of twelve cranial nerves, nerves that emerge directly from the brain, linking the brain to other parts of the body. **The vagus nerve stretches all the way from the brain stem to the colon, connecting your brain to your gut.**

En route from the brain to the colon, the vagus nerve interacts with several organs in both parts of the autonomic nervous system. It can impact both the sympathetic (arousing) and the parasympathetic (calming) of the body.

But trauma inhibits the signals sent by the vagus nerve and interferes with the gastrointestinal process. The vagus nerve also reacts to signals in the environment, and there are ways in which you can stimulate this nerve, something referred to as "improving vagal tone."

Stimulating the vagus nerve can help regulate your body's calming functions. This underscores the importance of the vagus nerve in resolving trauma. In Chapter Seventeen, we will offer some ways in which you can improve vagal tone.

The gut also houses a complex ecosystem known as the microbiome. When your microbiome is healthy, it contains a balanced diversity of bacteria and other microbes that help you absorb nutrients. **A healthy microbiome also influences your mood, helping you to maintain a positive outlook by sending messages to your brain that all is well.**

When you experience trauma, though, many parts of your nervous system send signals to your gastrointestinal system. This triggers your gut to panic and

---

41   bit.ly/Gut-BrainCommunication

disrupt your microbiome by killing off good bacteria. In this way, the brain and gut impact each other. We call this the **trauma-gut link**, and this powerful link helps explain how **your gut health impacts your overall mental health** and how important it is to consider gut health in trauma resolution.[42]

The Vagus Nerve

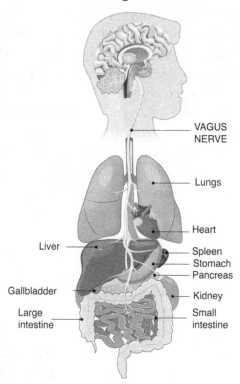

Stretching from the brainstem to the gut, the vagus nerve interacts with many organs on both parts of the autonomic nervous system, thus impact- ing both sympathetic nervous system (arousing) and the parasympathetic nervous system (calming) of the body.

---

42 Once the balance of your microbiome is disrupted, it must be addressed. There are several wellness components that contribute to a healthy microbiome and trauma recovery. Some of these are eating good nutritious food, probiotics and prebiotics, sound and restful sleep, movement, and exercise. Once incorporated, being consistent with these practices is important in reminding the body that all is well and safe. Consider talking with your medical doctor or a nutritionist about ways in which you can restore good gut health and create a healthy and vibrant microbiome.

Your Endocrine System

The endocrine system is made up of glands throughout the body that produce and regulate hormones. The hormones produced by your endocrine system regulate metabolism, growth and development, tissue function, sexual function, reproduction, sleep, and mood, to name but a few.[43]

In general, a gland selects and removes materials from the blood, processes them, and secretes the finished chemical product for use somewhere in the body.[44] When this system encounters a traumatic experience, it increases its production of cortisol. As the so-called stress hormone, cortisol makes you more reactive to stressors, and this state of heightened reactivity can lead to your body producing even more cortisol.

Cortisol provides the energy you need to endure trauma and prolonged stress. You might think that if the trauma or stressor is resolved, your body's hormones would return to balance. It is not that simple. Once your body is re-exposed, it produces more cortisol.

While this is helpful in the short-term, having elevated cortisol levels in the long term can be toxic. It can cause heart disease, chronic fatigue, depression, and immune disorders. And, as pointed out earlier, high levels of cortisol could also strengthen your memory around the traumatic experience.

Remember Zoe? Part of her recovery and healing experience was to first get her to safety. This meant she had to share with investigators, attorneys, and doctors the details about her abuse. Every time she would meet someone for an interview, her cortisol levels would rise.

Although Zoe was safe, the situation was very stressful. And because of the stress, her body produced cortisol so she could deal with the difficult situations. However, the increase in cortisol kept her in that heightened state of alert.

———•———

While the GI system and endocrine system play key roles in resolving trauma, they do not always succeed in that task. Unresolved trauma can impact other systems within the body, including your heart, lungs, muscles, and your reproductive system.

---

43 The endocrine system includes the glands that secrete their products into the bloodstream instead of externally (like sweat, tear, or saliva glands do). bit.ly/TheEndocrineSystemOverview

44 bit.ly/EndocrineSystemFacts

Your Cardiovascular System

When your body senses danger—whether real or perceived—it releases adrenaline, norepinephrine, and cortisol to help you conquer the threat. This causes your heart rate to go up and blood flow to increase so that your body can get oxygen to all the parts of the body that may need to respond to the trauma. This elevates your blood pressure, which could lead to a heart attack.

Your Respiratory System

Because your body is sending oxygen to parts that might need it to respond to the trauma, you may experience either shortness of breath or rapid breathing during or after a threat. This may cause anxiety or panic attacks, giving the impression you may be dying.

When you experience a threat, you might even hold your breath. This creates low oxygen flow to the brain, which can result in headaches, memory loss, an inability to concentrate, and fatigue.

Your Musculoskeletal System

In addition to your heart racing and your breathing getting shallow, your muscles tense up as they ready for impact. Your muscles will remain taught until the threat has been resolved—or until you have manipulated them to relax by getting a massage. This muscle tension may cause headaches as well as pain in the neck, shoulders, back, lower back, and feet.

Your Reproductive System

Stress can create challenges in both the female and male reproductive systems. Stress can make it difficult for women to get pregnant, and it can cause changes in menstruation, sexual desire, or cause the body to go into early menopause.

For men, stress can affect their reproductive system by either decreasing or increasing sexual desire, causing erectile dysfunction, or leading to other challenges with reproduction.

———•———

So, when you encounter trauma, your essential functions are on hyperalert as they scan and prepare to handle further threats. This vigilance helps keep you alive; however, it also keeps you from accessing internal resources[45] and accessing the brain's high-level executive functioning. And it can have a significant effect on your emotions.

How Does Trauma Affect Your Emotions?

Now that you know how trauma affects your body, you may have a better understanding of how the release and suppression of various neurotransmitters and hormones can do a number on your emotions.

Your heart rate controls your emotional energy. When your heart beats fast, you feel anxious, and when your heart rate slows down, you feel calm. But your emotional state can also influence your cardiovascular system.

Not all the time when your heart beats fast will you experience emotions like nervousness, fear, or anger. Sometimes you might experience your heart beating faster because of a relationship crush, or exciting news. **Your emotions indeed can cause heart rate changes, which in turn can influence your ability to transition from one emotional state to another.** Once your heart rate is regulated, you can go from a state of euphoria or fear to a state of calm.

Your change in heart rate can also affect your coherence—a state where your body, emotions, and your mind are in energetic alignment and cooperation. According to the HeartMath Institute, your heart has neurons that are similar to your brain neurons, and that your heart and brain are in constant communication.

Your heart communicates more with the brain than the brain with the heart. And when your brain sends a message to your heart, your limbic system can interfere and change or distort the signal.

Some feelings—anger, frustration, anxiety, and insecurity, for example—cause your heart rhythms to become erratic. This not only stresses out your body and causes you to physically feel exhausted, but it also keeps you from thinking clearly. As a result, **your level of coherence is significantly disrupted by trauma.**

When your body experiences emotional stress, it seeks ways to resolve it so you can return to a state of homeostasis. But when an emotional stimulus activates your heart and it communicates back to the brain, the reptilian brain and

---

45 Examples of internal resources are vitality (energy), a positive outlook, perspective, engagement, and finding meaning and stability through secure relationships.

the limbic system react before the message can reach the neocortex, keeping it from discerning what the appropriate response would be.

When trauma is present, your body and brain send stimuli which dysregulates your emotions. This keeps you from emotional regulation and from resolving the traumatic response and coherence. As a result, it keeps the traumatic response going.

———•———

As you can see, trauma affects every single part of your body. It is important to understand that while you did not have a choice in how trauma hurt you, you *do* have a choice in understanding your trauma, and you are responsible for your healing process.

When you unlock the power of choosing to understand and be responsible for your healing, your trauma recovery journey will begin, and you are on your way to discover the wealth of resiliency that lies within you!

**You did not have a choice in how trauma hurt you,
but you do have a choice in your healing.**

Once you understand what trauma is, how it affects your body, heart, and mind, you can begin to appreciate the monumental effect trauma has on individuals, family systems, and communities at large. **Turning a blind eye to your trauma or someone else's will only allow the trauma to perpetuate, thereby creating more trauma.**

Once your body is engaged, ready to protect you, getting it to relax can be tricky, especially if it has a long history of having to protect you against this specific kind of trauma—or anything that resembles it or reminds your body of that trauma.

When it comes to responding to trauma, your body is the first to arrive at the party and the last to leave. It is the first to react to a threat, and it is the last part of you to believe you are safe, that the danger is gone. Remember, its main role is to keep you alive. And it is *committed* to fulfilling that role.

When your body keeps interpreting signals as your life being in danger, like it did with Brandon and Pete, you are experiencing a trauma loop.

What Happens During a Trauma Feedback Loop?

It is common for folks who are trying to sell their house to pull out warm cookies from the oven just before potential buyers walk through the door. The smell is intended to evoke good memories and a feeling of you being right at home.

In the same way, smells and other triggers can stir up memories of trauma. And when something reminds you of a traumatic event, the memories stored in your body can cause your body to believe that you are reliving the trauma in the moment. Although the inciting trauma happened in the past, possibly even before you can remember, your body can be triggered to relive it as if it were happening now.

The reptilian brain and the limbic system's trauma response make it hard for you to be present and aware of what really is happening in and around you. Instead, you re-experience the trauma in real time. You can even anticipate it happening again in the future.

Trauma loops are highly sensitive to triggers. A trauma trigger is something felt that can be magnified, including loud, distinct, or different tones of sounds, certain smells, a specific time of day or season, a certain sensation or feeling, and repetitive thoughts you felt while going through your trauma.

Examples of triggers that can be felt and magnified
- *loud, distinct, or different tones of sounds*
- *some smells*
- *a specific time of day or season*
- *a certain sensation or feeling, and*
- *repetitive thoughts you felt while going through your trauma.*

Case in Point

Jenni Getting "Kicked in the Gut" by a Song

Jenni had a monster of a grandfather. Ralph had sexually abused her from before she could remember. The first time Ralph sold his granddaughter to a colleague, Jenni was just four years old. On the ride home that day, Ralph played "How Great Thou Art." Most times after that, when Ralph would take

Jenni back to her parents' house after having sold his granddaughter to men in his community, he played the same hymn over and over.

"My grandfather intended to keep me bound in captivity for life," Jenni says, "and [that hymn] provided him with the chains he would use to accomplish his purposes."

Jenni was able to escape when she was seventeen, and today, more than thirty years later, she and her husband work internationally to help young victims escape being trafficked.

Despite much healing, for years when Jenni heard the song, she had to get up and leave the room, her body trembling. Today, she no longer has to rush out of a room when she hears it, but she says that the song still "kicks me in the gut and leaves me gasping for breath."[46]

———•———

Once triggered, more than just causing a temporary response like Jenni gasping for breath when she hears a specific song, the trauma loop could even create longer-term symptoms in your body.

It can cause changes in your appetite, disrupt your sleep, it can lead to fatigue, muscle tension, stomach aches, and headaches. It can even cause you to feel isolated, suspicious, hopeless, angry, frustrated, numb, and anxious. If that is not enough, it can impact your thinking, causing you to replay bad memories and worst-case scenarios and make you hypervigilant.

Case in Point

The Mendocino Complex Fire

Victims of the Mendocino Complex Fire experienced a significant trauma feedback loop. The fire burned for more than three months in the summer of 2018, destroying 280 homes and other structures. Victims were displaced for many months, suffering symptoms from the trauma. Then, in August 2020, another massive fire—starting as thirty-eight separate wildfires—ravaged Northern California again and destroyed 935 structures in the area.

---

46 Jenni S. Jessen. *The Lucky One* (Colorado Springs: Compass 31, 2016) 7.

Despite having survived the fire in 2018, the renewed threat to their physical safety, their lives, the threat of losing their homes, and the threat of displacement held the victims captive to trauma triggers.

Even the smell of burning leaves or the smell of barbecues would trigger them, as would the feeling of being stuck in traffic, the sound of sirens, or not having access to their phone or personal belongings.

——•——

Once you recognize trauma, you can offer compassion and understanding to the victims whose safety and trust were compromised. Now that you better understand their reaction to what their five senses are telling them and why fear or sadness follow what they smell, hear, taste, touch, or see, you can better understand how the trauma of losing everything to a fire might affect them even years later.

Can Unresolved Trauma Be Dangerous?

When trauma goes unresolved, it becomes the breeding ground for headaches, stomach aches, heart disease, susceptibility to colds and illnesses, changes in sleep patterns, chronic fatigue, and immune disorders. It also leads to decreased mental health, including poor decision-making, addictions, anxiety, depression, PTSD, nightmares, flashbacks, outbursts of anger and rage, self-blame, and survivors' guilt.

To make things worse, it is not like your trauma goes to the grave with you. In many cases, it is passed down from one generation to the next. Until you deal with it.

Unresolved trauma begets more trauma for generations that follow.

But without assistance from a trusted outsider, it is common for people who have experienced trauma to not even recognize the trauma. Sometimes, the inability to recognize trauma is due to the symptoms being masked by medication, unhealthy coping mechanisms, repeated trauma, denial, or fear.

How Do You Resolve Trauma?

Though we had mentioned this earlier, it warrants being repeated. You did not have a choice in how trauma hurt you, but you *do* have a choice in your healing.

Once you understand trauma, you can address it with the appropriate interventions and with self-compassion. This paves the way for resilience, healing, and recovery. And it provides hope, not only to you, but also to your friends, family, colleagues, and your community.

Since trauma is a multidimensional experience, resolving trauma requires a multidimensional approach—not only talk therapy. When triggered, your body shuts down functions it deems unnecessary for survival—including logic and executive functioning. And talk therapy requires those to be intact for the therapy to be effective.

Trauma resolution requires you to integrate what your body senses with your emotions and beliefs. And *that* requires an approach that starts with the body. **This holistic approach to trauma recovery starts by using therapeutic exercises and interventions and is referred to as embodied trauma resolution work.** (As a reminder, embodied trauma resolution refers to working with the body to integrate experiences from your five senses to find safety and reason.)

It is best that you do trauma resolution work with the help of a professional. We highly recommend you seek treatment from an experienced trauma-informed clinician. However, there are steps you can take on your own to begin your healing. **It is some of the most important work you can do to heal yourself.**

But first, it helps to understand the role your personality type—your Enneagram type—plays in your healing. As you better understand your type, you can utilize specific trauma intervention practices to reclaim your resilience.

CHAPTER TWO

We All Handle Trauma Differently

In our work as trauma counselors, we have found that different personality types respond differently to the exact same therapeutic approach. Yet as we implemented insights based upon clients' personality types—their Enneagram number—we found that they tended to respond better to therapeutic interventions.

The Enneagram is an ancient personality typology depicted as nine (*enéa* in Greek) interconnected points on a diagram. It has evolved from several ancient wisdom traditions.

The study of the Enneagram is a study of nine distinct patterns of doing, feeling, and thinking along with the underlying motivation for *why* each type behaves, feels, and thinks the way they do.[47] These actions, emotions, thoughts, and motivations reflect a person's personality; hence, it is also referred to as the "Enneagram of Personality."

---

47   Typically, we refer to *think, feel,* and *behave*—in that order. This is rooted in cognitive behavioral therapy (CBT). In CBT, thoughts are addressed to change the way you feel, which in turn will impact the way you act. However, research has shown that **behavioral change starts by addressing memories stored in the body, which impacts how you feel, and finally how you think.** We will go into this more throughout this chapter. However, you will note throughout that we use the changed order to *behave, feel,* and *think.*

While the precise origin of the Enneagram is unknown, the diagram used to depict the nine types was developed only approximately fifty years ago by the Chilean psychiatrist, Oscar Ichazo.

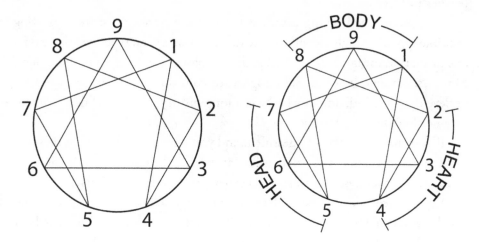

While you naturally relate stronger to one type, the connecting lines indicate fluidity in movement from one type to another. This movement occurs as your stress level and your coping skills shift. (More about that in the next chapter.)

Studying the Enneagram description of your type allows you to better understand yourself. As you learn about your internal world and that of others, it creates room for you to be yourself while also allowing room for others who do not necessarily see the world as you do.

Once you identify your Enneagram type—and yes, you only have *one* type, and it does not change, even after trauma—you will discover that others of your type behave, feel, and think in many of the same ways you do, but everyone is still different.

Your Enneagram type does not change—even after trauma.

Determining Your Type

"Where can I take an assessment to find my type?" This is a question we are often asked. After hearing about the Enneagram, it is indeed tempting to want to simply take a test to learn what your type is.

While there are several assessments available in books and online—some free and others at a substantial fee—please consider the following: Some types look a lot alike, so it is challenging to determine your type by answering just a few perfunctory questions.

Also, even when taking a test, you will likely receive a score suggesting multiple types. Though you may relate to aspects of several types, you have only one primary Enneagram type. And each type has several levels of development. Most assessments, however, are designed to confirm type at the average level of development. Individuals who have a long history of personal development may not look like the average type.

If you choose to take an assessment and you have a long history of personal development, you may want to consider answering the questions as if you were in your early twenties, that is, as a less experienced version of yourself.

If you have taken a test and the result suggested several types, consider which center of intelligence you naturally default to. (More about that later in this chapter.) Also consider the numbers either side of your possible number(s)—called *wings* in the Enneagram world—to see if you can relate. Plus, there are lines that connect your type to two other types. If it also feels like those types represent some of who you are, you may be on the right track to finding your number.

Another way to be typed is by reading descriptions of various types as presented by certified and experienced Enneagram teachers.[48] (We offer descriptions in Chapter Three.) Then follow the same process as outlined above, checking if you relate to the wings and lines connecting your possible number to others.

Whether you already know your type or not, it will be helpful to consider the insights we offer into the **three centers of intelligence** so you can identify *your* center of intelligence. From there, you can consider the patterns, core beliefs, and worldview of each type, which would help you determine your Enneagram type.

We also describe where each type tends to place their attention, how the type performs under stress, what they tend to avoid, what their unmet child-

---

48   We strongly urge against basing your number on haphazard descriptions posted on social media. Though some of those are descriptions provided by Enneagram-certified professionals, many are not.

hood needs were, their natural defense mechanisms, and their natural gifts of resilience.

Along with the gifts of resilience of each type, we will also point out each type's vulnerability to trauma at the end of each of the stories in Part Two.

If you prefer someone else to help you discern what your type is, you can consider doing a typing interview with a certified Enneagram professional trained in conducting such interviews. Those can be done in person or online.

Typing During Trauma

If you are in the midst of trauma, accurate typing can be very difficult. Since your executive functioning is often inaccessible during trauma, what might *appear* to be true for you might not represent the real you. Learn what you can about the nine types, then return to discerning your type when you are in a better place.

Trauma Intervention and the Enneagram

The Enneagram, when it intersects with trauma recovery, offers promising results. As you better understand the patterns of your type, you can utilize specific trauma intervention practices to access the resilience within. The practices we offer in Part Two are based on the nine types' worldviews, their current sense of safety, how trauma is showing up in their life, and a host of other factors.

This method of integrating trauma knowledge with Enneagram wisdom is what we describe as Enneagram-informed trauma resolution.

In Part Three, we offer multiple intervention practices that you can try on your own or with the help of a trusted other. Implementing these practices begins with you cultivating inner observation. Simply noticing what your body, emotions, and thoughts are trying to tell you is the first step to growing in self-awareness.

**The road to healing starts with observation.
Noticing what your body, emotions, and thoughts
are trying to tell you is the first step to growing in
self-awareness—and the first step toward healing.**

Throughout, we will explore the power of the Enneagram in trauma recovery. In doing so, one large goal is to help you reclaim your resilience. By practicing trauma resolution strategies considering each of the nine types, we believe there is a higher likelihood of trauma integration and healing.[49]

What is Enneagram-Informed Trauma Resolution?

Based on your personality, you respond to trauma and trauma resolution in unique ways. Like everyone else, you have developed one of nine personality patterns. In *The Essential Enneagram*, Doctors David Daniels and Virginia Price say that **we acquire these patterns "to protect a specific aspect of the self that felt threatened as our personality was developing."**[50]

These personality patterns are helpful predictors regarding your response to the initial experience of trauma *and* to what the best ways are to access the gifts of resilience. But the strategies you developed early on to manage life may no longer serve you in the way they initially did. In this way, studying the Enneagram provides you with insight and compassion.

You will also learn why you respond to trauma the way you do based on understanding how trauma affects you biologically as well as how it affects your personality style.

Best of all, looking at trauma through the lens of the Enneagram offers you a roadmap to resilience. It offers you insight, self-compassion, and responses to activate the relaxation response system during trauma and while recovering from trauma.

A trauma-informed approach to recovery recognizes the role trauma has played in impacting your reactions, emotions, thoughts, and the relationships with those you love.

Taking an **Enneagram-informed** *approach to recovery recognizes that your personality type could make you more vulnerable and also more resilient to various types of trauma.*

Looking at trauma through the lens of the Enneagram offers you a roadmap to resilience.

---

49 As described earlier, trauma integration occurs when you can acknowledge that you have the necessary strengths within you to overcome the trauma so that all the systems of your body (physical, emotional, and cognitive) function as they should.

50 David Daniels, MD and Virginia Price, PhD. *The Essential Enneagram: The Definitive Personality Test and Self-Discovery Guide* (San Francisco: HarperOne, 2009), 1.

There are three biological instincts identified in the study of the Enneagram. These needs are primal, that is, they *must* be met for you to function well, feel safe, secure, certain, loved, appreciated, heard, and to become independent. All humans experience these. Without them, you cannot thrive.

These are the need for **self-preservation** (also referred to as the need for **survival**), the need to be **social** (the need for **bonding**), and the need to be **sexual** or **one-to-one** (the need for **intimacy**). Each instinct is strong and arises from the body center—from your gut—and is a biological imperative.[51]

- The need for **self-preservation/survival** is the need to have enough provisions, that is, food, shelter, and safety.
- The need to be **social/bonding** is experienced as a need for belonging, that is, to a group, a family, a tribe, or being a part of a community.
- The need to be **sexual** or the **one-to-one**/the need for **intimacy** is experienced as a need for closeness or intimacy.

However, trauma keeps you from getting these biological imperatives met. Trauma keeps you from feeling safe. Trauma keeps you from truly bonding with yourself and others. Trauma also keeps you trapped and unable to function both independently and interdependently.

To deal with the trauma you have experienced, you tend to cultivate resilience skills. Each of the nine Enneagram types has unique resilience skills. (We will explore these in the next chapter.)

These skills include having the energy to handle life challenges, positivity, having a sense of vibrancy and vitality, reaching various achievements, knowing your life is filled with purpose and meaning, knowing and following up with priorities, having close connections (with friends, colleagues, and family), and more.

As you develop a greater understanding of how trauma interferes with you leading a normal life, you can also appreciate how important resilience is for healing and how the Enneagram can be a helpful guide. It provides the lens to see you as a unique person, especially as it relates to the trauma you have experienced.

The Enneagram also helps you understand your natural coping mechanisms. As you grow in understanding about your type, you will be able to tone

---

51 Once each of these instincts engage with the type, a sub-type arises. There are therefore twenty-seven subtypes. For more information, refer to the work by Peter O'Hanrahan.

down those protective coping mechanisms that used to work and develop new healthy coping strategies that lead to resilience.

Before we go into each of the nine types: A foundational component of understanding the Enneagram as more than simply a personality typology is to learn about the three centers of intelligence.

The Three Centers of Intelligence

You learn about yourself and the world around you through observing, noticing, listening, understanding, and taking action. Not only do you receive and process this information through your intuition (that is, through your body), but also by responding emotionally (that is, using your heart), and by collecting data and thinking about what you are observing (that is, using your head).

> **You gather and process information through...**
> **your intuition (your body)**
> **your emotions (your heart)**
> **and from data (your head).**

In Enneagram language, we refer to these—the body, heart, and head—as the centers of intelligence. Each of these three centers provides us with valuable information.

Your body center offers you **sensate information** through the five senses: sight, sound, smell, touch, and taste. It also offers a sense of autonomy, justice, and right action.

Your heart center offers you **emotional intelligence,** including being relational, engaged, and connected to others.[52]

Your head center allows you to make meaning of the information coming from all the centers, including language, memory, imagination, planning, and more. You **mentally map and strategize** using this center.

Although you have access to all three centers, if you are like most people, you naturally default to or rely heavily on just one or two of the centers. And the more you use just one or two centers, the more those develop and are, therefore, more easily accessible than the others. However, when you operate in an

---

52   The *heart* in *heart center* refers to the emotional nature of humankind. Emotions are connected to the limbic system in the brain, not the blood-pumping organ. We go into more detail into that later in this chapter.

integrated way, that is, by accessing all three centers, your response to life events is more balanced, which allows your life to run more smoothly.

Your Enneagram type is often reflected in which center you rely on the most.

> **When you operate in an integrated way, accessing your body, heart, and mind, your response to life events is more balanced. This allows your life to run more smoothly.**

The Three Centers and Trauma

Trauma interrupts your ability to fully use each of your centers. For the body center, the trauma response puts your body functions on hyperalert, keeping your heart beating, your lungs breathing, and **your basic body functions going while other body functions, like hunger, are being suppressed.** The focus is purely on keeping you alive. (This is true even if your Enneagram type is in the heart or head center.)

For the heart center, the trauma response **interferes with your relationships** with yourself and others, keeping you from fully connecting and engaging by potentially acting frenzied or numb.

And for the head center, the trauma response **interferes with your ability to use logic,** discernment, and reason by attending to other body functions that are necessary for survival.

But just as trauma can interfere with certain functions offered by each of the centers, these centers also specifically give you access to resiliency.

The Three Centers and Resiliency

Some of the resilience skills associated with each of these centers are:

- The **body center** or gut offers you existence, identity, grounded presence, confidence, action orientation, endurance, and strength.
- The **heart center** gives you access to connection, love, empathy, comfort with relationships, positive outlook, and emotional self-regulation.
- The **head center** allows you access to remaining calm, dispassionate observation, objectivity, situation-specific reasoning and logic. It also offers the capacity to sustain attention, have clarity and focus, and plan for the future.

Each of the centers also has a core motivation that drives you.

The Core Motivation of Each Center

Body types (Eights, Nines, and Ones) employ autonomy, personal justice, position, power, and attempting to bring life back to the way it should be as a strategy to assure being heard and to minimize discomfort. This can also be referred to as **instinctual intelligence**. This core motivation is rooted in their unmet childhood need for autonomy, justness, and fairness. The body types respond by seeking to **manage life through power and control**.

Heart types (Twos, Threes, and Fours) process life through the lens of how they are receiving—or *not* receiving—affirmation and validation, whether they are liked and seen by others, and the quality of their connections with those around them. This can be referred to as **emotional intelligence**. The unmet childhood need of heart types is to be seen and for acknowledgment, approval, and validation for who they are, and they respond by seeking **esteem and affirmation** by using connection and relatedness as their strategy for managing life.

Head types (Fives, Sixes, and Sevens) use planning, mapping, and strategizing as a means to manage life. This can be referred to as **mental intelligence**. Due to their unmet childhood need for consistency and predictability, these types respond by seeking **safety, security, and certainty** so they can know that life is predictable and that potential danger is being dealt with.

——•——

While the types within each of the centers are concerned with the same unmet childhood needs, each type expresses their response strategy in a slightly different way.

Also, regardless of your type, we *all* need and use power and control, esteem and affirmation, as well as safety, security, and certainty. It simply is that one of those core motivations moves front and center, influencing how you manage life, and developing strategies to help you manage trauma in a stronger way than the other centers of intelligence do.

The Body Center and the Brain

As we pointed out in the previous chapter, in the development of a baby, the first part of the brain to develop is the brain stem, often referred to as the reptilian brain. It is responsible for governing functions like respiration, heartbeat, and temperature regulation.

The body center has a strong connection to the reptilian brain. Regardless of your Enneagram type and preferred center of intelligence, though, when you experience trauma, your body center is the first to react. One example are the changes in your heart rate and respiration. Several other body functions are impacted, as described in the previous chapter.

The body center also has a direct connection to the immune system of the body, the gut. Many body systems are regulated within the gut. It is not surprising that your gut health impacts your emotional and mental health as well as your physical health.

Even if you naturally default to processing the world through your heart or head center, the body center and its connection to the reptilian brain plays an integral role that cannot be ignored. For this reason, in an Enneagram-informed approach to trauma resolution we begin by addressing the body center. It is also for this reason that throughout this book, we consistently lead with the body center, followed by the heart and the head centers.

> **Regardless of your Enneagram type and preferred center of intelligence, when you experience trauma, your body center is the first to react.**

The Importance of the Body Center in Resolving Trauma

Your body offers you sensate information. As a result, when it comes to trauma resolution, almost all types respond to *some* body-based intervention, but not all types would respond favorably to the *same* body-based intervention. Holding ice, for example, might work to calm some types but not others. Likewise, different breathing techniques work for some types and not for others.

Your sensate experiences can also elicit specific emotions and thoughts. Each of your senses provides you with valuable information that helps you manage your life. As a child you may have learned, for example, that it hurts to touch a hot stove. Do it once, and you likely never touched another hot stove.

The body center also offers other instinctual responses described as your "gut feelings." If you pay attention to the information your gut provides, these can guide your actions. Because your body provides you information in real time, that is, in the present moment, you are wise to listen to your gut.

The real-time information may be related to something you had experienced in the past; nonetheless, listening to what your body tells you means that you are learning from your instinctual intelligence. A statement like, "I just knew it—I felt it in my gut" is typical when accessing this type of intelligence. And if you are like us, you may have wished a time or two that you had listened to your gut.

The Heart Center and the Brain

The part of the brain that the heart center is related to is the limbic system of the brain. Simplistically stated, the limbic system sits atop the reptilian brain. Emotions are largely housed in the limbic system. This system regulates how you bond with others, even as a newborn.

Though the heart center is the center given the least credence, it offers you information about engagement, connection, and relatedness. Observing the engagement between a mother and her baby, we can learn about the heart center and co-regulation. An infant begins to learn about relationships through the quality of this connection.

Through experiencing various emotions, you can learn more about both your internal emotional experience and develop a greater sensitivity to the emotional experiences of others. This allows you to grow self-compassion as well as compassion for others.

But emotion is widely misunderstood. It is hard for us to truly know how someone else feels, and as a result, we tend to avoid discussions about emotion unless there is a strong basis of trust. Yet love, the most powerful of all emotions, is something you cannot live without.

Still, many cultures undervalue emotion and the contribution the heart makes in your understanding of the world around you.

The Head Center and the Brain

The head center is connected to the prefrontal cortex. This part of the brain is responsible for language, complex problem solving, integrating the other centers, along with several other functions. The very last part of the brain to develop, it does not operate to its full potential until you are well into adulthood.

It is the center that we are generally referring to when we talk about intelligence. The head center offers us maps, charts, patterns, logic, and strategies to manage life. You compare, imagine, plan for the future, and call on past memories as a means of accessing and processing information in this center. Some of the greatest inventions and science as we know it today are due to this center.

In stark contrast to the lack of value given to emotion, intellectual intelligence is the most valued intelligence in many cultures. We tend to give credit for solutions to problems coming mostly from this center, although we may find that all three centers of intelligence play a role in arriving at excellent solutions.

———•———

Ongoing research is being conducted on the distinct neurobiology of each type, helping to provide greater understanding of the body's looping reactivity to trauma. Information about each type is important, but practices designed to cultivate inner observation and to grow in self-awareness are the most helpful interventions.

These offer holistic help: awareness, insight, self-compassion, and responses to relax the nervous system while you are experiencing trauma or recovering from trauma.

You can cultivate inner observation and access resilience by something we call the Three-M Triad of resilience.

The Three Centers and the Three-M Triad™ of Resilience

Resilience is your ability to bounce back from the trauma response and return to a state where you are receptive, calm, and open. Only then are you able to access all three centers of intelligence.

We have developed a method we call the Three-M Triad of resilience that you can use to check in with your three centers using **movement, meaningful connections,** and **mindfulness.** Each of the m's in the Three-M Triad is related to an essential aspect of healing trauma.

Unique and powerful on their own, we will describe them separately. However, you will notice the overlap as they work in conjunction with one another, assisting you in your healing.

Although each of the m's in the Three-M Triad can be assigned to one of the three centers (body, heart, and head), there is an overlap in how they work most effectively.

Movement

When you are in a traumatic state, movement is impaired both internally and externally. Internally, certain systems move faster while others slow down to keep you alive. **The desired result of a movement practice is to return to**

a state where movement is not just keeping you alive but allowing you to thrive.

- Movement is *all* activity in the body. It includes internal as well as external movement of energy in the body. It is more than just exercise. Any practice that allows energy to flow freely through the body is considered movement.
- Movement also includes how you hold your body as you walk through life, for example your posture and the ability to be physically present and still.
- Movement also includes your sensate experiences—what you smell, what something feels like when you touch it, what you hear, what you see, and what you taste.
- Movement is about breathing as well as your physical health.
- Movement is also about the innate wisdom of the systems within your body working to keep you alive.

Meaningful Connections

In trauma healing, we often talk about the need for emotional regulation, that is, a person must learn to regulate their emotional response to trauma by themselves. However, all humans are interdependent. We need one another. In fact, we cannot survive without one another.

- Meaningful connections are about honoring yourself—your general needs as well as your need for others in your life. When you are building meaningful connections, you are clear about what is important to you, including that those you are reaching out to have your best interests at heart.
- Meaningful connections begin when you have learned to co-regulate through having safe, nurturing, and predictable relationships with others. Only then can you begin to self-regulate. If as a child you had inconsistent or poor early nurturing relationships, meaningful connections can develop at a later stage in life.
- Another part of meaningful connections is maintaining these connections by spending time nurturing them.

Mindfulness

Mindfulness is an essential part of the head center's contribution to healing from trauma. It helps identify where you place your attention, how you use discernment, and helps you find clarity. This helps to integrate stimulus from and with the other centers.

- Mindfulness is the ability to be present to what is. Being mindful requires gathering your attention and placing it somewhere. This is hard to do when you have been traumatized, as after trauma, your attention could be scattered—moving back and forth between several concerns—or it can be frozen, feeling like your attention is paralyzed. When traumatized or in a trauma loop, you may find it hard to shift your attention. Mindfulness often works best when distractions are kept to a minimum.

- Mindfulness works best when you have self-compassion while navigating the terrain between what is going on *inside of you* and what is going on *in your life* in real time. This can be tough as it is easy to get sidetracked and move more in one direction—either focusing mostly on your inner world or focusing mostly on the world around you. To be in a mindful state means being fully present in the *here and now*, something the trauma response makes it difficult to do.

> **Resilience is your ability to bounce back from the trauma response and return to a state where you are receptive, calm, and open. Only then are you able to access all three centers of intelligence.**
>
> **You can use the Three-M Triad (movement, meaningful connections, and mindfulness) to cultivate inner observation, access your three centers, and become more resilient.**

—•—

Just as it takes practice to access information from all three centers of intelligence at the same time, incorporating each of the m's in the Three-M Triad also takes practice. As you investigate how these practices work in your day-to-day life, you will need to constantly adjust how you use the Three-M Triad knowing that making adjustments is a fundamental part of being resilient.

But first, another word on physical and psychological safety.

> Benefits of using the Three-M Triad include stress reduction, enhanced performance, greater awareness and insight, better judgment, increased self-compassion, increased attention to your needs and the needs of others, and overall improvement in relationships.

Anchoring in Safety

Before you proceed with any method or exercise to resolve trauma, consider these three insights based on the Three-M Triad of resilience.

- **It is normal to revisit trauma. It is not normal or healthy to be retraumatized.** If you are retraumatized by any exercise, it is not the right type of work for you. Using interventions such as tapping, trauma-release exercises (TRE™), or a butterfly hug, or having a helping professional assist you with down regulating (that is, returning to a state of calm) is very important.

  Using such **movement** exercises is a way to check in for safety related to your **body center** of intelligence.

- **Decide if you can do it alone or need help**. Many individuals we have worked with over the years have tried to navigate their recovery on their own. However, you need other people to work with you.

  If you decide to reach out to a therapist, keep in mind that choosing just *any* therapist is different from choosing a qualified person to work with you. When you first get to know a new therapist, you may not feel completely safe with them. But if you have been working with them for a while and still do not feel safe or feel even *less* safe than at the start, trust yourself—you are not working with the right person.

  This is a way to check in for safety as it relates to your **heart center** of intelligence using **meaningful connections**.

- **Identify what your goal is.** Is it to lower your overall reactivity to a fight, flight, freeze, or fawn response? To feel safe more often? To identify or reduce the number of triggers? To feel more empowered? Reaching your goal may start with baby steps. That is fine.

  This is a way to check in for safety related to your **head center** of intelligence using **mindfulness**.

Once you have identified your goals, know whom you will turn to for support, and know that whatever interventions you choose should make you feel safe, you can try out some exercises. We offer several in Chapter Seventeen.

The Importance of Integration

The effectiveness of resilience is strengthened when you can integrate resourcefulness coming from your body (physical and sensate resources), your higher emotional states (positive emotions such as gratitude and contentment), and your thoughts (categories of planning, imagining, fantasizing, and remembering).

Many people who have difficulty finding a way to look for resilience in their bodies, feelings, and thoughts might turn to religious, spiritual, or faith-based practices they find comfort in.

In fact, at birth, before your personality begins to form, you possess certain attributes of spiritual resilience. Some aspects of spiritual resilience are the ability to find meaning and purpose, feeling connected to a higher power, and experiencing unity and oneness.

As you may have learned spiritual practices of prayer, meditation, and other faith or spiritual-based forms of resourcefulness, these may be easy for you to recall as a welcome addition on your journey to integration and resilience.

Through practicing resolution strategies based on each of the nine type-specific responses to trauma, there is a higher likelihood that you will be able to align your body, heart, and mind and reclaim your resilience.

Each type has gifts, challenges, and distinct ways of being resilient. In the chapter that follows, you will learn more about each of the nine Enneagram types.

CHAPTER THREE

The Nine Personality Types

Now that you have a better understanding of the three centers of intelligence, we can finally explore the nine types and the nine unique strategies people use to manage life. This includes the motivations for why they behave, emote, and think the way they do.

Each of the nine Enneagram types is distinct from the others, having unique gifts, challenges, and worldviews. Each type also has a distinct way of reacting, feeling, and thinking.

You may have encountered some Enneagram literature referring to types by names or descriptors. We choose not to do so. We intentionally use only the number as a descriptor as many of the titles commonly used can be misleading.

An entire section will follow where we provide more detailed information on each of the types. While there are also subtypes (twenty-seven in total), the focus of this book is to provide a solid understanding of the connection between the nine main types and trauma, hence we focus specifically on the nine types and their centers of intelligence.

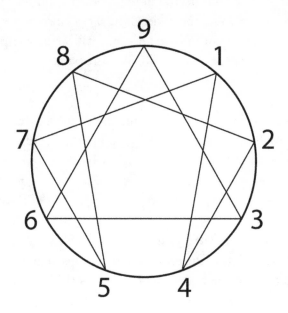

Wings

On either side of each type sits another type. These are referred to as the wings of the type, and the wings influence the expression of each of the types. Often, one of the wings is expressed more prominently. Both of your wings can complement your type, though, so the goal is to develop each of your wings.

For example, as a Two, Renée has both a One and a Three wing. She is constantly working on expressing her One wing but is naturally more comfortable expressing her Three wing. Sharon, meanwhile, is a Three with access to both a Two and a Four wing, but she is more comfortable expressing her Four wing.

Lines

There are lines that connect each type to two other types. These lines illustrate the movement between the types. Some Enneagram illustrations have arrows at the end of each line, further describing how each type moves from one type to another under stress and integration. It might also indicate that one might be more likely to be reactive in one direction and more responsive in the other.

Stress and integration may be misleading when we speak about trauma, though. When you are exposed to a traumatic event, your actions, emotions, and thoughts are focused on survival in the moment, and they may not reflect what would be true for your type under normal circumstances.

In our graphic we do not show arrows, nor will we be going into depth on movement between types as that can fill an entire book.

The Circle

The circle of the Enneagram represents the wholeness each of us has, and the connection we have to aspects of all types. In other words, even though you are only one type, you have some aspects of each of the Enneagram types. The more integrated you are—that is, the more access you have to all three centers of intelligence—the greater your ability to access aspects of all types.

Descriptions of the Nine Types

As we have made clear in the previous chapter, an exploration of the Enneagram always starts with the body center as that is the part of your brain that developed first in utero. And we start our descriptions with type Eight as Eights are the first type of the body center.

As we explore each of the types, we focus on the following characteristics of each type:

- Center of Intelligence
- Type Description
- Core Belief
- Worldview
- Where Attention Is Placed
- How the Type Performs Under Stress
- What the Type Avoids
- Unmet Childhood Needs
- Defense Mechanism
- Gifts Toward Resiliency

There are many more characteristics to explore, and we encourage you to do so in other literature.

> **Each of the nine types has a particular unconscious strategy to manage what is unpleasant, deemed threatening, or unacceptable. These are called *defense mechanisms*. Each type is likely to use one**

defense mechanism more often than another but may also use more than one throughout the day.

Center of Intelligence: The Body

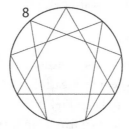

To assure protection and regard in a tough world, Eights believe you must be strong and powerful. Action-oriented, they have a lot of energy and may not be aware of their impact on others. Eights are not afraid to speak their minds and can be direct to the point of being blunt. They see themselves as powerful and protective. Eights seek justice and can be intense. They also can be overly impactful, excessive, and impulsive. They tend to make quick decisions and respect others who do the same.

Core Belief

- "The world is filled with injustice. Powerful people take advantage of others' innocence."

Worldview

- "The world is filled with injustice, and I am here to offer protection."

Where Attention Is Placed

- Power and control
- Justice and injustice
- Who has the power
- Who is deceiving who
- Helping those unable to defend themselves

Performance Under Stress

- Exerting power or dominance
- Dealing with a situation here and now
- Going full-out
- Denying fatigue and pain
- Intimidation

Avoidance

- Being taken advantage of

- Experiencing and expressing vulnerability
- Being seen as weak
- Not being respected by people they regard

Unmet Childhood Needs

- Need for autonomy, fair treatment, to be heard, and to feel empowered

Defense Mechanism

- Denial
  - o By disavowing its very existence, Eights unconsciously negate what makes them feel fearful.
  - o Denial serves to keep Eights from feeling fatigue, pain, or vulnerability while they live in an intense way and practice excess in much of what they do.

Gifts Toward Resiliency

- Self-confidant, decisive, assertive, direct, self-determined, just, big-hearted, and loyal

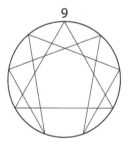

Nines believe that to be loved and valued, you must blend in and go with the flow. Consequently, Nines seek harmony and unity, are inclusive, amiable, easygoing, comfortable, and steady. They can also be self-forgetting, conflict avoidant, and stubborn. Nines are easygoing. They go along to get along. They merge easily with the ideas and needs of others, often forgetting their own. Nines often have difficulty identifying a particular idea or opinion they have, and they can easily fall asleep to what is important to them.

Core Belief

- "So that life is more comfortable and flows with more ease, I blend in with the beliefs of others."

Worldview

- "The world treats people as relatively unimportant for what they are and requires them to blend in to be comfortable. By blending in, I will find a sense of comfort and belonging."

Where Attention Is Placed
- Comfort, peace, and harmony
- Other people's agendas

Performance Under Stress
- Passive-aggressive expression of anger and stubbornness
- Resistant to others
- Some explosive outbursts of anger when they feel pushed too far

Avoidance
- Conflict
- Taking action regarding what is truly essential and supportive of self
- Their own ideas and feelings, especially if they perceive it will cause conflict

Unmet Childhood Needs
- Need for autonomy, fair treatment, to be heard, and to feel empowered

Defense Mechanism
- Narcotization
  - Nines unconsciously numb themselves to avoid something that feels too large, complex, difficult, or uncomfortable to handle. Examples of numbing might include watching TV, eating, sleeping, drinking, or gambling.
  - They narcotize to avoid conflict and maintain a self-image of being comfortable and harmonious.

Gifts Toward Resiliency
- Receptive, can see many sides of an issue, inclusive, willing to be part of the collective, reassuring, fair, patient, unassuming, diplomatic, gentle, kind, and down to earth

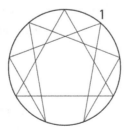

Type Ones believe they must be good and right to be worthy. Consequently, Ones are conscientious, responsible, improvement-oriented, and self-controlled, but also can be critical, resentful, and self-judging.

Core Belief

- "You must be good and right to be worthy. I can do this by being conscientious and doing things the right way."

Worldview

- "There are so many things in the world that need improvement, and I am here to notice them and improve them."

Where Attention Is Placed

- What can be corrected or improved
- What is right or wrong
- What *should* be

Performance Under Stress

- Feeling overburdened with changes that need to happen
- Being anxious and resentful as my inner critic takes over
- Becoming easily frustrated with perceived wrong

Avoidance

- Being wrong
- Making mistakes

Unmet Childhood Needs

- Need for autonomy, fair treatment, to be heard, and to feel empowered

Defense Mechanism

- Reaction formation
  - Ones try to reduce or eliminate anxiety caused by their behaviors, feelings, or thoughts that they consider unacceptable by responding in a manner that is exactly the opposite of their real responses.
  - This allows Ones to believe they are right regardless of their behavior. For example, a One may have strong ethical beliefs that cheating or stealing is very wrong and yet might cheat or steal.

Gifts Toward Resiliency

- Self-controlled and disciplined, quality-minded, precise, thorough, fair, ethical, upstanding, organized, responsible, and having integrity

Center of Intelligence: The Heart

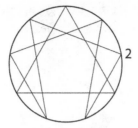

Twos like to help and believe you must give fully to others to be loved. Consequently, Twos are caring, helpful, supportive, generous, and relationship oriented. They also can be prideful, intrusive, and demanding.

Core Belief

- "To get what I need in life, I must give. To be loved, I must be needed."

Worldview

- "People need my love and support. I am here to give it to them."

Where Attention Is Placed

- On the needs and concerns of others
- Supporting and serving others
- Giving to get

Performance Under Stress

- Feeling indispensable
- Tendency to give too much
- Being confused about self-care and attending to their own needs
- Upset about having invested too much in relationships that do not work out, leading to becoming resentful

Avoidance

- Knowing and attending to their own needs
- Disappointing others

Unmet Childhood Needs

- Need to be seen, need for acknowledgment, approval, and validation

Defense Mechanism

- Repression
  - o Twos hide information about themselves from themselves that is too difficult to acknowledge consciously.
  - o This allows the Two to continue to give relentlessly believing they are just being helpful although they are repressing feelings of resentment for doing so.

Gifts Toward Resiliency

- Generous, helpful, friendly, caring, supportive, generous, encouraging, optimistic, nurturing, and warm-hearted

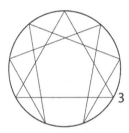

Threes are doers and believe they must perform successfully. They believe you must accomplish and succeed to be loved. Consequently, Threes are industrious, fast-paced, efficient, and goal-oriented. They also can be inattentive to feelings, impatient, and driven based on what others may think and believe about them.

Core Belief

- "People are rewarded for what they do and not who they are."

Worldview

- "The world is a contest, and I can win if I work hard. Winners are valued."

Where Attention Is Placed

- All the things that must be done—tasks, goals, future achievements, efficiency, and being the best

Performance Under Stress

- Wondering if they are doing enough or a good enough job
- Being out of touch with their feelings
- Working too hard toward the goal of prestige

Avoidance

- Losing face
- Failure

Unmet Childhood Needs

- Need to be seen, need for acknowledgment, approval, and validation

Defense Mechanism

- Identification
  - o Threes unconsciously incorporate attributes and characteristics of another person that they deem desirable as a means of bolstering their self-esteem.

o   It allows the Three to see themselves as successful by imitating successful people or behaviors.

Gifts Toward Resiliency

- Adaptable, persevering, self-driven, energetic, dynamic, efficient, pragmatic, ambitious, productive, and they present well

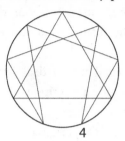

4

Fours are individualistic and romantic. They believe you can regain the lost ideal love or perfect state by finding the love or situation that is unique, special, and fulfilling. Consequently, Fours are idealistic, deeply feeling, empathetic, and authentic. They can also be dramatic, moody, and self-absorbed.

Core Belief

- "There is always something missing. I will ultimately be abandoned because of an original loss of connection."

Worldview

- "We are all here to be authentic and seek a deeper understanding of life."

Where Attention Is Placed

- What is missing, that others have something that they do not have
- What is beautiful and aesthetically pleasing
- Finding love, meaning, and fulfillment
- In the future *or* in the past

Performance Under Stress

- Problems with emotional regulation
- Feeling constantly misunderstood
- Deep envy of others

Avoidance

- Being rejected or abandoned
- Resisting change for fear of losing themselves
- Feeling that they do not measure up or there is something inherently wrong with them

Unmet Childhood Needs
- Need to be seen, need for acknowledgment, approval, and validation

Defense Mechanism
- Introjection
    - o This is a counter intuitive defense mechanism. Instead of repelling critical information about themselves or an experience, Fours take the information and internalize it, taking it on as their own.
    - o This allows the Four to deal with self-inflicted information rather than respond to criticism or rejection from others.

Gifts Toward Resiliency
- Expressive, creative, sensitive, original, intuitive, perceptive, and unique

Center of Intelligence: The Head

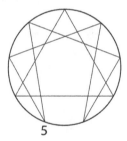

5

Fives like to observe. They believe they must protect themselves from a world that demands too much and gives too little. Consequently, Fives seek self-sufficiency and are non-demanding, analytic, thoughtful, and unobtrusive. They also can be withholding, detached, and overly private.

Core Belief
- "The world demands too much from people and gives them too little."

Worldview
- "Life is imposing and complex, and understanding the complexity gives me a sense of safety."

Where Attention Is Placed
- The intellectual domain
- Facts, analyzing, and thinking
- Being self-sufficient
- Maintaining privacy and boundaries

Performance Under Stress
- Feeling fatigued

- Setting firm boundaries
- Withdrawing

Avoidance
- Strong feelings, especially fear
- Intrusive people
- Too many requests
- Depletion

Unmet Childhood Needs
- Safety, security, and certainty

Defense Mechanism
- Isolation
    - Fives withdraw into themselves. This could be by physically removing themselves or mentally withdrawing into their thoughts.
    - Isolation helps Fives keep themselves from experiencing emotions and dealing with the demands of others.

Gifts Toward Resiliency
- Perceptive, innovative, observant, logical, knowledgeable, reasonable, curious, analytical, self-reliant, and dry-witted

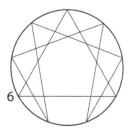

Sixes believe you must gain certainty and security in a hazardous world that you simply cannot trust. They often scan their environment for danger. Sixes are intuitive, inquisitive, trustworthy, good friends, and problem-solvers. They can also be doubtful, accusatory, and fearful.

Core Belief
- "The world is threatening and dangerous, and people simply cannot trust one another. It is essential to be prepared to meet or to avoid the potential hazards of life."

Worldview
- "The world is a dangerous place. Truth is hidden. Appearances are suspect. People cannot trust one another."

Where Attention Is Placed
- What could potentially go wrong
- Playing devil's advocate
- What is dangerous
- Difficulties
- Hidden meanings

Performance Under Stress
- Balancing the need they have to trust others with the basic mistrust they have
- Once the stress or pending danger is real, they tend to push through it well

Avoidance
- Feeling fear directly[53]
- Untrustworthiness
- Betrayal
- Being cornered or controlled

Unmet Childhood Needs
- Safety, security, and certainty

Defense Mechanism
- Projection
    o Sixes unconsciously attribute their own unacceptable, unwanted, or disowned thoughts and emotions onto another as if they were the other's.
    o This functions for Sixes by creating a false sense of making their world more predictable.

Gifts Toward Resiliency
- Engaging, responsible, reliable, prepared, dutiful, sensible, loyal, trustworthy, truth-seeking, and faithful

---

53 To avoid fear, Sixes vacillate between *phobic* reactivity to fear and a counterphobic reactivity to fear. These are not two distinct sub-types among Sixes. Instead, Sixes can respond either way to fear. Some simply lean toward one response more than the other. When in phobic reactivity to fear, a Six gives in to fear and becomes mistrusting, apprehensive, and tense. In counterphobic reactivity to fear, a Six confronts the fear and/or denies it. In that case, the Six can look like an Eight.

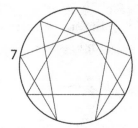

Sevens look for options and opportunities. They believe you must stay upbeat and keep your possibilities open to assure a good life. Consequently, Sevens seek pleasurable options, and are optimistic and adventurous. They also avoid pain and can be uncommitted and self-serving.

Core Belief
- "The world limits people, causing them pain and frustration."

Worldview
- "To avoid pain, I will explore all the exciting possibilities."

Where Attention Is Placed
- Options
- Interesting, fascinating, and pleasurable ideas
- New projects
- The interrelatedness or interconnectedness of ideas and options

Performance Under Stress
- Anxiety rises as the Seven realizes pain is inevitable
- They can also feel anxious when they feel trapped or when they have overcommitted

Avoidance
- Pain
- Frustrations
- Feeling trapped or being constrained

Unmet Childhood Needs
- Safety, security, and certainty

Defense Mechanism
- Rationalization
  - Sevens makes excuses for what they do, feel, or think.
  - It works for Sevens because they can reframe what might be negative or painful into something positive.

Gifts Toward Resiliency

- Spontaneous, versatile, optimistic, visionary, charming, light-hearted, friendly, innovative, and enthusiastic

———●———

Although these are brief explanations of the nine Enneagram types, you may have found it interesting to notice how the qualities and the worldviews differ by type, underscoring the fact that we are all intrinsically different and yet we are all human.

Studying the Enneagram helps you grow in compassion for self and for others—and the world is a much better place when you can be kinder to yourself and to others in your life. It can help you grow in acceptance, tolerance, and respect.

Understanding what each type avoids can also give you a better understanding of how one type might be more susceptible to a particular type of trauma than another, and how some may be more resilient.

Now that you have a basic understanding of trauma, the three centers of intelligence, and the nine Enneagram types, we will offer you ways in which you can learn to be resilient.

CHAPTER FOUR

Resilience and Recovery: Interrupting the Trauma Response

Your body is hardwired to guard you against any potential threat. Day in and day out, your body looks for ways to keep you alive. Once it experiences a threat—or what it believes to be a threat based on a memory of a traumatic event in the past—it does all it can to protect you.

Your body responds to the trauma by shutting down functions it sees as nonessential to your survival—things like reason, logic, and discernment. Those get shoved to the back seat while responses from your brain stem and limbic system take the driver's seat.

Depending on which part of your nervous system has been affected by the traumatic event from your past, your body either goes into an altered state of fight (to defend yourself), flee (to run away from the perceived threat), freeze (to stay still and become invisible), or fawn (to please the person who is a threat in order to avoid conflict).

Your body sees this trauma response as crucial to your survival, and it does not necessarily make sense. In fact, logically the trauma response often makes no sense at all. Say something triggered you and all you want is to be held so you feel safe and connected. But instead, you act aggressively, and you push the person away who is wanting to help you. (You will notice this happening in Thomas's story in the next chapter.)

The response to fight is rooted in your strong sense of fear due to past unresolved trauma. As a result, you cannot discern if the person wanting to help—the one you are now pushing away—is a safe person.

If you are someone who has unresolved trauma, it is likely that you experience this type of response every day. Your body keeps responding in ways to keep you alive—even when those strategies are not helpful, as they rarely are. This causes the trauma response to repeat itself, becoming another way of moving into a trauma loop. This is referred to as you being in a state of reactivity.

Not only does this occur in a truly traumatic situation, your body can respond in this manner anytime it feels overwhelmed or experiences a sensation that is a reminder of past traumatic experiences. And the more your body reacts to what it perceives to be a threat, the more ingrained the trauma loop becomes. This makes it harder for you to break out of reactivity.

It is like you are being held hostage to this trauma feedback loop, and until you intervene effectively, your body will hang on to the trauma response.

Remember the mini neuroscience lesson from the first chapter? The trauma response from the brain stem and limbic system interrupts the communication between your body and the cortex. If you want to break out of the trauma loop, it is crucial for you to learn how to restore the communication between the body, the emotions, and the higher functions of your brain.

What Is Resilience?

Restoring communication is a function of resilience. Resilience is more than being able to simply bounce back from difficult situations. It is about bringing the body back to a balanced state, to homeostasis, to healthy communication with your emotional and mental systems.

For many reasons, this is a complicated process, and it is a process that is unique to each person.

When functioning at its best, resilience is about finding the internal resources that best fit the situation at hand, then utilizing them with as little effort as possible to interrupt the trauma feedback loop so you can cope with the challenges, stress, and trauma you are facing.

Internal resources include energy, a positive outlook, perspective, engagement, and finding meaning and stability through secure relationships. They also include hope, faith, motivation, and the ability to grieve.

> *External resources include developing and using support systems, accessing finances, food security, safety, and education.*

The Importance of Internal and External Resources

Access to external resources—or a lack of access—can impact your capacity to be internally resourceful. If you have access to safety, food, clothing, and shelter, for example, you will have more energy to access internal resources like hope, belief, grief, or motivation. But if you are constantly in danger or looking for your next meal and you are not sleeping consistently, your energy will be focused on worry, hunger, safety, or fatigue. In the latter case, you are merely surviving—physically surviving.

Healing from trauma is an exhausting experience, so when you have access to supportive friends, family, and/or a therapist, it offers you more shoulders to help carry the weight. Having a support system is another external resource that allows you to reclaim your resilience.

Interrupting the Trauma Feedback Loop

In the first chapter, we referred to what happens during the trauma feedback loop, causing you to experience a past trauma as if it is happening in the present. We suggested that an awareness of what triggers the trauma loop is a helpful first step in beginning the process of recovery.

There are many ways by which you can interrupt the trauma loop. These interventions or practices may include working with what your body senses, how you feel, or what you think.

Throughout the rest of this book, we will offer you different practices based upon the Three-M Triad of resilience. Depending on your Enneagram type, your center of intelligence, and the details of your past trauma, you may find some practices more helpful than others.

Try as many practices as you need until you find the key to interrupting the trauma loop. Doing so will allow you to access all three centers of intelligence.

The Importance of Self-Compassion

Compassion means to "suffer with." Hence, to have *self*-compassion requires you to first notice that you are suffering. Sometimes, based on your type, history, or environment, you might not see the need to extend yourself compassion. You might choose to push through any suffering, not necessarily desiring self-compassion.

Because healing from trauma is an arduous road, the last thing you need is the inner critic pointing out all your failures and inadequacies. By enacting self-compassion, though, you allow yourself to move away from self-judgment and be kind to your weary soul.[54]

Self-compassion allows you to see your hurt and pain as something all humans experience rather than something that is wrong with you. It does not lead to isolation. Instead, self-compassion either moves you toward other human beings or toward solitude. And it allows you to slow down, becoming mindful of your limits, and celebrating your wins in recovery. Self-compassion is a must on the journey toward resilience.

> *Self-compassion moves you toward other human beings or toward solitude—not into isolation.*
>
> *Self-compassion allows you to see your hurt and pain as something all humans experience rather than something that is wrong with you.*
>
> *Self-compassion allows you to slow down, becoming mindful of your limits, and celebrating your wins in recovery.*
>
> *Self-compassion is a must on the journey toward resilience.*

Learning to be Resilient

Recovering from trauma is a slow process, yet when you begin to engage in slowing your **reactivity**—the behavior that you think is keeping you safe—and you begin to practice **receptivity**, you will experience healing and hope.

Receptivity is the invitation to be kindly or tenderly curious in life, but to be receptive, your nervous system must be calm. It signals elements of thriving.

Trauma steals your joy, humor, peace, and curiosity. It places you in a state of numbness. As your mind, body, and heart begin to heal, though, you will once again have access to joy, humor, peace, and curiosity. This is the fuel to receptivity, and receptivity offers you a doorway to resilience.

Receptivity is the invitation to be curious in life.

---

54   While we will go into detail on the different Enneagram types' response to events, it is worth pointing out here that self-judgement is a battle all types engage in one way or another. Ones, however, are *highly* attuned to their inner critic and will often find themselves in that space faster and sitting there longer.

The Power of Resilience

Resilience is the ability to bounce back, recover from, or adjust easily after stress, challenge, misfortune, or change. Resilient people can turn to their internal resources, scan them, and choose which is the best way of addressing specific situations integrating the behavioral, emotional, and mental possibilities.

Resilience requires awareness—a higher-level executive function—and is dependent on the status of the body and nervous system.

Your path to resilience will include learning about trauma, knowing your resilience skills based on your personality type, and incorporating practices that allow for a calm integration of your bodily sensations to enable you to regulate your emotions and discern your thoughts.

Enneagram-specific practices offer a holistic method to increase awareness, insight, self-compassion, and responses to relax your body and nervous system during or while recovering from trauma, providing a portal to receptivity in your recovery.

On your journey of recovering from trauma, moving from surviving to thriving depends on your ability to access skills of resilience. The good news is that these skills can be learned.

> **Resilience is the ability to bounce back, recover from or adjust easily after stress, challenge, misfortune, or change. Moving from surviving to thriving depends on your ability to access skills of resilience.**

Skills Needed to be Resilient

In Chapters Two and Three, we offered you an approach to resilience by integrating trauma-informed care and an Enneagram-informed approach to healing. Using these approaches, you can learn the skills you needed to be resilient, including:

- having self-awareness, that is, cultivating inner observation
- noticing where you place your attention
- calming your body and finding ways to return to a state of calmness
- being able to exercise emotional regulation and co-regulation
- being able to access higher mental capacities
- being able to integrate the trauma so all the systems of your body (physical, emotional, and cognitive) function as they should.

> *The keys to an Enneagram-informed approach to trauma resolution are:*
> - *accessing specific resilience skills according to your Enneagram type, and*
> - *incorporating practices that allow for*
>   - *a calm integration of your bodily sensations (incorporating body work through **movement**)*
>   - *regulating and co-regulating emotions (by developing **meaningful connections**)*
>   - *and discerning your thoughts by getting executive functioning back online (through **mindfulness**).*

In the next part of this book, we offer twelve stories that represent the nine Enneagram types. Each story portrays a different type of trauma. With each person, we will share their story, facts about the trauma, what resilience looks like for that type, and how each of the nine types might experience both vulnerability and resilience when exposed to this type of trauma.[55]

Although we have highlighted a particular trauma in each of the stories, you may notice more than one type of trauma in each story. This is common. Even when one trauma has been resolved, once a *new* trauma is experienced, residue of the previous trauma can show up. This is due to the deep rootedness and the embodied nature of trauma. As a result, unresolved trauma can pile up, making it more difficult to get through the next trauma. We might call this residual trauma or complicated trauma. However, the resilience you gained from a *previous* trauma can be instrumental in resolving *future* traumas.

**The resilience you gained from a previous trauma can
be instrumental in helping to resolve future traumas.**

---

55 Research is being conducted on the distinct neurobiology of each Enneagram type. This is aiding mental healthcare professionals in deepening their understanding of the body's looping reactivity to trauma.

At the end of each story, we share a practice specific to the type in the story that might be helpful to break the trauma loop. These are based on the Three-M Triad of resilience.

Please note that although each story is told through the lens of a particular Enneagram type, any type can experience any kind of trauma.

We acknowledge this is a brief overview and that there is much more to discuss to understand and resolve trauma. It is our hope that you can listen to each person's narrative, learn something about yourself and others impacted by trauma, and find the resilience within.

Part Two

Moving from Trauma to Resilience

*We start our stories with Enneagram type Eight
as that is the first type in the body center of intelligence.*

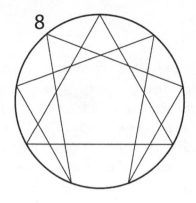

8

CHAPTER FIVE

Thomas's Story of Classic Post-Traumatic Stress Disorder

By the time seventy-two-year-old Thomas turned to us for help, his wife was ready to leave their marriage. She complained that her husband was unable to connect on an emotional level. He was neither willing to own his emotions, nor was he willing to or ask for her help in any situation.

Although Thomas was adamant that people who ask for help are weak, he turned to us for help at the insistence of his wife—his fourth in just fifteen years. When she gave him an ultimatum to get help or she would leave too, Thomas came for what would turn out to be months of therapy.

This was not his first try at seeing a therapist. Prior experiences had failed, he said, because he had difficulty respecting people, and he would test those around him to see if they were strong enough to handle his intense energy.

Previous therapists simply could not handle him, Thomas insisted. What he would not admit, though, was his fear that if he fell apart in therapy, the therapist would not be competent or strong enough to help him put himself back together.

Thomas's wife had complained that he was unable to emotionally connect with her. Thomas admitted he was comfortable with only *one* emotion: anger.

And Thomas's anger frightened his wife to the point that she often left their home, seeking safety with friends.

For Thomas, though, anger was his friend. He described it as somehow helping him feel powerful and in control. Plus, it allowed him to avoid dealing with all the things he was unable to control during his experience in the Vietnam War, where he had served for three years.

Thomas had never dealt with the trauma he had experienced in combat, and it did not take long for this to surface during his counseling sessions.

"They wanted to talk about the war," he complained, referring to his previous attempts at therapy. "I am *done* talking about the war."

He insisted that, unlike other veterans, he did not have PTSD. Instead, he was seeking counseling advice for what he described as "my inability to make intimate and emotional lasting connections in my life."

Thomas and his wife had no issues with physical intimacy. Their physical connection and chemistry were what kept them feeling alive as a couple. If only they could have the same emotional connection, things would be fine.

Though he might not have wanted to talk about the war, the impact of the war on Thomas was still very much alive within him, triggering him more often than he cared to admit.

Living close to an airfield, Thomas had flashbacks from the war whenever a helicopter flew by too close to his home. The same thing happened when he was surprised by loud noises. His body would tighten, his breathing would become shallow, and he would feel disoriented.

And then came the anger. When he got angry, Thomas got loud—really loud.

He would smash his fist through a wall. If he was in the car when he got triggered, he would start driving recklessly. This rage would be followed by bouts of insomnia, nightmares, night sweats, even self-criticism as he would beat himself up as being weak and helpless.

Still, he lacked any sense of fear, believed he was invincible, and insisted he did not have a problem.

Despite no longer being in the military, when we talked about the war, Thomas shared facts with eloquent detail yet with no apparent emotional connection. It was as if he was merely the observer recounting the facts and did not personally participate in the war. But his words were incongruent with the innocence in his eyes as he spoke about the devastation he had observed.

Still, there were signs of the trauma he had experienced. At times, Thomas's breath shifted from relaxed to almost gasping for air as he shared his words. Occasionally his eyes would tear up, and he would wipe the tears with his arm as though by doing this, no one would notice the emotion.

His eye contact varied, too. At times, his gaze was intense, but then he would stare into the distance for several minutes as he described some of his experiences, talking as if it happened to someone else. This was a coping mechanism that Thomas employed when he felt vulnerable to the information he was recalling.

Through it all, Thomas avoided any vulnerability and denied that he was impacted by the traumatic experiences of war.

Resilience in the Face of PTSD

Introducing Thomas to the Enneagram and giving him the power and control to identify his personality type was instrumental in his treatment. He liked that we were not the ones to tell him what his type was.

It did not take long for Thomas to identify that he was an Eight. He also appreciated discovering that there were others like him who had the same challenges, that he was not "defective."

As Thomas started trusting us more—something that took a long time—he shared about his past and began to soften.

He described a history of wanting to rescue others. Thomas also described how others had come to him to deal with problems they did not want to face, knowing they could count on him. Although he liked this some of the time, he often judged others as weak, something he insisted he would never be.

When describing his parents and his relationship to them, it was as though Thomas was talking about strangers. He told of growing up as an only child with a fair share of behavioral challenges. Thomas's parents did not know how to handle him, so by the second grade, they sent him off to a boarding school. But even there, Thomas acted out and got in trouble. He was finally sent back home.

Whenever Thomas misbehaved, his father beat him with a belt. Meanwhile, his mother—who drowned her cares in alcohol—responded by drinking more than usual. Thomas begged his mother to get help, but his requests were to no avail.

Thomas's father was a military officer and his role had them attend important events. Naturally, Thomas's mother attended these events, but she would get drunk at these events and publicly humiliate Thomas's father. This led to constant fights.

———•———

Thomas recognized that he made many decisions based on his gut instinct, and he knew he could count on most of them being spot on. He also said he could tell right away if someone was being honest with him or not.

As a young adult, Thomas had been a bodybuilder, and he was still pretty in tune with how his body felt. Although he struggled with emotions, he was able to recognize feelings in his body through his senses. This gave him reliable information about what was going on with him.

As we discussed basic information about traumatic responses, Thomas could relate to the fact that people who had experienced trauma were often not in touch with their bodies. He was able to identify how while in the past he could accurately sense what his body was telling him, he could no longer discern it as well as before the war.

Once he understood the trauma response and how this caused him to lose touch with his gut instincts, Thomas seemed to open up about the war, his service, and his past. He even began looking at his early boarding school experiences, where he could identify some of the trauma of being taken from his parents and placed in an environment where he felt powerless.

Due to Thomas's parents being emotionally unavailable to him and the fact that he was an only child, he came to believe that he could not count on anyone but himself. This was aggravated by the lack of understanding and support he experienced in school and by being bullied by other boys in the neighborhood.

Thomas developed a strong belief that any type of vulnerability was weak and that the weak would be annihilated. These beliefs were firmly in place well before Thomas was drafted into the Vietnam War at the age of eighteen. When he left for Vietnam, he had already lost two friends to the war.

When describing any part of his service in Vietnam, Thomas would sweat, his breathing became shallow, his focus would be distant but intense, and he would fidget. Initially, he was unaware of these reactions. He was only aware that he had to straighten his posture and all but hold his breath.

Through a series of body-awareness exercises, Thomas developed a way to check in with his body and his senses whenever he discussed anything about the war. He also identified some specific triggers of smell, sound, and touch that he associated with trauma.

With practice, Thomas learned to acknowledge his discomfort and not see it as being weak. He learned to ask for a moment to turn his attention to his body, scan it, and to deliberately breathe in a deeper way.

A father of two industrious children who served as first responders during the COVID-19 pandemic, Thomas saw his children going through some really tough times. He was able to recognize that they were experiencing symptoms of trauma similar to what he did after the war.

Thomas shared that once he understood his type and the way PTSD controlled his life, his response to his wife and children was different from before. Today, it brings him a great deal of comfort to listen and support his family. He no longer feels the need to jump to their protection or evaluate their competence. When they share their experiences with him, Thomas now is able to simply bring his strong presence as an Eight to be with them as an active listener without feeling a need to take over.

"It's funny how often I tell them to breathe," he told us with a twinkle in his eyes.

———•———

Being in touch with your body is a wonderful tool of resilience for trauma resolution. Because trauma is often first recognized in the body where it impacts functions like breathing and heart rate, your body awareness can be helpful in trauma resolution. But most people are not very aware of what is happening in their body when they experience trauma or a trauma feedback loop.

Having been a bodybuilder, Thomas was accustomed to noticing what was going on with his body. Hence, working with Thomas to develop even greater awareness of his body and how it was impacted by PTSD was easier than with many other clients.

For Thomas, the fact that he could wield some control and influence over his body was very appealing. He grew in awareness of how his bodily functions were impacted when trauma showed up.

Thomas implemented several types of breathing and stretching exercises into his trauma recovery. He also chose to employ the practice of walking in nature daily to begin his day, finding pleasure in being aware of how he placed his feet on the ground and being mindful of how his feet hit the earth. He was aware of how much power and control he had to adjust his gait, that he could choose to walk lightly or stomp, if he so wanted.

Thomas reluctantly agreed to his wife joining some sessions. The couple benefited from Thomas's wife learning more about PTSD and the differences between Enneagram types. As a result, their relationship has been strengthening.

> *Thomas began his healing by starting with the **body center** to ground himself and feel like he had control, then moved into the **heart center** to co-regulate with the help of his therapist, after which he could move into the **head center** where he put together all the pieces. By incorporating all three centers, Thomas found a greater understanding of what he needed to continue to manage the lack of predictability in his life.*

The Nine Types and PTSD

Body Types and PTSD

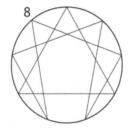

Vulnerability
- Because denial is the primary defense mechanism of Eights, it deters them from admitting that there is any problem that they cannot solve. As a result, Eights believe they are invincible.
- Eights avoid being vulnerable, seeing it as a weakness.

Resilience
- What helps is that Eights have an innate ability to push through and persevere when most other types would give up.
- They believe their bodies are invincible, thus they embrace an embodied approach to healing from trauma.

Vulnerability

- In a desperate attempt to calm their nervous system so they can avoid acknowledging the trauma of PTSD, Nines withdraw to a point of disappearing and participating in self-sabotaging behaviors.
- While others in their lives may express concern about the effects of PTSD, Nines remain unaware.

Resilience

- When Nines become aware of repetitive or self-sabotaging behaviors, they can more easily switch to other less self-sabotaging and regulating behaviors.
- Practiced over and over again with an accountability partner, even the most elementary of embodied interventions work well for a Nine.

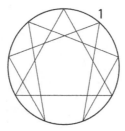

Vulnerability

- Through reaction formation—a disowning of their contradictory thoughts or actions—Ones will identify in those around them the very behavior they do not like about themselves.
- For Ones, the focus of attention is more on the need for reform than on what is going on with themselves and others. This keeps them from engaging in compassion for self and others.

Resilience

- When Ones recognize their powerlessness in regard to their symptoms and own it as a part of the trauma loop, they lighten up on self-judgment and can practice self-compassion.

- Once aware of their self-judgment, Ones can move into more compassion for self and others suffering from PTSD.

Heart Types and PTSD

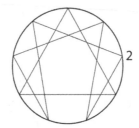

Vulnerability
- Twos will return to traumatic situations if they think they can be helpful to someone else. By returning, they can easily re-expose themselves to PTSD.

Resilience
- Twos are hardwired to seek connections, and they avoid being alone. This assists them in finding a person or community to co-regulate with and begin the healing process.

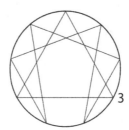

Vulnerability
- The fast-paced movement of all that needs to get done is a distraction that keeps Threes in a trauma loop until they are no longer able to complete a task.
- Threes often focus on a task with little regard for the impact it has on their health. This keeps them from acknowledging PTSD.

Resilience
- Once a Three realizes that mental health challenges require slowing down and that doing so does not reflect doing something wrong or

inefficiently, they are more likely to embrace the slower pace and will feel successful in accomplishing the task of slowing down.

- When accessing their own sensitivity, it is easier for Threes to reach out and connect with those around them, empowering their journey of healing.

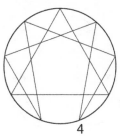

Vulnerability

- Prone to romanticization, staying in the PTSD trauma loop may be comfortable to Fours. Romanticizing may deter them from seeking help.
- The heaviness of the Fours' despair can keep them stuck in the trauma and may make it more difficult to move to resilience.

Resilience

- Fours have the innate capacity to hold and maintain intense emotion, hence they are not deterred in their recovery journey.
- Fours can be attracted to a community of support for survivors when other types may have some resistance to joining this type of group.

Head Types and PTSD

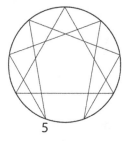

Vulnerability

- Fives' body center is often shut down and their head center is usually very active.
- They can become mentally paralyzed by gathering facts about the problem of PTSD.

Resilience

- Once Fives find evidence that interventions other than mental ones are the best trauma intervention, they are likely to give them a try—providing that they believe their findings.
- Fives will stay up to date on information about PTSD.

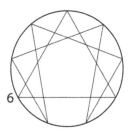

Vulnerability

- Constantly scanning for danger, Sixes are most susceptible to engaging in a trauma loop of any sort.
- Second-guessing and self-doubt may keep Sixes wondering whom they can trust and keep them from finding help.

Resilience

- When Sixes determine a situation to be dangerous—regardless of whether it is actually dangerous or not—they can break the trauma loop.
- Finding a trusted source of information is often the first successful intervention for a Six. If they experience success through a suggested process, Sixes are likely to continue to comply with the recommendations.

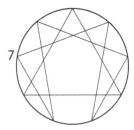

Vulnerability

- Sevens look for many other options to participate in, keeping them from addressing symptoms of PTSD.
- Despite their focus on avoiding pain, pleasurable activities may incite a trauma loop.

Resilience

- Sevens place optimistic attention on options and possibilities. This allows them to try new and exciting interventions.
- They have a general hardwired tendency to reframe events, which helps Sevens tolerate many difficult situations.

A Movement Intervention

The introduction of temperature change is helpful as a trauma intervention for Eights. Sensations arising in the body of Eights often feel warm to hot rather than cool, and they are often familiar with some level of anger.

When you find yourself in a situation where you become aware of your trauma response, remove yourself from the situation. If possible, find a bathroom or some privacy.

With your hands or a washcloth, briefly splash icy water on your face—as cold you can tolerate. If there is access to ice, you may even try wiping your face with ice water.

Alternatively, you could drink something ice cold or hold an ice cube in your hand. Notice what changes occur as you become more aware of the present.[56]

Facts About PTSD

Contrary to what many believe, anyone can develop PTSD: veterans and non-veterans, men and women, the very young, and the elderly. About 7 to 8 percent of the U.S. population will have PTSD at some point in their lives—that is up to twenty-five million people, based on current U.S. population estimates—and many more are affected by a loved one's PTSD. Chances are that someone you know has PTSD.[57]

Matthew J. Friedman, MD, PhD
Senior Adviser and former Executive Director, National Center for PTSD

PTSD is a term that was coined after the war in Vietnam. It was officially recognized by the American Psychiatric Association in 1980 when included in the third edition of the *Diagnostic and Statistical Manual of Mental Disorders*.

56 For additional interventions, please see Chapter Seventeen.
57 bit.ly/RaisePTSDAwareness

Beginning in the 1970s, a set of symptoms seen as similar to those from previous wars was prevalent with most returning service members who had been in combat in Vietnam.

These symptoms include agitation, irritability, hostility, hypervigilance, self-destructive behavior, social isolation, flashbacks, fear, severe anxiety, mistrust, loss of interest or pleasure in activities, guilt, loneliness, insomnia, nightmares, emotional detachment, and unwanted thoughts.

To add insult to injury, due to the amount of controversy surrounding the Vietnam War, returning military veterans were not welcomed home as heroes to be celebrated as those returning from other wars.

Members of the US military forces continue to encounter trauma not only during combat but also post combat. More than four million veterans or active-duty personnel serving since 9/11 report experiencing heartbreak, frustration, and confusion over the US withdrawal of troops from Afghanistan in 2021.

As for those having served both in Iraq and Afghanistan, 40,000 veterans received a post-deployment diagnosis of PTSD. We know that this population is notorious for having difficulty sharing their concerns. Still, there has been an uptick in concerns from veterans following the withdrawal from Afghanistan, and a 7 percent increase in calls to the Veterans' Affairs crisis line since the withdrawal. Some were impacted by images shown on the news, magnifying memories that these veterans might or might not have been working through.

The cost of the first year of treatment for PTSD is more than $2 million, or $8,300 per person, which is three and a half times higher than the VA spends on those without PTSD in the first year of their return.[58]

Signs/Symptoms of PTSD
- Your behavior might be agitation, irritable, hostile, hypervigilant, self-destructive, or you might move into social isolation.
- You might experience flashbacks, fear, severe anxiety, mistrust of those around you, or a loss of interest or pleasure in activities.
- Also common is feeling guilt, loneliness, insomnia, nightmares, or emotional detachment.

---

58 bit.ly/PTSDcost

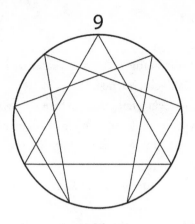

9

CHAPTER SIX

Amy's Story of Dealing with Family Violence

A my loved her life—all of it. Except for her marriage. At thirty-five, she began to realize how weary her body, heart, and mind were. She had been married for fifteen years, had two elementary-school boys and a third on the way.

As a child, Amy had been a quiet, sweet girl. She grew up in a two-parent home, her father a pastor and her mother a stay-at-home mom. Amy never caused any problems.

Growing up, Amy was very aware of the church's expectations of her family. Often, she would overhear her parents expressing their frustration to one another over the time and effort the church demanded of them, the lack of financial reward, and how hard it was to please the church members.

Her ears became attuned to the subtle conflict between her father, mother, and church elders—not that her parents were the only ones to suffer the wrath of the elders. She was at the local playground one day when an elder pulled her aside, berating her for how dirty her clothing was.

The man's words made her body feel hot and her heart beat faster. Amy ran and hid in her dad's office. But instead of comforting her, Amy's dad asked her to apologize to the man for being rude. She remembers being unable to get a word out and that her stomach churned.

Since that time, whenever she stood before men, Amy felt trapped and disappeared inside herself. Years later, Amy still identified with the sensations of becoming hot, her heart racing, and feeling like she was disappearing—the same sensations she had as a little girl. Her innovative way of retreating inward would become an effective coping mechanism in her marriage to an abusive husband, Jim.

When Jim would yell or slam the doors, Amy would disappear. She would lose track of time reading, playing her vinyl records for hours, or shopping mindlessly.

Fortunately, Jim was a touring musician whose job had him out of town most weeks from Wednesday through Sunday. This gave Amy the reprieve she needed. Those five days, life was peaceful. She and her sons had a rhythm that was simple and easy. It was when Jim was home that life became complex.

Amy would walk on eggshells, carefully managing every detail of the day to ensure there would be no conflict. Sometimes, she was good at it. But other times, she would miss something, and that would cause Jim to explode. He would yell at Amy and berate her. Other times, Jim would hurl his wife across the bedroom into a wall or slap her across the face.

If Amy sensed an explosion coming on, she would get the boys to their rooms so they could not see the mayhem. But more often than not, Jim's outbursts were unexpected and left her helpless on the floor while the boys witnessed their father's rage and their mother's pain.

By the time Amy was around six months into her pregnancy, she had less and less energy to stay on top of things, and the abuse became more frequent.

One morning, while she was unloading the dishwasher, a coffee mug slipped out of her hand and shattered, startling the boys and herself. The three of them began to laugh, but with Jim being home, Amy quickly silenced her boys. The laughter woke Jim up, and he stormed into the kitchen yelling obscenities at the three of them.

Amid Jim's rant, he grabbed dishes from the dishwasher, smashing them on the floor, and throwing them at Amy. As a mug hit Amy's back, her oldest son (then ten) ran and stood in front of his mother. He begged his dad to stop. Jim spewed a vile sentence into the young boy's face, stormed out of the kitchen, and went back to bed.

In shock, Amy and her boys sat on the floor among the broken plates and mugs, stunned. Amy felt anger rise in her body. She felt in her gut that this was the final straw. Jim had crossed a line by attacking their son.

Resilience in the Face of Family Violence

Amy's Nineness helped her survive intimate-partner abuse, and yet it kept her from leaving her toxic marriage. By avoiding conflict, she was kept somewhat safe. Still, Amy lived in silent terror, merely surviving.

She began secretly seeing us. In seeking counseling, Amy felt the gift of being believed and validated. We helped her understand the pseudo peace she had been living in by choosing not to rock the boat, how she had been ignoring her needs in order to manage Jim's rage.

This strategy was effective until it became utterly ineffective.

Amy began learning about the symptoms of family violence. In the process, she reclaimed her resilience by paying attention to her needs, finding a support system, and strategizing her exit from the marriage.

Amy started a journal where she listed things she needed in life—the basics such as food, clothing, shelter, a job, and emotional and physical security. Keeping her diary in the trunk of her car so her husband would not find it, the journal became a helpful reminder when she lost track of herself and her needs.

Amy admitted that for years, she had been asleep in the marriage. As she emotionally and physically awoke to the tragedy of it all, she realized her boys had seen her being choked, thrown across the room, and slapped in the face.

The greater Amy's awareness of her pain, as well as the pain her boys were experiencing, the greater her grief. Still, she utilized her skill of being diplomatic, patient, and kind to Jim until she could leave safely.

Amy's motivation behind her behavior reflects her type Nine personality: **Keep the peace at all costs.** Other Enneagram types will have different reasons for the way they respond to violent family systems. There will also be differences in how each type has access to resilience and begins the healing process.

*Amy began her healing by moving into the **body** center to reconnect with her intuition, then came back into the **head** center to access her discernment around the safety of herself and her children. Only then could she move into her **heart** center to truly grieve the loss.*

The Nine Types and Family Violence

Body Types and Family Violence

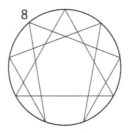

Vulnerability

- Prone to avoid vulnerability at all costs, Eights will not ask for help, even if they are trapped in intimate-partner abuse.
- They move to action quickly, often out of protection for self and others. As a result, family violence can escalate quickly. Due to their innate level of aggression, a type Eight victim may even be mistaken as being the perpetrator.

Resilience

- Eights are likely to respond to assist others less capable as they have the innate ability to focus on injustice. Stepping up for the sake of someone weaker than them (for example, a child) can help an Eight find a way out of a situation where family violence is prevalent.
- Eights can weather a storm; they have an innate capacity to reset and move on rather than staying trapped in an abusive relationship.

Vulnerability

- Nines are conflict avoidant and often make excuses for unacceptable behavior.
- Due to their motivation to "go along to get along" and not wanting to rock the boat, Nines might be more tolerant of family violence than other types.

Resilience
- With an innate capacity to de-escalate, Nines can become aware of their own needs and seek a way out of a relationship marked by intimate-partner abuse.
- Nines' capacity to defuse a rising conflict allows awareness for better self-care and the need to develop a strategy to attend to their own needs.

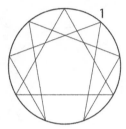

Vulnerability
- With an inner critic stronger in Ones than in any other type, they have a moral dilemma with leaving a primary relationship.
- Judging leaving as an incorrect decision, Ones may turn the focus to what they can personally do to improve the relationship.

Resilience
- With greater awareness, Ones can turn their focus to the fact that family violence is unacceptable, and they can take a deeper look at what needs to be changed in the relationship.
- Once their tendency to judge relaxes, it is easier for a One to do the next right thing.

Heart Types and Family Violence

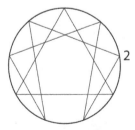

Vulnerability
- Twos see the potential of who people can become. Combined with their lack of healthy personal boundaries, this makes them especially vulnerable to family violence.

- They believe they can help others—often the abuser—even when they cannot.

Resilience

- As a Two grows in self-awareness, love of self becomes as important as love of others.
- Self-love helps Twos set healthy boundaries and make changes that reflect personal concerns.

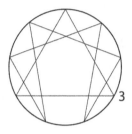

Vulnerability

- Fear of failure holds a Three captive to not making changes. They tend to stay trapped in a marriage due to their focus on what others would think of them if they left.
- Threes are often unaware of their own emotional and physical discomfort, thereby entering a state of numbness that causes them to check out emotionally.

Resilience

- Once Threes realize that the abuse is not a reflection of them being defective or having done something wrong, they can focus on their own change, needs, and recovery.
- Once shame has been illuminated, a Three can find a successful path out of shame.

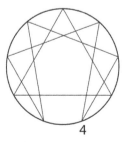

Vulnerability

- Fours are comfortable with reactivity and can resign themselves to the abusive relationship being familiar territory.

- For a Four, returning to the abuser is part of the dramatic experience of life. They may even subconsciously feel that returning makes the abusive relationship more alive.

Resilience

- As Fours become receptive to their internal emotional landscape, they can begin to identify that the way some emotions are expressed is not necessarily healthy.
- They have the ability to access equanimity. This calmness allows them to be present to what is going on in the moment, that it simply is what it is. Having access to equanimity also allows a Four to make an appropriate move out of an abusive situation.

Head Types and Family Violence

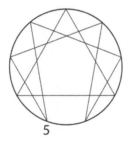

5

Vulnerability

- Fives find solace in solitude and in their own thoughts. This makes them vulnerable to staying trapped in abusive relationships.
- It is unlike them to trust others or ask for help. Instead, Fives might find themselves trying to research their way out of the abuse.

Resilience

- Fives could use their ability to research and gain knowledge about family violence. This knowledge can amplify their awareness of the danger they are in and help them to find a safe way to leave.
- Fives value internal resources like solitude. They may benefit from spending time alone practicing self-care and healing. As safety is secured, they will begin to grow emotionally, physically, financially, and spiritually.

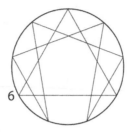

Vulnerability

- Sixes' propensity to loyalty and their value of authority cause them to doubt their intuition and question their role in the violent relationship, wondering whether they did something to cause the violence.
- They tend to replay what they are experiencing over and over in their head, leading to more doubt and inaction. This is the very essence of being paralyzed or stuck.

Resilience

- As Sixes develop, their courage to secure safety and certainty works to their benefit.
- Once they begin to trust their intuition, Sixes will plan their exit strategy. This strategy is often centered around their safety, wellbeing, and daily routine.

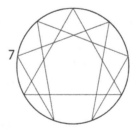

Vulnerability

- The positive outlook Sevens have and their avoidance of painful experiences cause them to defend the silver lining in challenging times. This can keep type Sevens in a risky situation, always hoping for and believing the best of their abuser.
- A Seven's ability to reframe situations can create an illusion that the violence will go away or that the abuser will change.

Resilience

- Always hopeful for a positive outcome, Sevens never lose faith in their family members.

- Their ability to reframe is used to Sevens' advantage, allowing them access to forward movement in life and to participate in life with humor and levity.

A Movement Intervention

 If, like Amy, you are a Nine, you can use grounding techniques to connect you to the present by bringing your awareness to quieting stressful behaviors, feelings, or thoughts.

Nines ground themselves by first noticing when they have disengaged or checked out. Becoming aware of when you are *not* present is vital to your practice of reengaging—that is, checking back in.

You may not be aware of the stress your body is holding until you begin to check back in with your body and your environment. Begin your practice with deep breathing. Inhale through your nose counting to four, hold for four, and exhale while counting to four. Repeat this at least three times.

Continue breathing deeply as you begin to engage your senses. Check in with your senses and identify what it is that you notice. What do you hear? What do you see? What do you feel? What do you taste? What do you smell?

If you are having trouble with this exercise, be more intentional with your five senses. Try holding a piece of ice, lighting a fragrant candle, or turning on some music. As you become more aware of the stress while you tune in to your body, allow yourself to continue to breathe through that awareness.

Facts About Family Violence

Family violence is also called domestic or intimate-partner violence. This type of violence destroys your sense of self, no matter your Enneagram type or family role. Family violence can include various kinds of abuses: physical, sexual, emotional, verbal, spiritual, or financial.

The closer the victim is to the abuser, the more significant the negative impact is on their self-worth. And while both men and women can be victims of family violence, women are at higher risk. The Centers for Disease Control and Prevention and the National Coalition Against Violence report one in four women will experience physical violence by their intimate partner at some point during their lifetimes, while for men, it is one in seven.[59]

---

59 bit.ly/FamilyViolenceFacts and bit.ly/NonFatalDomesticViolence

In 2017, the World Health Organization reported that abusers had intentionally killed 87,000 female victims that year alone. Of those women, 50 percent of their killers were intimate partners or family members.[60]

An abuser...

- controls who you are, who you are with, and what you are doing,
- destroys your belongings,
- threatens to hurt you, your children, other loved ones, and/or your pets,
- hurts you physically through hitting, beating, punching, pushing, kicking, or by using a weapon,
- forces you to have sex when you do not want to,
- blames you for their violent outbursts, and
- prevents or discourages you from going to work or school or from seeing your family and friends.

Often with physical abuse comes emotional or psychological abuse. This type of abuser...

- might stalk you,
- checks your phone, email, or social networks without your permission,
- controls your birth control or insists that you get pregnant,
- decides what you wear, eat, or how you spend money,
- purposely humiliates you in front of others,
- unfairly accuses you of being unfaithful,
- threatens to hurt themselves because of being upset with you,
- threatens to report you to the authorities for imagined crimes,
- says things like, "If I cannot have you, then no one can," and
- uses derogatory names to shame you.

Many victims show emotional signs, including disorientation, numbness, fatigue, delayed emotional development, social withdrawal, depression, and low self-esteem. Often victims experience debilitating doubt about who they are or how to make decisions.

If you, a family member, or a friend is a victim of domestic violence, remember: **Safety first**. The physical safety of a victim or their children is the primary concern. Seek expert advice in these situations.

---

60 bit.ly/GenderRelatedKilling and bit.ly/FactsAboutViolenceAgainstWomen

Signs/Symptoms of Domestic Violence

- Your behavior changes when you are with family and friends, often turning toward isolation, or describing a false picture of the intimate relationship.
- You might feel anxious or afraid of your partner most of the time, and often feel like you are the one who is crazy.
- Fearing your partner's anger, you avoid certain topics or situations.
- You check in often with your abuser or receive frequent harassing calls.
- You feel emotionally numb, trapped, or helpless.
- You feel intimidated or threatened.
- Physical signs include frequent injuries, use of a lot of clothing to cover up the injuries, and frequently missing work or school.

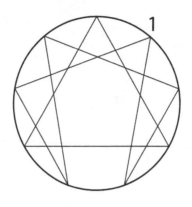

CHAPTER SEVEN

Saman's Story of Dealing with a Natural Disaster

Natural disasters leave people feeling helpless. Such events—tsunamis, hurricanes, tornadoes, floods, fires, volcanic eruptions, or derechos—often appear suddenly, creating the perfect storm for a trauma environment.

To navigate the ongoing, ever-changing landscape of the victims' physical and emotional lives, post-recovery efforts require flexibility from individuals as well as from their community.

This was the case for Saman who was born and raised in the beautiful country of Sri Lanka, an island nation in South Asia.[61] Sri Lanka has beautiful mountains intermixed with deep valleys, and it is surrounded by sandy beaches and the Indian Ocean.

---

61   While this is a story about resilience in the face of a natural disaster, it is also about more than
     that. It includes chronic, complex, and acute traumas. Saman and his wife's journey—growing
     up in Sri Lanka during a civil war, immigrating to the United States, and experiencing the
     2004 tsunami—is full of perseverance, tenacity, and resilience. Despite chronic stressors, they
     discovered the grit to carry on.

The island is diverse in religion and home to over twenty million people representing two ethnic groups, the majority being Sinhalese and the minority being Tamil.

Saman is Sinhalese, but his mother had raised him to support humanity over civil unrest, something Sri Lanka had plenty of. He recalls how he and his brother would intervene when their Sinhalese community would chase their vulnerable Tamil neighbors.

It was not just that one group would spew comments at the other. The tension between the country's people groups was rooted in discrimination and violent persecution.

By 1993, Sri Lanka had two full-on civil wars. There was the culture-based war in the north between the Sinhala and the Tamil Tigers, while the south was being ravaged by the People's Liberation Front (the JVP), a Marxist revolutionary group composed of disaffected Sinhalese university students and school children acting as domestic terrorists.

This was the environment Saman and Nirmala—the Sinhalese woman he would eventually marry—grew up in. The sound of gunshots was all too common in their cities. Something as simple as going outside would not be safe. Instead, they would receive announcements under their doors stating when they could leave their homes.

Both Saman and Nirmala recall not only hearing bombings but also seeing buses being blown up. Saman was even threatened with his life for not joining JVP protests, and one of Nirmala's family members was executed for flying the national flag.

Each in their own way, Saman and Nirmala learned that silence kept you safe. Speaking out got you killed. Nevertheless, both had a desire for justice and peace in their country.

Saman talks about having two options to move through those challenging times: study hard and get a decent job or become a part of making change through violence. He chose to focus on his studies and get a decent job. This offered his family more opportunities and allowed him to help in ways that led to positive changes for them.

During their time spent in their war-torn country, Saman and Nirmala each experienced anger, yet it surfaced quite differently. For Saman—who would during his conversations with us years down the road discover that he was an Enneagram type One—his anger lay beneath the surface, fueling action to make things right, correcting the injustices around him, and participating in causes while focusing his attention on the details and trajectory of his education.

Nirmala's anger—when she was attuned to it—was hot and fiery. As a Nine, she quickly moved into peacekeeping conversations, desperately trying to see all the angles of the war.

After more than twenty years of living amid the civil wars, Saman and Nirmala left their homeland. A few years after becoming citizens of the United States, Sri Lanka was hit by a devastating tsunami.

Waves as high as a four-story building ravaged Sri Lanka's shores on December 26, 2004, while many Sri Lankans along with foreign tourists were packing the beaches and resorts around the country. Two hours before the tsunami hit, a massive underwater earthquake had occurred in Indonesia.[62]

To focus on recovery efforts, the warring factions in Sri Lanka signed a ceasefire agreement. However, in the northeastern part of the country, hundreds of landmines had been uprooted and moved by the wave, posing threats to those who were trying to reach communities in the area to provide medical and humanitarian support.

The civil war had impacted the country's infrastructure and morale, and it had caused thousands of people to be displaced, further amplifying the devastation caused by the tsunami.

While Saman and Nirmala were thousands of miles away, it did not take long for them to start receiving one phone call after another from family back in Sri Lanka. Horrified yet powerless, they watched live news coverage and listened to stories.

They were told of how the ocean at first receded significantly. Curious, many people ran to the receding water. Then came the horror. The enormous wave caught people off guard. Curiosity and the lack of a tsunami warning signal brought many to their deaths. (Interestingly, animals instinctively fled into the hills.)

---

62 This tsunami was triggered by an underwater earthquake off the coast of Indonesia. The earthquake measured 9.0 or more on the Richter scale and lasted almost ten minutes, the longest quake ever recorded and the most violent of the twenty-first century. It raised the seabed by several meters, which displaced massive volumes of water. This triggered a massive tsunami that was centered mostly in the Indian Ocean.

   The worst waves were in Aceh, Indonesia, measuring almost 100 feet. More than 1,000 miles from the epicenter, Sri Lanka's coastline was battered by waves as tall as forty-one feet. In Sri Lanka alone, more than 90,000 buildings were destroyed by the tsunami. bit.ly/The2004Tsunami

As the day wore on, Nirmala learned of the death of her grandmother who had been enjoying the Christmas holiday with Nirmala's sister and husband. She was relaxing by the pool when the wave hit their resort.

Resilience in the Face of a Natural Disaster

Although far from their family, Saman and Nirmala found meaning in their Sri Lankan roots. While feeling overwhelmed and powerless, both experienced a lot of anger in the wake of the tsunami. They were each able to access and manage their anger in a productive way, though, harnessing the power anger can bring if managed and understood.

Their anger moved them into action, helping them to find solutions for their friends and family back home. Understanding the reality of how vulnerable they were even before the tsunami, the couple fought hard for the victims, asking for help by seeking the engagement of their community. Several Sri Lankan American communities came together as a source of social support and strength. With his brother, Saman created a non-profit organization so they could provide the support and organization to build hundreds of new homes.

Because of their long-term encounters with hardship, Sri Lankans are generally filled with vitality as a way of living. This was true for Saman and Nirmala. And although the war had caused feelings of entrapment, fear, grief, and anger, the couple had a shared perspective on trauma recovery from the war. After the tsunami, this became their guide for resilience.

While they had come to appreciate the political, social, and infrastructure stability in the United States, they were well aware of the stark contrast in Sri Lanka. There, the roads had been difficult to travel on even before the tsunami, and the emergency efforts to reach people after the disaster were treacherous.

Between Saman's value for humanity and Nirmala's unconditional positive regard for people, the couple devoted their energy and awareness to social action while the injustices back home gave them the energy to keep going.

Considering past experiences of overcoming war trauma, they maintained a positive attitude that their homeland would recover over time.

> Saman began his healing by moving into the **heart** center to sit with his grief for his country, then came back into the **head** center to engage in strategy around how he could help his country. This allowed him to finally move into his **body** center, putting action to his strategy.

The Nine Types and Natural Disasters

Body Types and Natural Disasters

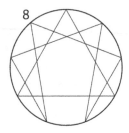

Vulnerability
- Eights are either all in or not in at all, so if they choose to disengage, they will take no action. But if they choose to engage, they may over-react and expose themselves to danger. This is due to their power to overcome challenges combined with the adrenaline rush.
- Despite a crisis unfolding around them, Eights are unlikely to recognize their limits and may resist asking for help as this can feel vulnerable.

Resilience
- Eights' innate leadership qualities can help them weather the storm.
- They naturally want to protect others and have the capacity to maintain their energy in the long term.

Vulnerability
- During a disaster, Nines can lack awareness of the specific impact the event has had on them and others by narcotizing—indulging in activities that are not helpful.
- Nines' tendency not to take action can keep them trapped in the crisis of a natural disaster.

Resilience
- Once awakened, Nines find power in hearing what their and others' needs are.

- They have a strong desire to help others and bring the community together, which can unite others in the grip of a natural disaster.

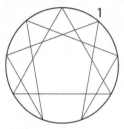

Vulnerability

- When facing a natural disaster, Ones can get stuck in all that needs to be fixed. As a result, they can become inflexible and unable to adapt.
- Ones tend to need to do things right, which is often not possible amid a disaster. This can lead to them becoming stuck due to frustration around the chaos and all that is needed for recovery.

Resilience

- What can help Ones get through a disaster is their innate attention to getting things back in order. They tend to use proven ways to recover rather than reinvent the wheel, which can speed up recovery.
- Conscientious and driven to make the situation better for everyone, Ones are naturally drawn to addressing the injustices and disparities that arise in the community after a natural disaster.

Heart Types and Natural Disasters

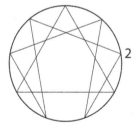

Vulnerability

- Twos' desire to help others can lead to them overextending themselves, which can lead to exhaustion. This can exacerbate the impact of the disaster.
- After a disaster, a Two can get stuck in the emotions surrounding the events and not know where to start the cleanup and recovery process.

Resilience

- Twos have an innate desire to be helpful.
- They intuitively know where help is needed, are generous with their care, and focused on the needs of others.

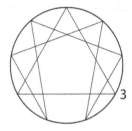

Vulnerability

- The impact of a natural disaster might cause a Three to become frenzied in their behavior, looking for the normal flow of life to return. This frustration over the lack of flow might exacerbate the impact of the disaster and impede recovery efforts.
- During disaster recovery, Threes can overextend themselves by working around the clock.

Resilience

- With their strong desire for communities to recover and function efficiently and productively, Threes are always ready to work.
- They tend to have the capacity to develop talent, which can help the community to build and recover.

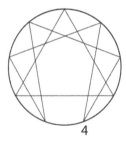

Vulnerability

- When facing a natural disaster, Fours might get stuck in the emotionality of the experience.
- Fours are self-focused and lack global awareness. They can also get trapped worrying that they will never recover and that life will always be this way.

Resilience

- Fours do not avoid difficult situations, and they have the capacity to sit with others' pain.
- They can see all the victims are going through, allowing authenticity of the hurt to be seen and heard.

Head Types and Natural Disasters

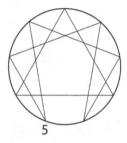

5

Vulnerability

- During a natural disaster, Fives can be overwhelmed by the chaos. Being overwhelmed, they will retreat inward and quit engaging emotionally.
- Fives will turn their focus to the fact that they do not know what is going on. Trying to make sense of the events, they will focus on gathering information instead of taking action.

Resilience

- Fives' ability to detach from the emotional impact of events can make them resilient to disasters. It also helps that they are adept at gathering accurate information.
- Fives can show immense dedication to recovery efforts.

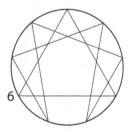

6

Vulnerability

- Sixes are prone to second-guess which actions to take. This is intensified during a natural disaster.
- Their tendency to either move away or plunge through is a fear reaction to the events unfolding around them.

Resilience

- With trusted, authoritative information, Sixes will take brave action.
- They have a dutiful commitment to taking action. Examining strategies and seeing the reality of what is, Sixes will break free from the grip of trauma of a natural disaster.

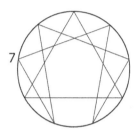

Vulnerability

- Sevens are experts at avoiding pain in all ways, including when dealing with natural disasters. They anticipate the scenario will improve.
- Because they are moving so fast, Sevens might create a safety hazard by not paying attention to what is going on.

Resilience

- Sevens' positivity provides hope for all, even amid tragedy.
- Naturally prone to strategize and look for options, Sevens come up with innovative ideas for resolution. They genuinely care about every-one getting help.

A Movement Intervention

Type Ones are in the body center of intelligence. Quieting your body during times of stress is very helpful. As a One, you carry your stress and heartache in your body, especially in your face, shoulders, and hands, and are often unaware the stress is just beneath your skin.

Quiet your body by slowing your breathing. Tune in to where you notice the stress in your body. Now notice your facial expressions. Is your face at rest? To determine your face's level of rest, try face "scrunchies."

Scrunch up your face or tighten it. Hold for five seconds then release. Alter-natively, you can blow air into your cheeks, and hold for five seconds, and release.

You may also try shoulder shrugs if you notice tension or tightness. Raise your shoulders to your ears, hold for five seconds, and relax. Do shoulder shrugs until you feel the release of your shoulders to a resting state.

The same goes for your hands. Make tight fists, hold for five seconds, then stretch out your fingers as far as you can. Repeat this until your hands are relaxed.

Facts About Natural Disasters

The 2004 Indian Ocean tsunami was unexpected and had a global impact. Worldwide, 250,000 people were killed by the freak wave while thousands more who survived were left homeless, injured, and suffering illnesses.

In Sri Lanka alone, over 30,000 citizens died in the tsunami, and countless more were added to camps already overflowing with internally displaced people.

Much like with Saman and Nirmala's story, Sri Lankans living abroad were also impacted by secondary trauma, compassion fatigue, and running out of resources to support their communities back home.

The impact of the natural disaster on Sri Lanka was compounded by the demographics, culture, geography, civil unrest, as well as the lack of structure, organization, and preparedness. The racial disparities and the country's prior concerns with economic and educational systems further contributed to the impact of the tsunami.

What's more, the twenty-five-year civil war in Sri Lanka had killed as many as 100,000 people and caused around 300,000 to be stuck in camps around the country, leaving much of the population with little to no hope.

To make things worse, many Sri Lankans do not have birth certificates, driver's licenses, or property deeds. This contributed to an inaccurate accounting of deaths.

On a positive note, the lack of structure, organization, and order allowed for non-governmental organizations and governments from other countries to respond quickly with there being no political red tape. As a result, the country was easily accessible to anyone who wanted to come and assist.

As for other natural disasters:

- Seventy percent of survivors typically do not get mental health related services after they experienced a natural disaster.
- In the last decade, forty natural disaster events have cost the US government at least $1 billion.
- Sixty percent of survivors report five or more types of emotional challenges in their first year after the disaster. [63]

---

63 bit.ly/DisastersAndMentalHealth

To recover from a natural disaster, the most basic external resources—clean water, sustainable food sources, and adequate medical care—are vital. It is crucial to attend to these basic needs before focusing on emotional or mental recovery.

Once the victims' physical and safety needs have been met, they will have the energy to focus on needs such as employment, finances, health, a sense of connection and intimacy, friendship, freedom, respect, strength, and self-esteem.

Signs/Symptoms of Victims of Natural Disasters

- Victims of natural disasters might experience intense or unpredictable feelings. They may also see changes to thought and behavioral patterns.
- Their sensitivity to environmental factors heightens. They might find sirens, loud noises, burning smells, and other environmental sensations to stimulate memories.
- There might be strain in interpersonal relationships or stress-related physical symptoms like headaches, nausea, chest pain, or muscle tightness.

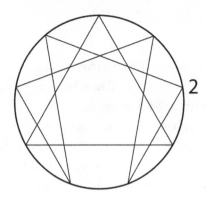

CHAPTER EIGHT

Remy's Story of Complicated Grief

Remy is a direct and soft-spoken woman in her late sixties. Articulate and warm, she was educated as a marriage and family therapist—a field she had personally struggled in, having been married twice and been in other less-than-ideal relationships.

By the time she came to see us, Remy had recently gotten married for the third time. "This relationship is very different," she insisted. "Zachary and I are supportive of one another. We have good communication, and we are both able to address any conflict and to walk through it with grace and respect."

———◆———

Remy decided at a young age that she would never marry someone like her father. In addition to being addicted to benzodiazepines and sex as well as being openly unfaithful to his wife, he was a man with a terrible temper.

Remy and her three younger siblings never knew when their dad would explode. He was verbally and physically abusive, and he frequently ridiculed his wife. He even incited the children to join him in berating their mother.

Remy's grandfather, whom she called "Poppy," was her safe person. She spent hours with Poppy every week and was devastated when he passed away.

Not long after Poppy's passing, her best friend's dad was murdered by the Mafia. The secrecy around his death led to Remy believing that you could neither be honest nor truly expressive about grieving.

She met her first husband, Fimm, when they were in high school. When Fimm went off to college, Remy skipped her senior year to follow him. Soon, they got married and moved to yet another part of the country. Remy worked two full-time jobs and took care of their home, all while studying.

But Remy was homesick. After they both completed graduate degrees, they finally moved home. Soon after, she got pregnant. While pregnant, it became apparent to Remy that they had sexual problems. She thought it might be that Fimm was frightened of being sexually intimate with Remy during her pregnancy, but Fimm's avoidance of Remy continued well past the birth of their child.

That was when Remy sought therapy for the first time. She internalized their marital problems, believing that her husband's disinterest in sexual intimacy was her fault, that she might have too strong a sexual appetite, like her father had.

During her second pregnancy, Remy learned she was a carrier of Tay-Sachs disease (TSD), a deadly condition that affects children. Fimm also tested positive as a carrier of TSD, so there was a 50 percent chance their baby would not only be a carrier, but she would be affected with the disease. Babies with TSD are born looking healthy, but they live only about two years before their organs begin to fail, leading to a slow death.

Despite worrying about this potential loss, Remy believed she could not express her worry or sadness. Instead, she focused on other things, leaving her unprocessed grief and worry unresolved.

Fortunately, their baby daughter ended up only being a carrier of TSD. Remy experienced a different kind of death in that season, though. Shortly after the birth of their daughter, Fimm came out as being gay. Rather than leave her, Fimm wanted to have both her and his lover in their life.

Remy knew there were many things that could change with therapy, but it was unlikely that one of those things would be her husband's sexual preferences. With that realization, she was finally ready to let Fimm go. After many years of putting up with Fimm's behavior, Remy had finally had it and filed for a divorce.

It took less than a year for her to fall in love again and get married to Harry. They had also known each other since high school.

Harry, with whom she would end up having two more children, was a successful business professional. But he was also needy and narcissistic, and he had a gambling problem. Still, Remy argued that gambling was not as bad as, say, alcohol or drugs.

But then her car was repossessed, and next, their home went into foreclosure. Meanwhile, Remy worked hard to take care of her four children while also having a full-time job.

As hard as her marriage was, Remy did not want to fail at another relationship, let alone go through another divorce. So, she worked hard to save the marriage. But when she was held legally responsible for Harry's debt and civil legal charges were filed against her, she called it quits.

Within months after her second divorce was granted, Fimm died of AIDS. And six months later, Harry passed away from a heart attack.

There was no time to grieve, though. Remy had too many things to take care of legally, financially, and personally.

Although Remy's life seemed less chaotic than while her spouses were alive, she continued to function in survival mode because of the unresolved grief and trauma.

It would take ten years before Remy would date again.

———•———

Remy's story is about the type of complicated grief where early unresolved grief intersects with new losses and with a series of traumatic events coming too fast and furious to be resolved.

She showed up for therapy after she learned about the Enneagram, fascinated with how it might help those she served in her counseling practice. True to her type, a Two, Remy was eager and focused on helping others while paying little attention to her own needs. During her Enneagram training, though, her mentors encouraged Remy to do her own work before trying to help others. They encouraged her to identify her needs, express them to others, and relax the self-judgment that followed for having needs.

"I don't think I knew how to live without taking care of others," Remy admitted. She was mildly aware of being overwhelmed and resentful, but it did not occur to her that she could say no to others and set boundaries.

It was not until she was introduced to the Enneagram and identified as a type Two that she was able to see her pattern of focusing on others, not attending to her own needs, and being overwhelmed and resentful.

In our times together, Remy went on to investigate her life. She began with early childhood messages about gender expectations, intergenerational trauma, complicated and delayed grief, abandonment, and betrayal. And for the first time, she addressed the fact that she was an adult child of an addict.

Resilience in the Face of Complicated Grief

When Remy first met Zachary and considered marriage, she knew she was no longer simply looking for someone to take care of her and her children or for a partner she could care for.

As she told us her life story with all the loss, betrayal, and codependency, Remy began to grow awareness of how resilient she was. She was aware she had experienced complicated grief in addition to various other types of trauma.

"The richest insight of all," Remy told us, referring to the sensate interventions we were using during sessions, "is that I must begin by calming my nervous system. I learned to do this with different breathing techniques and various body practices. Even though I am a Two, a *heart* type, resilience starts by working in and with my *body*."

Remy's early history revealed a strong appropriate secure attachment with her mother. As the firstborn, she was attended to with strong intergenerational support from several family members. She was validated and acknowledged for her ability to relate and connect with others. She was also praised for her kindness, her ability to be present with others, and her ability to articulate her thoughts.

Remy had a solid early childhood foundation to support bonding, connectivity, and wanting to show up and be present in relationships.

> *Remy began her healing by moving into the* **body center** *to ground herself and physically express emotions such as strong anger, then came back into the* **heart center** *to embrace her own emotions more fully. Finally, she could move into her* **head center** *to set boundaries that kept her on track with self-care.*

The Nine Types and Complicated Grief

Body Types and Complicated Grief

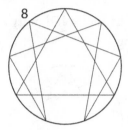

Vulnerability
- Although Eights are typically very present to being with others (through active listening, for example), they are often not present to loss. Much like Threes, they focus on what needs to be done instead.
- Eights attend to the details and not the emotional requirements of the experience, which makes them more vulnerable to the impact of complicated grief.

Resilience
- When in touch with vulnerability and their personal sadness, Eights can move through the grieving process and access their innocence.
- Once in touch with the vulnerability of human suffering, Eights can be tender and move toward the grief.

Vulnerability
- Nines may remain asleep to their emotional experience as they encounter grief. In doing so, they function much like Twos by focusing on the needs of those around them.
- They can easily get distracted by other issues that need their attention in the moment, especially if there is conflict between others.

Resilience

- Nines innately move to a peaceful awareness, allowing for acceptance of loss as a natural part of life. This is an exceptional gift in dealing with grief.
- The innate virtues of harmony and unity allow Nines to bring together those who are grieving.

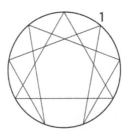

Vulnerability

- Ones live with a level of dissatisfaction and a sense of loss. When grief gets complicated, it magnifies the loss already present, causing them to feel that the world and everyone in it could be better.
- When they encounter a personal experience with loss, Ones may reach an even deeper low.

Resilience

- Daily wanting a better world, Ones innately grieve. Loss is a normal experience for them, something they can grieve daily.
- Ones will attend to the mores and values of others who are grieving. This can help them move through their own grief.

Heart Types and Complicated Grief

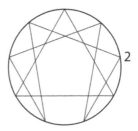

Vulnerability

- Focusing on the needs of others, Twos often postpone their grieving process. In fact, Twos may not grieve until they are overwhelmed.
- Twos might become resentful of taking care of others.

Resilience

- Twos who are in touch with their own sadness become more aware of their own emotions and not just the emotions of others.
- Once they learn to offer the same love and support to themselves as they offer others, Twos can move through the grief process.

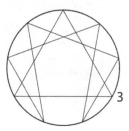

Vulnerability

- Threes often ignore their internal emotional landscape and may get caught up in the to-dos.
- They do not process their emotions in real time. As a result, others may see Threes as cold.

Resilience

- When Threes slow down enough to allow the arising emotions, they have access to a wealth of compassion and grace that they can extend to both self and others.
- Threes are able to attend to details, such as a funeral, setting their feelings aside and showing up for others.

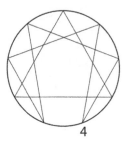

Vulnerability

- Fours romanticize loss and grief to the point of sometimes loving the experience of grief.
- Their affinity for grief can lead to an extended grieving process which can keep them from moving forward.

Resilience

- Fours do not resist the process of grief.

- They have the innate capacity to tolerate the intense emotional roller coaster and unpredictability of how and when sadness shows up.

Head Types and Complicated Grief

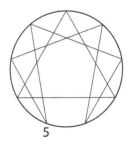

5

Vulnerability
- Following multiple losses, Fives may be drawn to focusing on the existential nature of loss.
- To move through their process of grieving, they may resist support and engagement from others.

Resilience
- By compartmentalizing, Fives can handle multiple instances of grief without creating a domino effect.
- Truly sensitive by nature, Fives want others to reach out to them but not in an intrusive way. They are also innately comfortable with solitude, making it easier to move through grief without being involved in support groups.

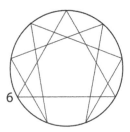

6

Vulnerability
- When Sixes feel blindsided by multiple losses, they might spiral into a deeper fear than is typical for their type.
- Their fear response might be the freeze response, which could perpetuate the experience of grief.

Resilience

- Sixes are often prepared for loss, constantly anticipating what might be—especially if someone is sick or the loss is expected.
- They innately access the courage they need to move through difficulties associated with complicated grief.

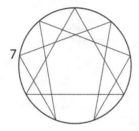

Vulnerability

- Sevens tend to avoid the experience of anything painful.
- As loss is associated with pain, Sevens will go out of their way to find ways to avoid this natural experience of life, often in self-destructive ways.

Resilience

- Sevens are experts at reframing situations and finding the good or the silver lining. This allows them to move from sadness into a more pleasant experience.
- They are skilled at planning celebrations of life and keeping positive memories alive.

A Movement Intervention

Twos are part of the heart center. Like Remy, Twos may be sensitive to the sensations, emotions, and thoughts of others, yet they are not necessarily present to their own.

One way you can discern what *your* sensations, emotions, and thoughts are, is to do some investigating. Have a pen and paper handy so you can jot down what you become aware of. There is no right or wrong, no good or bad. You are simply invited to pay attention.

Take time away from others and away from distractions. Turn your attention inward and find a comfortable pace to your breathing. Think of a situation that happened recently—not a traumatic one but something that was significant.

With your attention focused internally, record any bodily sensations that occurred as you considered the situation. Then record any emotions you were aware of about the situation. Finally, record any thoughts you had about the situation.

Once you have completed writing, review what you wrote, and confirm that these were *your* sensations, emotions, and thoughts—not those of others.

While this practice starts in the body center, it moves to the heart center, and finally to the head center.

Facts About Complicated Grief

Complicated grief is typically grief that is unresolved. It has the following symptoms:

- Never-ending focus on the loss to the exclusion of everything else
- Feelings of intense, daily longing
- Numbness and feelings of detachment
- Depression
- An inability to manage daily affairs because of the overwhelming nature of the grief
- Constant feelings that life is meaninglessness
- Irritability
- Inability to co-exist with others
- Replaying aspects of the person's death over and over in the mind
- Lack of involvement in the world, spending all non-working hours at home, usually alone
- Bitterness and anger toward the world
- Withdrawal from family life or social activities
- Lack of trust in others and cynicism about people's good intentions
- Either intense attachment to or a total rejection of reminders of the departed person
- Negative emotions that are constantly triggered by exposure to those reminders or by memories of the lost loved one
- Suicidal thoughts, feeling like death is the most attractive alternative

Signs/Symptoms of Complicated Grief

- Symptoms of complicated grief can include intense sorrow, pain, and rumination over the loss of your loved one, focus on little else but your loved one's death, and extreme focus on reminders of the loved one.
- It can also include intense, persistent longing or pining for the deceased.

- Numbness and detachment can also be seen. You might also have trouble carrying out normal routines and may isolate from others or withdraw from social activities, even to a point of excessive avoidance.
- It is also common to experience depression, deep sadness, guilt, or self-blame.

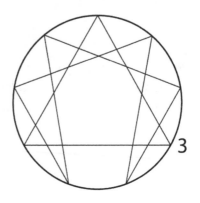

CHAPTER NINE

Clint's Story of Growing Up in Poverty

The youngest of two boys, Clint is a Black man who grew up in a struggling single-parent home on the outskirts of Richmond, Virginia. But what Clint's mom, Martha, lacked in financial resources, she made up in a multitude of ways.

When Clint was just a baby, his mom used to take him and his brother, Carl, to the local Women, Infants, and Children Program where they were given milk and cheese in exchange for a blood donation. Their mom also supplemented their food supplies with donations from the local food bank.

Judging by the way they looked, you would never know they were poor. Martha taught her boys how to take really good care of what they had—including taking good care of themselves. And though their outfits were from the Salvation Army, Clint and Carl were always clean and well-dressed.

Martha ruled the house with order and demanded respect from her two young boys. Not having a car, she took two buses to and from work. She had a full-time job at a local manufacturing plant and a side job on Saturdays clerking at the corner grocery store.

As far back as Clint could remember, his mother would wake them while it was still dark out, hastily give the instructions for breakfast, and run to the bus stop.

Every evening, Clint would be at the small apartment window, watching for his mother. He knew he would have her for one hour before he needed to go to bed. He strategically planned every homework question, concern, or story he wanted to share with her.

Clint learned early on that the better the stories, the grades, or the sporting events he could win, the bigger it would make his mom smile. To him, it seemed as if it made his mom's day better, and he felt a sense of pride when he worked hard and achieved something. As a result, Clint made it a point to be the best at all he did so his mom would be very proud of her son.

That sense of pride when he achieved something drove Clint to do more and work even harder—something he was not afraid of at all. In fact, due to his socioeconomic and racial background, Clint knew that if he wanted to get ahead, he had to work harder and perform better than all his friends at school.

He dreamed about the day when he could work and take care of his mom. He knew, though, that the world was unfair and harsh. He got bullied a fair share, and in his mind, everyone around him had it better than him.

As he grew older, Clint would watch his white friends' easy way of life and wonder what it would feel like to live so free of cares. He studied their every move, how they talked, walked, and how they got attention.

Clint's mom had taught him to keep his home life private, not to speak about the differences in lifestyle, neighborhoods, or the fact that she had to work so much. By being private about his life, acting like the other kids, and excelling in sports, Clint blended in more and evaded being bullied.

Clint's friends had no idea how poor he was. Nor did they know anything about the neighborhood from where he was bused in every day. To them, Clint was just another kid.

Resilience in the Face of Poverty

Clint came to see us when he was already in his sixties. He still lives in the South, and much of his way of life is the way it had been growing up, except for the fact that he is now financially secure.

He still lives humbly, though, driving a beat-up truck. "I don't want a new car," Clint explained. "People might think I'm too rich." People's opinions matter to Clint, especially their first impressions of him. Despite driving an 80s truck, Clint is meticulous about how he dresses.

When Clint learned about the Enneagram, he easily recognized that he was a type Three. As a Three, Clint faced his childhood challenges with a positive outlook and was able to fit in.

Looking back at his childhood, Clint described his mom's reliance on faith as an underpinning to their little family of three. To this day, his faith continues to keep him strong and give him meaning.

Another plus was his ability to make friends while picking up on societal norms. While growing up, this provided Clint with a large social circle. His natural charm and inviting spirit also kept him on his teachers' and youth ministers' radars. Clint used the relationships he was able to foster, along with his achievements, to help him overcome the obstacles of growing up in poverty.

Clint was able to identify how he had found ways daily to compartmentalize his hunger pains, the used clothes he had to wear, and the limited time he had with his mom.

He was also able to see how, despite his mom working two jobs and being a single parent, she provided stability, consistency, discipline, and a sense of belonging. This was what had given him a level of confidence to believe he could do anything.

It was not until he was older that Clint realized that achievement became what drove him, that he always wanted to feel like he was succeeding at whatever he was doing, and that his relationship both with himself and with others was rooted in his achievements. As he learned to connect with himself, Clint was finally able to foster authentic connections with others.

Some might say Clint has had a hard life, but Clint would say that life is what built the hardworking, goal-oriented, resilient man in him.

> Clint began his healing by moving into the **body** center to bring awareness to being present with himself, then came back into the **heart** center to access his authenticity and the honesty of his needs. Finally, he could move into **head** center where he could find a better pace of life and work, allowing him to be himself and to be successful.

The Nine Types and Poverty

Body Types and Poverty

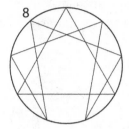

Vulnerability

- Due to the sense of powerlessness that they experience in situations where they lack resources, Eights develop a strategy to find resources. Often these resources are not legal, and they find themselves involved in criminal activity.
- By denying the obstacle of poverty and pushing through challenges, Eights develop an even tougher exterior. This prevents them from allowing anyone to see their struggles.

Resilience

- As a body-based type, Eights use their strength to push through challenges, gaining strength as they go.
- They use this strength and anger to find solutions, even when it comes to poverty.

Vulnerability

- Nines might see the challenge of poverty as never-ending.
- They will find ways to escape the pain and discomfort of poverty by overindulging in food and alcohol, and they may lose motivation to make changes.

Resilience
- When Nines realize that they can work with others to resolve poverty, they will exhibit relentless perseverance and engagement with their community to bring about change.
- Nines will often assist in community-based efforts to eradicate poverty within the community.

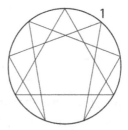

Vulnerability
- When facing poverty, Ones might become hyper-focused on being a good person and on toeing the line.
- They want to improve what is within their control but in doing so, Ones may lose sight of the poverty needing to be addressed.

Resilience
- The attention of a One is placed on improving situations and seeking better outcomes, which can help them break the grip of poverty.
- Their motivation for a more ideal situation will lead them into career areas like education, healthcare, fitness, nutrition, or government—places where they can make a difference.

Heart Types and Poverty

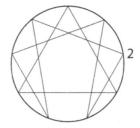

Vulnerability
- Sometimes stuck in appreciation and gratitude, Twos may be unaware of the dire situation they are in.
- Twos' innate pride may keep them from asking for help.

Resilience

- Their ability to connect with people provides Twos with silver linings, resolving their journey of pain.
- Rather than being trapped by scarcity, Twos are intuitive people who can find resources, especially if they feel like they are helping others.

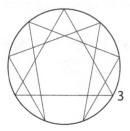

Vulnerability

- Threes feel shame for not having what others have. This might move them into overachieving ways in order to move the spotlight from their lack of food, clothing, or shelter.
- Asking for help might expose their poverty, so Threes will mask their vulnerability, even regarding the basic needs of life.

Resilience

- Once Threes realize that their overachieving is a result of taking the spotlight off their lack of basic needs, they can begin the journey out of shame.
- Threes can connect to themselves without a need for success or approval from others, thus freeing them to be who they truly are—separate from their resources.

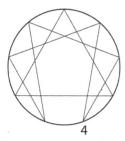

Vulnerability

- Feeling misunderstood, Fours constantly yearn for everything that they believe to be missing from their lives. This makes them susceptible to constantly feeling impoverished.

- Fours can accept the tragedy of being raised in poverty. This can prevent them from seeking change.

Resilience

- Once Fours can understand the importance and impact of gratitude and appreciation, they organically move out of a poverty mindset.
- By accessing equanimity, Fours appreciate what is.

Head Types and Poverty

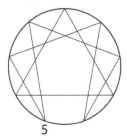

5

Vulnerability

- Fives have a minimalistic view of the world and require very little to begin with. This may keep them from feeling impoverished and can keep them from finding a better way of living.
- They may also isolate and compartmentalize their experiences, withholding and living in a world of secrecy.

Resilience

- With a true desire to learn and be self-sufficient, a Five might gather information and resources that can help them move out of poverty.
- They will make changes at a pace that works for them, allowing for sustainability.

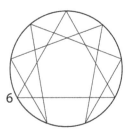

6

Vulnerability

- Sixes' worry and rumination about the lack of resources is part of who they are, and they may have a hard time breaking free from that cycle.

Resilience
- Sixes are realists. When they can see what is, they can implement prudent and pragmatic strategies to get them out of poverty.

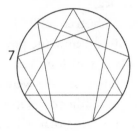

Vulnerability
- Sevens find a silver lining of abundance, even amid extreme poverty.
- Often Sevens do not recognize the reality of their circumstances. This might keep them from seeking change.

Resilience
- Once they face the reality of their situation, Sevens have an innate gift of examining options.
- A realistic reframing to a positive mindset allows a Seven to maintain forward momentum in moving out of poverty.

A Movement Intervention

 Threes are typically on the move, so slowing down to connect with your feelings can cause stress. If you are a Three, like Clint, a good grounding practice is to do walking meditations.

Begin with walking. As you are walking, focus on your breathing. Take a deep breath, inhaling through your nose while counting to four, holding for four, exhaling while counting to four, then waiting for four before inhaling again. Repeat this at least three times.

As your breathing becomes rhythmic, notice your feet walking on the ground. Do you feel the pressure of each step you take? What does that feel like to you? Can you feel the earth, the pavement, or the asphalt beneath your feet?

Continue the rhythmic breathing as you engage your five senses. What do you hear? What do you see? What do you feel? What do you taste? What do you smell? Check in with all five senses and identify what it is that you notice. Challenge yourself to walk, breathe, and notice all that your five senses are bringing to you.

Facts About Poverty

More than 10 percent of the world—almost 700 million people—are living on less than $2.00 a day. And of all the children living in poverty, 75 percent live in Asia and Sub-Saharan Africa.

In the United States in 2018, thirteen million children—that is 18 percent of all children in the nation—lived below the poverty line with their parents earning $26,000 or less for a family of four, half of what is needed for basic financial security.[64] Of these, children of color were affected significantly more. This is a higher poverty rate than in other developed nations.

Low income creates food insecurity, that is limited or uncertain access to nutritionally adequate food.[65] And a lack of proper nutrition during a child's development has lasting effects on their brain development. It contributes to low reading and math scores. It also leads to an increase in physical and mental health problems.

The pandemic created new food-insecure families, and racial disparities in poverty surfaced. As of May 2020, over twenty million families in the United States entered the $26,000 or less income bracket.[66]

Another subsection of the global population that is disproportionately affected by poverty is single-parent families.

- Eighty percent of single-parent families are headed by a single mother.
- In the United States, there are fifteen million families headed by single mothers—three times higher than in 1960.
- A typical homeless family in the United States consists of a single mother and two underage children.
- There are nearly three million single parents in the United Kingdom.
- In Canada in 2017, close to 20 percent of all children lived with single parents.
- Globally, the percentage of children living with a single parent varies by race and ethnicity, but not necessarily by religion.
- Nearly 60 percent of children of African descent live with a single parent, and of those, close to 80 percent live with a single mom.

---

64 bit.ly/DefinePoverty
65 bit.ly/DefineFoodSecurity
66 bit.ly/DefinePoverty

Signs/Symptoms of Poverty

- Growing up in poverty can lead to ongoing financial stress.
- It can also lead to depression, anxiety, psychological distress, and sometimes suicide.
- Growing up in poverty can result in nutritional deprivation, which can cause hypothalamic-pituitary-adrenal (HPA) axis changes as well as other brain-circuit changes such as challenges with language processing and executive functioning.
- Family-level signs include parental relationship stress, parental mental stress, low parental warmth or investment, hostile and inconsistent parenting, and low-stimulation home environments.

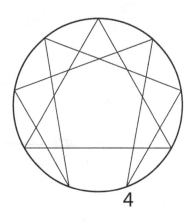

4

CHAPTER TEN

Georgette's Introduction to Racism

Georgette is a striking and articulate woman. Born in Panama, she is the daughter of immigrant parents. They moved to New York City when Georgette was young, joining her grandparents in the home they had purchased in an upper-middle-class area of the city.

When Georgette came to us for counseling, she told us she had been studying the Enneagram and identified with the type Four. She told stories of her parents and grandparents who spoke and understood only Spanish. In her thick New York accent, Georgette spoke of her mother and grandparents being her caregivers. Her father served in the military and was away much of the time.

She also told of how their family was targeted by white neighbors who would drop trash on their doorstep every day. And every day, Georgette's mother would simply go out to clean it up.

Eventually, Georgette came to understand that these were acts of racism.

———■———

Georgette was light skinned, but she lived under the same roof with darker-skinned, wealthy Panamanian relatives who were all simply seeking to live the American Dream. While the difference in skin tone was no issue in Panama, in the United States, it added an element of complication and confusion that young Georgette tried to understand and unpack.

At school, she coped by developing a strong spiritual life. She also joined a church where she assumed people of all races would be treated equally. But she was mistaken. Still, instead of being disillusioned and turning away, Georgette's spiritual life grew. It became a major source of her coping and resilience.

Georgette married Ruben—a Black man raised in the Deep South who had experienced racism across several generations. Ruben was very different from Georgette and angry much of the time. He drank a lot and often raged when he was drunk. Over time, she grew to fear Ruben. When he was sober and trying to communicate with Georgette, he would make statements about how mistrustful he was of others at work and in their surrounding white community.

She did not understand how Ruben had such a different experience of being brown skinned than she had. She did notice, though, how she was forced to shift and present herself differently at work and among the white community.

Being away from her family of origin and raising her children with Ruben who was much darker skinned than she, Georgette was more directly exposed to racism in the United States. Ruben wanted to teach their children about protecting themselves against racism. Still naive about the issue, Georgette did not agree. At times, she argued with Ruben about the merits of teaching their children about ways to protect themselves, and at other times she simply withdrew. Their two oldest children went on to have a lot of academic and disciplinary problems in school and were in and out of jail.

Increasingly, Georgette withdrew into her spiritual world, becoming less available to her children and husband. By the time their youngest daughter, Somarah, was born, Georgette was getting ready to leave Ruben. She could no longer handle the violence, and she perceived Ruben as a victim, destined to have problems, and unwilling to seek help.

———◆———

When Somarah was six years old, Georgette left Ruben and moved to Oakland, California with Emerald, whom she married. Somarah stayed with her father for a few years, only spending summers with her mother. Eventually Somarah moved to California to be with her mother full time. The two grew closer.

Somarah was a beautiful, creative young woman, just a little darker skinned than her mother. Still, she was light skinned enough to be exposed to discrimination within the brown-skinned community. It seemed that Somarah was too dark to be white and too light to be Black.

Away from Ruben and through her daughter's varied experiences, Georgette grew a much deeper understanding of racism in the United States. At Somarah's school, racism led to almost daily physical fights between the girls. She felt powerless to protect her daughter. Each day her daughter returned home from school alive was another momentous day in Georgette's life.

Somarah was more prepared than her mother to face and deal with the racism, though. Between her father's honest discussions about life as a brown-skinned person in America and Somarah's good street sense, she found a way to survive and, ultimately, to thrive. She did this through an activity she found that helped her to hold on to her heritage. Somarah had started doing Indigenous dancing—dances from various tribal cultures throughout the world—when she was ten. As she grew into her teenage years, she not only found immense pleasure in it, but she was also quite good at it.

At the beginning of Somarah's high school years, she, her mom, and her stepfather, Emerald, moved to Tucson, Arizona where they moved into a predominantly white neighborhood. Rather than being part of the majority like she was used to in Oakland, Somarah had to get used to being part of a small minority. This brought about additional challenges, including making friends and having her friends' parents accept her. To make things even harder, Emerald's business had mostly white patrons, and Somarah's dance community was no longer a part of her life.

To this day, Somarah works on finding her way honoring her heritage in Tucson, Arizona. She has found a social network of people of all colors and backgrounds. She also joined a new dance community and has other creative outlets. Still, she is aware that she is the minority and is prepared for negative comments and judgmental stares.

Resilience in the Face of Racism

Georgette describes her three children—each almost ten years apart—as being raised by three different mothers, each in a different developmental phase of her spiritual life. Georgette's faith grew daily due to her devotion and commitment to her spiritual life and practices, so each consecutive child received more nurturing from their mother. She also became progressively more self-aware, compassionate, and available. As a result, Georgette developed stronger and more secure attachments with each child.

Through Georgette's commitment to her spiritual life, she found meaning and purpose, and an earlier tendency toward depression dissipated. She developed a strong social network by forging friendships with people at her church. Georgette even explored spiritual teachings from other religions and looked to ancient wisdom traditions from societies of long ago, increasing her capacity to see the world through the lens of others.

At home, Georgette's female role models remained strong. Her family laid a solid foundation with positive relationships. They encouraged her to persevere.

She was firmly identified with her own culture and open to learning about others. She was proud of who she was—a Panamanian American woman. This is a different dynamic than most Black women raised in the United States, particularly the South.

By growing up in Panama, Georgette was not carrying intergenerational racism trauma as many black-skinned and brown-skinned people she met in the United States were. As a result, her perspective and worldview were not impacted in the ways many people of color are, allowing Georgette to have a more objective view of the dilemmas of racism in the United States.

When faced with dilemmas related to systemic racism—being asked to camp in a different area than her white friends from church, for example, or being asked to give up a seat on a bus to accommodate a white person—Georgette could observe her thoughts as well as observe how she felt both physically and emotionally. She could use discernment to choose her response, always taking the high road because of her spiritual principles and values. Her culture and family system supported this view, even in the face of adversity.

Georgette was comfortable with being by herself, even back when she was a teenager. Throughout, she was able to resource solitude, using it as a way to integrate her varied experiences. She was also able to comfortably navigate spending time in her community and with her family.

She was also quite curious by nature. She had so many questions she was unable to answer through her readings and prayer. Hence, she was intentional about seeking mentorship and guidance from qualified others. She chose to pursue additional education to improve her status. She stayed her course with purpose. She chose to reframe all situations as spiritual learning experiences.

By the time she began to face trauma in her life, Georgette had a relatively solid foundation. Her trauma began when she married a Black male raised in the Deep South, and it continued to unfold as she had children of her own through whose experiences she had to face systemic racism.

*Georgette cultivated a strong spiritual life early on. She began her healing by moving into the **head** center to see the reality of what racism is and find safety, security, and dependability. She then came back into the **heart** center to grieve, after which she could move into her **body** center to take action.*

The Nine Types and Racism

Body Types and Racism

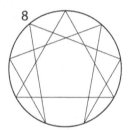

Vulnerability

- For Eights, the nervous system often defaults to fight rather than to flee, freeze, or fawn.
- When facing systemic racism, Eights can get trapped in a loop of constant reactivity while holding on to the injustice. This can keep the Eight from moving to solutions.

Resilience

- Eights are changemakers, even when fighting systemic racism. They have the capacity to notice racism yet not be held captive by it.
- Eights' focus tends to be on assisting the underdog rather than focusing on themselves. They have an innate appreciation of the innocence of all living beings, which helps them stand up to racism.

Vulnerability

- Not being aware of their own needs feeds into Nines being complacent to the powers that be and accepting that living with racism is how life will always be.
- To keep harmony, Nines can dismiss racial microaggressions, while their tendency toward passive-aggressive behavior keeps them recycling their suppressed anger.

Resilience

- Able to see all sides of a situation, Nines have an innate ability to mediate for others, which can help them and others move through racist experiences.
- They also have an innate desire for unity and healing of all. A well-developed Nine will push through the discomfort of conflict to reach a place of unity.

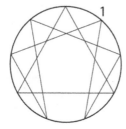

Vulnerability

- When dealing with systemic racism, Ones are gripped by a constant frustration at not being able to correct the situation, and they repress their simmering reactivity to injustices.
- Ones can be rigid regarding what needs to be done to make things right. They can find it difficult to collaborate with others in reaching those goals. As a result, they can get stuck on what needs correction while not getting anything done.

Resilience

- Ones who are working on personal growth will check themselves for how they may be contributing to racism.
- Ones are conscientious around the desire to correct injustices. They persevere to come up with fair and just ways to deal with dilemmas—including racism.

Heart Types and Racism

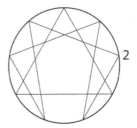

Vulnerability
- Twos tend to be people-pleasers and in their desire to be liked, they can be inauthentic.
- Twos are good at avoiding the concerns at hand as well as the part they play in them.

Resilience
- Like Nines, Twos have a strong and authentic desire to heal the differences between people as they want all people to be connected.
- Seeing the good in all, they easily forgive and move forward.

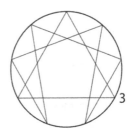

Vulnerability
- Seeking approval and respect, Threes may not be honest in their interactions with others.
- The appearance of resolution may be more important to them than the actual work done to achieve resolution.

Resilience
- Once Threes have connected with their authentic self, they can have honest, open dialogue about racism.
- Threes engaged in authenticity will build connections and will draw people together, often promoting courageous conversations about racism.

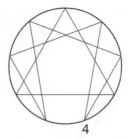

4

Vulnerability

- Fours can get stuck in seeing racism as just another frailty of humanity.
- While appreciating the dilemmas of those impacted by racism, they might stay in sadness and not do anything to seek change.

Resilience

- When Fours are moved to action, they have the capacity to sustain a conversation about a difficult topic, even engaging in the topic authentically while leaving room for others to do so as well.
- Fours can use their deeply felt emotion and heartache to bring about transformation.

Head Types and Racism

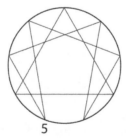

5

Vulnerability

- Fives may avoid getting involved in addressing racism due to their concern of the energy they will need to expend.
- Thinking they are not ready, they may delay entering the conversation or taking action around racism.

Resilience

- Fives will not simply accept what others say as the truth. They will keep gathering information that is current and applicable.
- Becoming the holders of the history and facts, they do not allow the reality of what is happening to be forgotten.

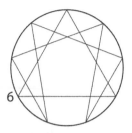

Vulnerability

- The dance between avoiding fear and plunging into fear head on can get Sixes into lots of trouble.
- They may fear taking a stance against racism but then jump into a street fight to deal with the sense of injustice.

Resilience

- Sixes are good at strategizing and planning ways to address racism, such as with rallies, demonstrations, or by supporting local agencies.
- They have a global awareness of social justice and will move intentionally into taking action around the injustices.

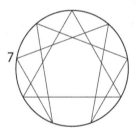

Vulnerability

- Due to their aversion to having difficult conversations, Sevens may ignore racism.
- They may even minimize the impact and reality of racism, as if we live in a world where something such as this does not exist.

Resilience

- Once they grasp the reality of a situation, Sevens will work hard to find solutions and advocate for healing.
- With a cheerleader-like quality, Sevens are hardwired for innate optimism while others might have a sense of hopelessness.

A Mindfulness Intervention

 Type Fours are part of the heart center. Of all the types in this center, they are the most aware of their emotional state. But while they are hyperaware of their emotions, they tend to find too much comfort in their emotional state and can become attached to their intense emotions.

If, like Georgette, you are a Four, you need to intervene in the trauma cycle of racism by working toward emotional regulation/co-regulation. All humans learn to self-regulate, tending to their own emotions better if they have learned co-regulation from early caregivers as infants and young children. Many are not so fortunate to have had good modeling for co-regulation in their early years. **The good news is, later in life you can learn through safe and trusting relationships to co-regulate and self-regulate emotions.**

Deep emotional states happen when you examine the categories of your experiences including memories, your imagination, the past and the future, and your plans. This orientation requires you to consider something that has happened to you or something that might happen. What is held in the past or what might happen in the future keeps you from focusing on the present.

When facing trauma, your attention tends to move back and forth between the past and future, looking for a way out. While this is already the tendency of Fours, it can be exacerbated during a trauma response.

Strategies to move the focus of attention to the present are called mindfulness practices. Here is an easy practice that can include body sensations, emotions, and thoughts.

During a repetitive task—for example, when you are cooking or doing dishes—practice turning your attention to what is going on at that moment. Also, pay attention to any emotion you may be experiencing. Whatever the emotion, see if you can gently shift it from what it is to a different emotion. If you are unable to shift the emotion, see if you can stay with that emotion and lower the intensity.

Facts About Racism

Often a person's class, education, or whereabouts growing up will increase or decrease their exposure to racism. For many persons of color (POC),[67] their experience might be different from that of an immigrant such as Georgette.

---

67   In addition to POC, another acronym that is often used is BIPOC, referring to Black, Indigenous, and (other) Persons of Color. See bit.ly/WhatIsBIPOC and nyti.ms/3rm724X. However, some

The experience of racism for many POC growing up in the United States is both overt and covert. It undermines their very personhood, which is why racism is chronic and insidious trauma.

Racial battle fatigue is a phrase used to describe the effect of this type of racial trauma. Originally coined in 2008 by William Smith, it was used in regard to the experience of Black men in America.[68] However, it is also experienced by other POC and marginalized communities.

These negative racial experiences wind themselves into every area where POC live, from workplace environments, health care, and educational systems to everyday encounters with people of the dominant culture.

William defines racial battle fatigue as a "cumulative result of a natural race-related stress response to distressing mental and emotional conditions. These conditions emerged from constantly facing racially dismissive, demeaning, insensitive and/or hostile racial environments and individuals."[69]

Covert racism and subtle microaggressions cause the person of color to "gear up for battle" daily. This daily battle causes them to overthink everything they do, utilizing their executive functioning skills simultaneously while being alert. They meticulously pick out their clothing in the morning, change their way of speaking, and think and overthink everything they do in the work environment.

Hyper-vigilance becomes the norm. Running on empty becomes the norm. Their children are raised to meet that same standard in order to battle racism and microaggressions.

Racial microaggressions are a form of psychological warfare and are defined as:

- subtle verbal and nonverbal insults directed at POC, often automatic or unconscious
- layered insults based on one's race, gender, class, sexuality, language, immigration status, phenotype, accent, or surname
- cumulative insults, which cause unnecessary stress to POC.[70]

---

argue against that term saying that it creates division among the minority community rather than unifying them. See bit.ly/POCorBIPOC.
68 bit.ly/WhatIsRacialBattleFatigue
69 bit.ly/WilliamsRBF
70 bit.ly/WhatAreRacialMicroaggressions

Prolonged exposure to various forms of mental, emotional, and physical strain is considered trauma and can lead to psychophysiological symptoms. Racism has also caused physical trauma and can lead to death.

Anticipatory thinking is an increase of anxiety resulting from a real or perceived threat. This type of thinking requires significant internal regulation and slow reactivity, and it is exhausting. Experiencing racially motivated conflicts may cause rapid breathing, an upset stomach, or frequent diarrhea/urination. These racial stressors can lead to long-term health issues and erode confidence and self-worth among POC.

When racial battle fatigue goes untreated or dismissed, this stress-related psychological and physiological disease can be lethal. It can kill gradually and stealthily through hypertension and poor health attitudes and behaviors.

———•———

Racism is not limited to just Black and white. With various skin shades in the United States, brown-skinned individuals can face prejudice from their local, brown-skinned community as well as the white community.

"In the United States," Jemar Tisby said in his 2021 book, *How to Fight Racism,* "race has largely been defined in terms of physical appearance. … But skin color remains the essential feature of race … the darker skinned a person, the lower their position in society."

Tisby goes on to explain that "People of color have even bought into the social construct of race. Among various people groups, 'colorism'—a practice in which people of color discriminate among themselves based on skin color— remains a problematic issue."[71]

- The employment-population ratio for Black Americans has historically tended to fall quite a bit lower than for whites or Latinos.
- Just as Black employment has historically been lower than for whites, the unemployment rate among Black Americans has been higher.
- Systemic racism against Asian Americans and Pacific Islanders (AAPI) in the United States dates back to the 1800s, it escalated after World War II, resulting in Japanese internment camps between 1942 and 1945. While many other laws were instated and hate crimes committed against the AAPI since that time, the recent escalation of hate crimes

---

71 Jemar Tisby, *How to Fight Racism* (Grand Rapids, MI, 2021), 21.

against AAPI has been of great concern. Stanford University reports, "Since the pandemic began, 3,795 anti-AAPI hate crimes have been reported in the US (as of February 28, 2021), at least 708 of which took place in the San Francisco Bay Area, and this number is most likely undercounted."[72]

- In the past decade, anti-Latinx sentiments have grown along with the increase in immigrants from the south. This is not a new issue, though. Mob violence against Spanish-speaking individuals goes back as far as the late 1800s, after the Mexican–American War, including violence against those from Mexico, Cuba, Puerto Rico and more than twenty Latin American countries represented under the umbrella terms *Latino* and *Hispanic*.[73]

- The largest minority in the United States, at nearly 19%, the terms *Latino*, *Hispanic* and *Latinx* are often used interchangeably to describe persons with ties with more than twenty Spanish-speaking countries. While each group is unique, they have shared many similar experiences enduring racial violence and segregation.[74]

- There are more than three million migrant farmworkers in the United States with almost 70% being from Mexico. While activists like Cesar Chaves fought for workers' rights and protections in the state of California in the 1960s, farm laborers are one of just two groups of workers that are not protected by the National Labor Relations Act.[75]

- Black Americans are underrepresented in high-paying jobs.

- People of color are severely underrepresented at the top of the corporate hierarchy, and Black Americans and AAPI have historically been underrepresented in the highest echelons of government.

- Research conducted in Canada shows that racism is an experience acutely felt by many Indigenous people. For example, according to a 2005 report of the First Nations Regional Longitudinal Health Survey, 38% of participating First Nations adults experienced at least one instance of racism in the past twelve months, and 63% of them felt that it had at least some effect on their self-esteem.[76]

---

72 stanford.io/3480CBx
73 bit.ly/AntiLatinx
74 bit.ly/LatinxRacism; bit.ly/LatinxMilestones
75 bit.ly/MigrantFarmworkers; bit.ly/FarmWorkersUnion
76 bit.ly/RacismAgainstFirstNationsPeople

- People of color have historically earned far less than white workers—even when comparing salaries of white high school dropouts compared to Black college graduates.[77]
- Similarly, overall income for Black Americans was about 42% lower than for whites in 2018.
- There is a similar disparity at the household level. Lower incomes mean that the poverty rate for Black families is over twice that of white families.
- The aggregate wealth white households have held has historically far outstripped that held by the Black community. And while it has increased for white people since the 1980s, it has remained stagnant for Black people.
- A key part of the American Dream is leaving your children in a better economic position than you were in, but that dream is less attainable for people of color.
- Black American males and Latino men are more likely to be stopped by police than white American males.
- Black American males are more likely to be detained for no legal reason than white American males.
- Black American males constitute more of the prison population than white American males even though there is a greater percentage of crimes committed by white American males.

Signs/Symptoms of Racism

- Racial battle fatigue is real. It can lead to re-experiencing of distressing events, even to somatization when distressed, such as having stomach aches, headaches, or rapid heartbeat.
- Racial battle fatigue can also cause depression, anxiety, hypervigilance, and avoidance, that is, being less willing to take academic or work-related risks.
- You might also experience hypertension, respiratory complications, higher allostatic load (the wear and tear of the body caused by chronic stress), and digestive issues.
- It can also lead to feelings of isolation, self-doubt, and unworthiness.

---

77   bit.ly/EducationNotEqualizer

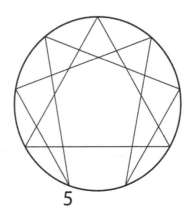

5

CHAPTER ELEVEN

Carter's Story of Complications from Addictions

Atenured professor well loved by his students, Carter is a man who carefully chooses his words. Thoughtful and pensive, Carter's eye contact moves away from you for extended periods as he contemplates and then back to you again as he presents his conclusion.

The product of a teenage pregnancy to parents who were from an ultra-religious community, the struggling trio was shunned by their families. This was but the beginning of Carter's traumatic early childhood.

His father was an out-of-control, raging alcoholic. The verbal rants and rages and the physical abuse was always targeted toward Carter's mother. Even as a young boy, Carter felt helpless. Still, he plotted ways he would help his mother stand up for herself.

Carter was just nine years old when he got a job, determined to help his mom so they could get out from under the abuse of Carter's father. When he realized she was not likely to leave, Carter kept his money, and he used it to get adults to buy him alcohol.

"Staying in an altered mood was how I coped," Carter admits.

He started drinking daily and was suffering blackouts by the time he was fifteen. By that time, he was also smoking pot daily and trying assorted drugs with his friends. He left home and camped in the desert while completing high school.

Carter came home one day to find his mother in a pool of blood, beaten by his father. He waited until his father came home, then he beat his father with a baseball bat. Then he left home for good.

Not long after, Carter met Julia and moved in with her. She would become his wife and the mother of his two children. Julia partied with Carter for many years, stopping only when she was pregnant. Carter's drinking escalated, leading to his first charge for driving under the influence at only twenty-one.

While working full time, Carter went back to college in the evenings and finished his graduate work by the time he was twenty-six. He immediately got a position as an associate professor at a local college.

———◆———

Watching his mother's strategies with his father, Carter learned that experiencing feelings—let alone sharing them—would be detrimental to his survival. Instead, he turned to alcohol, sex, love, and later gambling to bury his unprocessed feelings.

On the outside, everything looked normal, but Carter's drinking and lifestyle began to take its toll. He struggled with depression and started to pull away from his wife. To save his marriage, Carter agreed to an open marriage. This led to a blurry ten years of sex, alcohol, drugs, depression, and an unsuccessful suicide attempt.

Carter's children begged him to stop drinking, to which he agreed. He started going to Alcoholics Anonymous, and with some AA friends, he celebrated six months of sobriety by going to a casino. Winning big that first night got him hooked, even though he promptly lost what he won—and more.

Within two months, Carter was at the casino every night. He drained his savings account, his children's college funds, maxed out his credit cards, and was living paycheck to paycheck.

Still, it surprised Carter when Julia filed for divorce. "I wasn't even aware that she was that unhappy," he later shared.

Carter thought his luck had taken a turn for the better when he was offered full professorship at a large university. None of his colleagues—neither the old nor the new ones—knew he was drinking again, was gambling out of control, had significant financial problems, and that he was going through a divorce. They thought of Carter as somewhat of a loner but still a nice guy.

At the casino, Carter met the woman who would be his next wife. As they got to know each other, they briefly slowed their gambling. But within six months, they moved in together, married, and returned to their routine of drinking and gambling. It did not take too long for her to walk out on Carter. He never saw her again.

After two unsuccessful attempts at marriage, Carter became somewhat of a recluse. He buried himself in his job as a professor and found solace in books and his addictions. In doing so, his health and finances became riddled with problems.

Carter could no longer escape. His coping strategies were no longer working. At that time, his boss at the university invited Carter to attend an AA meeting with him.

At first, he was allowed to simply show up at the meetings and observe. Nothing else was required of him. Carter found a community of people who did not judge, did not want anything from him, and were always available.

Though he was able to break his drinking habit, Carter continued to gamble. As long as he did not drink, it seemed like he had some control of his gambling. His gambling became more frequent, though, and Carter soon found himself stealing from his handicapped mother—the one person he thought he would never harm, the one person he always hoped to protect. This led to his family and colleagues staging an intervention.

Carter joined Gamblers Anonymous where he not only found a sponsor who was a recovering alcoholic and recovering gambler, he also fell in love with a fellow GA member whom he married not long after.

Resilience in the Face of Addiction

When Carter was introduced to the Enneagram as part of his initial treatment, it took him a while to identify his type. This is, in part, because while in active addiction, a person's preoccupation with the addiction controls their thoughts, emotions, and behaviors. It also did not help that he could identify strongly with attributes of a type Four, Five *and* Six.

Once Carter identified that he was a Five (with strong Four and Six wings), he became aware of how dangerous it was to disengage, isolate, and mentalize his problems. He started to look for strategies to stay in the game. He found ways to be active in both the AA and GA communities, including sponsoring others. Carter also shared his background and fears with his daughters, and he began to make restitution to his mother.

When he was not using, Carter was able to observe his thoughts, feelings, and behaviors. He noticed certain patterns he would typically repeat. He was able to identify that these patterns were not only part of the reason he used but also of the resilience he could access in recovery.

As he grew in self-awareness, his periods of abstinence became longer. This, in turn, allowed Carter to identify some triggers and blind spots associated with his type.

The trauma recovery and Enneagram practices of inner observation and noticing can help you to grow self-awareness. For Carter, the Five's gift of discernment returned. He even began to look at himself differently.

Partnering with us, Carter grew aware of the trauma triggers in his body, including having heart palpitations, having a desire to run, and often finding it difficult to catch his breath. Carter also realized that he had been holding his breath off and on for most of his life.

He was able to see that all these patterns were not necessarily bad or good, they were simply strategies to manage life. It was part of his personality as a Five.

Through Enneagram-informed counseling, Carter learned that identifying what was going on in his body complemented the information he was learning about addiction recovery. He learned to calm himself through breathing practices, through carefully placing his attention on what was the next step necessary for recovery, and not to run.

> Carter began his healing by moving into the **body** center to inform him of how he was sensing (feeling) the world in his body, then into thinking about the world through the **head** center, evaluating what was safe and what was a threat. From there, he was able to begin to identify the name of various emotions. Only after that could he move into his **heart** center where he began to grieve and process other emotions.

The Nine Types and Addiction

Body Types and Addiction

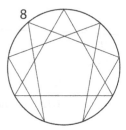

Vulnerability
- Given their lust for energy, Eights tend to see substance abuse and behavioral addictions through a lens of "more is better." This way, their lust for *more* places them at risk of developing an addiction.
- Likely addictions include anything where more is better: alcohol, action gambling, sex, amphetamines, and designer drugs that add energy.

Resilience
- Eights can embrace recovery with the same lust they have for their addictions, especially if they find someone or a community that can hold their intense energy.
- To move into a vulnerable space and be receptive to help, an Eight must embrace the concept of powerlessness and/or a higher power.

Vulnerability
- Nines naturally seek ways to go with the flow. This makes them susceptible to giving in to peer pressure and thus getting trapped in addiction. Addictions can also develop in response to seeking new and comfortable ways to narcotize to avoid conflict or pain.
- Likely addictions include alcohol, marijuana, escape gambling, and overeating. They are also prone to codependency.

Resilience

- Nines do well in communities of support—almost better than with an individual helping professional.
- Because of their open-mindedness, Nines can take in information from others and integrate it into self and recovery.

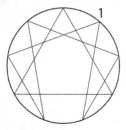

Vulnerability

- Finding it too difficult to deal with more than one flaw or imperfection at a time, Ones rarely have co-occurring addictions. Instead, they tend to have only one active addiction at a time.
- Likely addictions include alcohol, eating disorders, all types of gambling, pain medications, benzodiazepines, or marijuana.

Resilience

- Ones have an uncanny ability to focus on making amends and righting their wrongs.
- When it comes to following the steps of a recovery program or the suggestions of a helping professional, Ones can do what is required of them.

Heart Types and Addiction

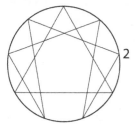

Vulnerability

- As a means of finding a way to relax, addictions often develop in Twos who have overextended themselves.

- Likely addictions include alcohol, pain medications, escape gambling, sleep medications, codependency, abuse of over-the-counter meds, and binge eating.

Resilience

- Twos are optimistic and have a positive outlook. They make easy connections with others, including those in recovery.
- Their ease in accessing gratitude and their strong desire to move through problems help them to stay engaged with others in recovery and with recovery communities.

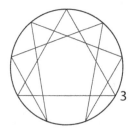

Vulnerability

- To cope with their need to stay in the *doing* mode and to sustain energy to complete tasks, addictions often develop in Threes.
- Likely addictions include alcohol, performance-enhancing drugs (such as steroids and amphetamines), and designer drugs (such as ecstasy) which enhance sexual experiences. They may also deal with sexual addictions as well as an addiction to diet pills, appetite suppressants, and action gambling.

Resilience

- Threes' competitive desire includes a desire to do recovery right.
- They may include as many recovery tools as necessary and champion the cause for recovery.

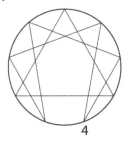

Vulnerability

- Fours prefer to focus on the past and future. To avoid their current state, they may develop addictions to intensify whatever mood they choose at that time. Because of the deep intensity of emotions, Fours may be ostracized by recovery groups.
- Likely addictions include alcohol, love and/or sexual addictions, abuse of sleep medications, heroin and other opiates, marijuana, and hallucinogens. Fours are also prone to a variety of eating disorders.

Resilience

- Fours have an innate capacity to not only tolerate but also resolve intense emotional concerns. This helps them to address the underlying causes of addiction.
- Having a strong desire to be understood, Fours can develop meaningful relationships in recovery and have artistic and creative outlets.

Head Types and Addiction

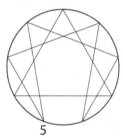

5

Vulnerability

- Addictions develop in Fives as a mechanism to cope with fear—sometimes existential fear. Believing that the world wants too much from them, addicted Fives isolate and withdraw, keeping them from getting the help they need.
- Likely addictions include alcohol, action or escape gambling, sexual addictions, hallucinogens, or other mind-expanding drugs.

Resilience

- Fives research and gather facts about recovery, providing them with resources about addiction and sobriety.
- With the support of others, they may be open to implementing evidence-based practices.

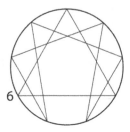

Vulnerability

- Moving between self-doubt and second-guessing, addictions develop in Sixes to help them cope with anxiety. The addictions will look different when in phobic and counterphobic reactivity to fear.
- Likely addictions for a Six in phobic reactivity to fear include alcohol, abuse of benzodiazepines, and escape gambling. For a Six in counterphobic reactivity to fear, alcohol, steroids, action gambling, and amphetamines are likely.

Resilience

- For Sixes, it is important to know that their sources of recovery options are respected and authoritative.
- Sixes innately comply with treatment protocols offered by authoritative and respected healthcare practitioners.

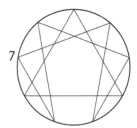

Vulnerability

- Sevens are driven to avoid pain and try new and varied experiences. This makes them prone to addiction, especially when transitioning into adulthood—a life stage when they are at higher risk of being exposed to addictive options and to peer experiences.[78]
- Sevens are vulnerable to *all* addictions—alcohol, amphetamines, opiates, hallucinogens, escape and action gambling, sexual addictions, eating disorders, and benzodiazepines.

---

78   Note that many adolescents transitioning into adulthood may look like Sevens but are not.

Resilience

- Generally, Sevens do well in self-help communities where they can access a variety of people and different ideas and experiences.
- Due to their openness to exploring options, Sevens may be more open to trying out different approaches to recovery, whether conventional or not.

A Mindfulness Intervention

 Fives are part of the head center. They manage their fear by gathering information, and they may do research so they know as much as they can about a topic.

Often, Fives are fascinated with information about their trauma, and they find it comforting to know how that trauma has hijacked some of their executive functioning or higher level of thinking. It makes it easier for them to understand that although it is not logical to engage in self-destructive addictions, it is their go-to so they can cope.

Fives are often good reporters and will give you feedback about what they observe. They are keenly aware of their thoughts, which makes it easy for them to report what they are thinking. However, Fives are less likely to be able to identify their emotions and bodily sensations.

If you, like Carter, are working on overcoming addictions, keep track of what you were thinking prior to using or engaging in addictive or self-destructive behaviors. You may even want to keep an inventory of what time the thoughts about using occurred in comparison to when you picked up the first drink, drug, or engaged in gambling.

From there, you can move on to investigate other thoughts that preceded the thoughts before the use. This will help you trace back to the triggering event.

Facts About Addiction

Addiction is a complex disease of the brain and body. It involves compulsive use of one or more substances or behaviors regardless of serious mental, physical, and social consequences.

Trauma, abuse, as well as predisposing mental health concerns are some of the major influencers in developing addictions. During the pandemic, alcohol consumption increased significantly, especially among individuals dealing with anxiety and depression.[79]

SAMHSA and the Foundation for a Drug-Free World provide these insights into addiction:[80]

- Addiction is a chronic disease that changes the brain and liver, thereby increasing risk of cancer.
- One in every three families is impacted by substance abuse. More than 10 percent of children in the United States live with a parent with alcohol problems.
- Employee substance abuse is estimated to cost businesses almost $200 billion a year.
- Substance abuse addictions include using substances that can alter moods through ingestion, inhalation, and injection. They differ from process addictions such as gambling, sex, eating disorders, and gaming, though these can also alter a person's state of mind.
- Alcohol is a drug.
- The average age children start experimenting with drugs is thirteen.
- Alcohol use during the teenage years could interfere with normal adolescent brain development and can increase the risk of developing alcohol use disorder.
- Alcohol kills more teenagers than all other drugs combined. It is a factor in accidents, homicides, and suicides—the leading causes of death among fifteen- to twenty-four-year-olds.
- Every year in the United States, at least 1.4 million drunk drivers are arrested.
- Of all domestic violence reports, 80 percent are related to alcohol and/or drug consumption.
- More than half of all traffic accidents involve alcohol and/or drugs.
- Half of all suicides can be traced back to alcohol and/or drugs.
- More than 50 percent of all violent crimes are committed by someone using alcohol and/or drugs.
- Substance addiction is the third leading cause of death in the United States.

---

79 bit.ly/DrinkingAndThePandemic2 and bit.ly/DrinkingAndThePandemic
80 The Substance Abuse and Mental Health Services Administration is a division of the U.S. Department of Health & Human Services. bit.ly/SAMHSAGov; bit.ly/Drug-FreeWorld

Signs/Symptoms of Substance Use and Process Addictions

- Most addictions, whether related to substance-use or to process addiction—gambling, eating disorders, and sexual addictions—have consequences in psychological symptoms as well as behavioral, emotional, and mental symptoms.

- Among several physical symptoms of addictions, users show signs of brief euphoria, decreased inhibition, combativeness, dizziness, nausea, changes in pupil size, slurred speech, poor coordination, irregular heartbeat, and a rash around the nose and mouth.

- As for process addicts, they tend to spend an excessive amount of time and energy thinking about or partaking in the behavior, and they continue to engage in a behavior despite negative consequences. They ignore occupational, academic, and family responsibilities in favor of the behavior, and they use the behavior to cope with difficult emotions while downplaying the magnitude of the problem.

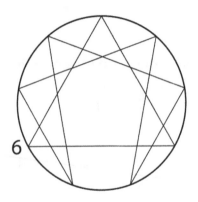

6

CHAPTER TWELVE

Brie's Story of Verbal, Emotional, and Spiritual Abuse

Brie came to us seeking treatment for a long history of anxiety. With her eyes darting between us and the office door, Brie admitted that she had been trying to calm her anxiety with meds and marijuana. At an early age, she was placed on several pharmaceutical medications to assist her with managing her anxiety, and she wanted to find healthier ways of coping.

Several years of anxiety in primary school led to Brie developing an eating disorder by the time she reached puberty. As Brie told us about her years of disordered-eating behavior, she shared that for the last six years, she had vomited daily. This daily vomiting led to severe gastrointestinal problems. Brie believed her eating disorder and the vomiting made her anxiety worse. On and off throughout our initial meeting, Brie clutched her stomach in pain as she shared her story.

When Brie sought treatment, she was attending a local university. Despite having a room at a dorm as per university requirements, Brie was too anxious to live with roommates she did not know or trust. Instead, she moved in with her grandparents who lived about forty minutes from her school.

Brie disclosed that she was especially fond of her grandfather. She described him as an incredibly wise and kind pastor, and the only healthy and stable long-term relationship with an adult male she had had to date. Brie spoke of the other male spiritual leaders she had met through her father, all of whom did not seem to live according to "the Word." She spoke of their hypocritical ways and how she wrestled with her concept of God.

When she was young, Brie's dad had a job in the entertainment industry and was gone most of the time. When he happened to be home, he was moody and unpredictable, having outbursts of rage. At the time, she had no idea of her dad's mental health challenges, but she was very clear about how frightened she was of his verbally explosive outbursts.

After her father quit touring as an entertainer, he bought a business in their town. Her parents divorced when she was nine. By that time, Brie had already had a couple of bouts with shingles, and she had severe gastrointestinal discomfort when stressed, which was most of the time.

When Brie was not with her mother, she had severe separation anxiety. This began in pre-school but continued for most of her primary grades. She did not want to visit with her father, but his prominence in the community, his legal ties, and his demands for Brie to spend time with him exacerbated her stress.

The local police even got involved, forcing Brie to spend time with her father. And if Brie did not comply with how her father expected her to behave, he would not only verbally and emotionally abuse her, but he would also punish her by locking her up in a room in his house, all by herself. She felt abandoned and neglected when she spent time with her father, and her anxiety worsened.

Brie and her mother were close—closer than her mother was with either of her two younger children. Through the difficulties each experienced through the tumultuous marriage and separation, Brie clung to her mother and her mother clung to Brie as a means of survival.

Due to Brie's mother being constantly shamed into believing she was the cause of all the toxic chaos and Brie's enmeshed bonding experience, Brie came to believe that toxic chaos was normal. Although she said she preferred a calm and peaceful environment, she sought out chaotic and difficult relationships as those felt normal to her.

Brie's teachers in primary school encouraged her to seek treatment to deal with her anxiety. She was diagnosed with attention-deficit/hyperactivity disorder and given medication for ADHD and anxiety. These strong medications had severe side effects for which she took several over-the-counter medications.

It seemed like at about that time, Brie developed an eating disorder to alleviate any discomfort with food in her stomach. She also began to develop a tolerance of and dependence on some of her medications.

By adolescence, Brie's well-developed inner critic judged herself harshly. She told herself that she deserved the pain and misfortunes that came her way. This judgment was rooted in her strict religious upbringing, which included harsh treatment by men.[81]

Though Brie had a strong and secure attachment with her grandfather, most of the other religious leaders she was exposed to preached from a platform of power, control, and misogyny, leaving her with a feeling that men were better than women.

When Brie moved away for college, she began to experiment with marijuana and alcohol. At the same time, she got involved with abusive and narcissistic men. Because of her beauty, she had no shortage of admirers. This made her boyfriends jealous. Some were even violent, and although Brie might break things off for a while, she would always choose to return to her abusers.

Resilience in the Face of Abuse

The first steps we took in working with Brie were to assist her in settling her physical symptoms of trauma and educating her about trauma loops and the enmeshed bond she had with her mother.

Next, her compromised gut had to be addressed. Under medical oversight and consultation, Brie was weaned off benzodiazepines. At the same time, Brie began a strong course of medical-grade probiotics and other nutritional supplements, and she made some dietary changes. We began to incorporate body scans, a simple technique that Brie used to identify where she was experiencing any discomfort in her body.

---

81 Brie still does not know for certain if she was sexually abused by her father. However, her father ended up being sexually involved with a trusted friend of Brie, someone who was barely older than her. Brie's father eventually married this girl.

Within two weeks, Brie stopped vomiting daily. After a month, she was no longer throwing up at all. She learned to use several body-based therapies—including various types of breathwork—to self-regulate her emotions and calm her nervous system down.

Early in her treatment, Brie had brief relapses using marijuana and alcohol, but she quickly noticed that this impaired her progress. She also did some brain mapping and biofeedback.[82]

Brie also learned how to observe her thoughts without impulsively taking action. In the past, she would either experience fear and be paralyzed by it, or she would plunge into a fearful situation and respond by impulsively attempting to rescue anyone she perceived to be in distress.

Gathering the resilience skills of a Six, Brie began to exercise greater discernment. She made lists and brought them to counseling sessions. She finally ended the destructive relationship with her longtime boyfriend. She decided to stay out of dating and relationships for a while as she became clearer about what was important to her.

Brie benefited from having an early secure attachment with her mother and maternal grandparents, and she continues to work on setting appropriate boundaries with all her loved ones.

> *Brie began her healing by moving into the **body** center noticing how she was sensing the world and feeling it in her body, then came back into the **head** center to make lists and strategies for finding safety. Only then could she access her **heart** center.*

---

82 Through brain mapping, the electrical activity of the brain is recorded, allowing trained professionals to observe the dynamic changes in the brain while processing tasks. Brain mapping helps them to determine which areas of the brain are fully engaged and which areas are disengaged so those can be targeted in treatment.

  Biofeedback therapy works by attaching electrodes and other sensors to the body to measure heart rate, brain activity, and muscle tension, measuring how your body reacts to various neurological states. Through biofeedback therapy, a patient can learn to control bodily processes that are normally involuntary.

The Nine Types and Verbal, Emotional, and Spiritual Abuse

Body Types and Abuse

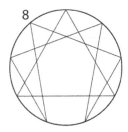

Vulnerability

- Eights rebel against any actions of power over or control toward them, causing them to react rather than pick their battles.
- As a result of aversion to vulnerability, if Eights encounter emotional, verbal, and spiritual abuse along with others, a trauma bond can develop quickly and is difficult to break.

Resilience

- Instead of being anxious, Eights are more prone to express anger. When they are older and less vulnerable, this can help to protect them from abuse and help them break out of the trauma loop of abuse.
- Their anger continues to help identify the injustices of all forms of abuse early on.

Vulnerability

- When faced with abusive relationships, Nines tend to "go along to get along" and lose any sense of autonomy and opinion.
- To avoid conflict in relationships, they might fall for a partner who will always call the shots.

Resilience

- Because Nines can see all sides of a situation, they may merge with others. But when they awaken to their own needs, they are able to move away from their abuser.
- They also possess the innate ability to hold on to harmony in other areas of their life, which could help them cope and respond to the grip of the abuse.

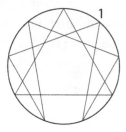

Vulnerability

- Ones might become fierce in choosing a partner whom they can focus on improving to complete what they could not as a young child.
- Ones raised in an emotionally, verbally, and spiritually abusive environment may see that as the correct way to live. And with criticism being hardwired in the One's core, noticing rigidity and fundamentalism could be difficult.

Resilience

- Naturally focusing on improving the world around them moves Ones to examine their environment and find ways to correct what is within their power to correct.
- They may more easily accept the responsibility to be a better person.

Heart Types and Abuse

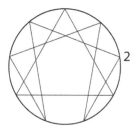

Vulnerability

- With the focus on the needs of others, Twos are vulnerable to codependent relationships and see it as their mission to stand by, assist, and aid their abuser.
- Twos minimize the effects of the abuse on them.

Resilience

- When Twos realize that they have needs and that having needs is okay, they realize that emotional, verbal, and spiritual abuse is not okay.
- They also realize the love and attention they are giving others is, in fact, more authentic when they learn to love, attend, and attune to their own needs first.

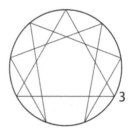

Vulnerability

- When they are young and encounter an abusive situation that they are powerless to fix, Threes might try to avert the attention placed on the problem and become performers who try to bring approval and a smile to anyone who holds power in their world.
- This is the budding root of shame that adult Threes might carry with them, keeping them stuck in abusive relationships.

Resilience

- When Threes realize that they can individuate without carrying the shame of the abuse, they might experience real feelings like anger, hurt, or sadness.
- As they begin to process these feelings, it gives rise to more authentic hope and truth.

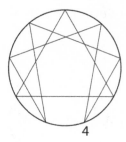

4

Vulnerability

- Fours can romanticize the tragedy and normalize the abuse, repeating unhealthy patterns so they can feel more deeply.
- Feeling misunderstood, Fours constantly yearn for the perfect relationship that does not exist. This can keep them stuck in any relationship that feels intense.

Resilience

- Fours can access a full range of emotions.
- With support and guidance from others, they can deeply grieve, process, and move forward in their recovery.

Head Types and Abuse

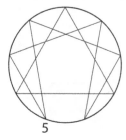

5

Vulnerability

- Fives retreat into their inner world, which makes them more vulnerable to abuse. They may isolate and compartmentalize their experiences, learning to withhold and live in a world of secrecy.
- Fives might even be drawn to cult-like situations due to the interesting nature of such environments.

Resilience

- With a true desire to learn and be self-sufficient, Fives might gather information and find a confidant they can trust and then make changes at a pace that works for them.

- Once a relationship or situation is proven to be abusive in nature, a Five will find a way out.

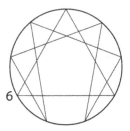

Vulnerability
- Having difficulty with trust, Sixes constantly doubt themselves.
- When wowed by authoritative figures, Sixes are very susceptible to abusive and cult-like relationships.

Resilience
- Once Sixes can see the reality of what is, they are able to use discernment and come up with a strategy to move to a healthy place.
- When Sixes move into a counterphobic reactivity to fear, they no longer doubt themselves.

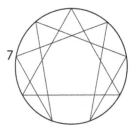

Vulnerability
- With an innate sense of optimism, Sevens may stay in the loop of chaotic and abusive relationships, believing it will all eventually work out.
- Being quite gullible, Sevens can easily be exploited.

Resilience
- Sevens are skilled when it comes to examining options and opportunities to remove themselves from harm's way.
- Their optimism allows them to reset and find the good in those around them and in their present experiences. It also helps that they are future focused.

A Mindfulness Intervention

 Sixes are part of the head center. They seek safety, security, and certainty. Being prepared for danger is important to them. They constantly scan for and attempt to prepare for danger, whether they are conscious of doing so or not.

Lists or worksheets are often helpful in assisting Sixes to identify, understand, and move forward from a place of flight, flight, freeze, or fawn.

Making a list of trauma triggers can help Sixes to either avoid triggers or be aware of their type's response to the triggers. The trigger worksheet can include triggers in your body or reactions, emotions, and thoughts.

Examples of **bodily triggers** include having trouble breathing or catching your breath, heart palpitations, trembling, or experiencing stomach aches.

Examples of **emotional triggers** are feeling irritated or agitated, angry, or sad without any clear reason. Sixes might also be having emotions that are not aligned with the current situation.

Examples of **thought triggers** include not feeling competent or good enough, not being able to make a decision or being unable to identify specific thoughts. It also includes suspecting danger and having paranoid thoughts with no real justification.

Making a list of all the body sensations, emotions, and thoughts that are particular to a Six's experience of trauma is helpful and personal. It can be used to help identify when danger is immediate and in the present, or whether fear is experienced as part of a trauma loop.

When Sixes are trying to discern danger or a fear-based trauma loop, it may be helpful to keep in mind the acronym *FEAR*, meaning "false evidence appearing real."

Facts About Abuse

Verbal, emotional, and spiritual abuse are internal experiences. Different from physical abuse and other types of trauma, these types of abuse leave no visible scarring.

With **verbal abuse**, words are used as a weapon to inflict pain, which often leads to the victim feeling inferior.

The goal of **emotional abuse** is to control someone. The weapons for wearing down a victim's mental wellbeing so they can be manipulated include words and/or actions through bullying, intimidating, criticizing, embarrassing, shaming, or blaming.

In the case of **spiritual abuse**, the abuse is often silent. A person in power misuses their position of influence for the purpose of meeting their own needs rather than the interests of the victim(s). Spiritually abusive leaders can use legalism and authoritarianism to exercise mind control.[83]

Emotional and verbal abuse from parents or early caregivers often interrupt your ability to successfully attach and attune to others later in life. These types of abuse negatively impact your relationships with friends, family, coworkers, and significant others.

The way that you interact with people early in life forms your core belief systems about yourself and others. It also impact your worldview.

Your core beliefs are fundamental to how you manage your life. Even after your circumstances have changed, your core beliefs, whether outdated or not, still run the show.

Signs/Symptoms of Verbal, Emotional, and Spiritual Abuse

- The symptoms of abuse are plentiful, including experiencing shame, fear, hopelessness, anxiety, depression.
- Victims' confidence levels decline, as does their self-esteem. They tend to disengage and self-isolate, and they can be disoriented about what is happening between them and the abuser.
- Denial, second-guessing, self-doubt, and feeling confused are also common. They might even have difficulty making simple decisions, and they could feel as though they cannot do anything right.
- In their various roles, whether as a child, a friend, a partner, or a parent, they may wonder, "Am I good enough?"
- They have difficulty concentrating, tend to be moody, and have many aches and pains that often cannot be explained.
- They tend to withhold information from loved ones and might start lying to the abuser in order to avoid the abuse, and they incessantly apologize. In addition, they frequently make excuses for their parent or partner while also being accusatory and casting blame.[84]

---

83 bit.ly/HealingSpiritualAbuse
84 For a detailed list of symptoms to help you identify abuse, visit bit.ly/SymptomsOfAbuse.

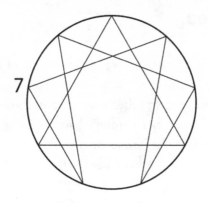

7

CHAPTER THIRTEEN

Avery's Story of Sexual Assault

Avery grew up on a farm, the eldest of eight children who worked collaboratively as equals running the family business. Their father was warm and respectful of his five daughters, reminding them they were the gender that "birthed all of life."

Avery's family was patriotic; many of them having served in the military. So, no one was surprised when at eighteen, Avery applied to join the United States Navy. She had always wanted to be a navy nurse.

When Avery left for the Great Lakes Training Center—a navy base in Chicago—her family was sad to see her go. Avery, however, was wide-eyed about beginning her new adventure, one she had always dreamed of. And having never lived in a city, even the idea of doing boot camp in the Windy City was an adventure Avery looked forward to.

She was thrilled about meeting women from all over the United States, imagining that they would exchange stories of their lives, and that she would make new friends and have a wonderful time.

But what Avery encountered when she arrived in Chicago was quite different from what she had expected. During the entire admission process, she encountered only men. Avery was greeted by a male officer-in-training who whistled at her and commented on how pretty she looked. She was given a physical exam by a male doctor and was given a tour of the campus and her lodgings by one man after another.

Avery would eventually meet other women, and those friendships and the camaraderie was what helped her through basic training. She had known it would be hard, but it couldn't be harder than working on a farm, could it? Life on the farm, though, had not prepared her for the cat calls she and her friends would receive.

After basic training, Avery started Officer Candidate School (OCS) for the Naval Reserve. The first morning of officer training, Avery was sent to meet her commanding officer whom she was told she would be working with as part of her training.

Each morning when Avery reported to her commanding officer, he would comment on her appearance. He would ask questions about her intimate relationships and would also find ways for them to be in confined spaces where he would intentionally rub against her. All of this made Avery extremely uncomfortable.

She approached another senior officer—also a man, as there were few female leaders she could talk to—and asked to be reassigned. Her request was denied, and the man seemed to share her concern with Avery's commanding officer. As a result, her boss became even more demanding. She began dreading coming into work.

One Friday, Avery asked her boss if she could speak with him before they left the office. She held little optimism that this conversation would go well, but she had to speak up. Her boss agreed to meet her, but as that day wore on, Avery became increasingly aware of her anxiety. She could feel her heart beating faster and her breathing become shallow. Avery even felt lightheaded.

By the time they were to meet, Avery's boss had told everyone they could leave early. He offered her a drink, and thinking it might help calm her nerves, Avery accepted it. Then, to help her relax, Avery began by telling her boss a bit about her family and how she missed them.

Instead of just listening, her commanding officer scooted up closer. Uncomfortable with his actions, Avery pulled her chair back. Her boss got up and commanded Avery to stand. She did as she was told.

"We both know you have been wanting me," her boss said as he leaned in to kiss her.

She told him to please stop, but he would not. With nobody in the building who could hear her even if she yelled, Avery was trapped. Her boss kissed her all over her body, then removed her clothes.

Avery remembers very little of the rest of the incident. She only vaguely remembers him taking off his pants and forcing himself upon her, taking her virginity.

Avery was half-dazed for the weeks that followed. She reported to work trying to pretend as if nothing happened. When she reported the abuse, she was reprimanded for speaking up and disrespecting a commanding officer.

She attempted to discuss the incident with one of her bunkmates, pretending it was something happening with another coworker. It did not help, though, as she learned that this woman was having a similar experience.

When Avery spoke with her family and they asked if she was okay, she denied anything was wrong. Meanwhile, her boss continued to take advantage of Avery every Friday and sometimes on other weekdays too.

Having no escape, Avery complied but dissociated during the assaults. She was physically present but described observing herself as in an out-of-body experience.

Avery sought counseling ten years after she left the navy. She had flashbacks of what had happened in OCS. She also had several failed relationships and was always dating men who were emotionally unavailable. She reported a long history of dissociation or disconnection from herself during sexual intercourse. Avery knew she needed help.

Resilience in the Face of Sexual Abuse

As a Seven, Avery was eager to regain the optimistic outlook she had had in the past. She longed to be present to the fun and the good times she used to have with others. She was also eager to develop a relationship with a man who would support and respect her, just like her father did.

Typical of a Seven, Avery was an eager participant, and she engaged in work that had her recall the experiences in her body and connect what was happening in her body to what was transpiring in her mind. She developed a stronger body awareness, though this took some time to reintegrate as she had disassociated with her body.

We had many of our sessions outside where her fear of entrapment was lessened. This had her confronting pain which she understood might be difficult.

Sevens avoid discomfort and pain, but Avery was so eager to get well that she knew it was worth it.

Avery had good early childhood experiences and a strong belief that she was supported by her family and the world at large. During her body work, we asked her to recall memories of an object that reminded her of her innocence and optimism as a young girl on the farm.

She had a strong positive Catholic background. During counseling, Avery's brother—a loving and kind priest whom she trusted, respected, and admired—supported her. Periodically, he even joined her in sessions and would remind her that she was not alone and that her spiritual life, established early in childhood, would see her through.

Her brother also reminded her of the chants, prayers, and smells of incense from church that she delighted in as a child.

> *Avery began her healing by moving into her **body** center to experiencing the sensations she could trust, then came back into the **head** center to map out her next move. Finally, she could move into co-regulating with her brother through her **heart** center.*

The Nine Types and Sexual Abuse

Body Types and Sexual Abuse

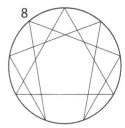

Vulnerability

- Seeing themselves as invincible, an Eight might verbally or physically engage in the abuse and may deny the experience.
- Eights often do not fathom their personal experience of being victimized. Without intervention and insight, Eights may recycle the abuse through intimidating others. This makes it even harder for them to seek help.

Resilience

- When Eights do the deeper work in healing, they identify the injustice and unfairness.
- They embrace their vulnerability and grieve the powerlessness and defenselessness of the experience.

Vulnerability

- To numb the pain, a Nine will merge with the perpetrator.
- Through the process of merging, the Nine loses their individuality and allows the abuse to go on until there is outside intervention.

Resilience

- When a Nine awakens to themselves as an individual who disagrees with what is going on, they take action.
- They are even likely to see the good in the other person, making it easier to forgive…yet not forget.

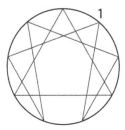

Vulnerability

- It is difficult for Ones to ask for help during or after the abuse.
- They may see themselves as being bad or wrong, and they may feel they should be punished because they must have done something wrong to deserve the abuse.

Resilience

- Once Ones understand they did not deserve the abuse, they will take action and find resources for themselves and others.

- Seeing the need for reform in certain systems, Ones might be the spokesperson against sexual assault, invest time and energy into a non-profit, or become an educator.

Heart Types and Sexual Abuse

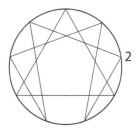

Vulnerability
- Twos often believe that they were the cause of the problem because they did not love the abuser in the right way.
- While they may resent their perpetrator in private, they may also believe that any sexual attention is good.

Resilience
- Always interested in connection, Twos are open to learning about positive and respectful connections.
- Twos who learn to spend time alone and develop the connection with themselves will learn to identify their own needs.

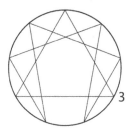

Vulnerability
- After a sexual assault, Threes might move into their *doing* mode, addressing all areas of life except their own heart.
- They might also be impatient with the recovery process, expecting more than what is possible.

Resilience
- Moving into their heart and slowing down to feel can help a Three to engage the healing process.

- Willing to try new approaches and implement new strategies, Threes will eventually find a way out, and they will not repeat the pattern. They are often emphatic, declaring, "This will *never* happen to me again."

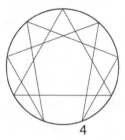

4

Vulnerability

- Tolerating the symptoms that one encounters in the aftermath of sexual assault, Fours can rationalize the assault as just another part of their difficult life.
- Due to how they process shame, it may be difficult for Fours to separate the wrongness and the violence of what happened to them.

Resilience

- When Fours realize how shame has fed into them dealing with the sexual assault, they can access their strong energy fueled by their emotional center. This allows them to follow through with a sound reset, carry on with life, and often not look back.
- Fours' expression of their pain through the arts is often a healing conduit for other victims.

Head Types and Sexual Abuse

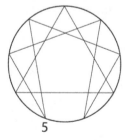

5

Vulnerability

- As victims of sexual assault, Fives become emotionally detached. They might even dissociate as they try to make sense of what is going on.

- Fives have a need for understanding before they can take action. This may allow the cycle of abuse to continue until the Five is armed with enough information to leave.

Resilience

- As Fives work with their ability to compartmentalize, they can slowly begin to integrate various traumatic episodes into their healing process. This allows them to find a comfortable rhythm for healing.
- They are generous with their knowledge and are often helpful and sensitive to others recovering from trauma.

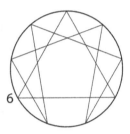

Vulnerability

- Depending on how a Six is processing fear in the moment, they may retreat as a victim or want to plunge through the fear and retaliate.
- They experience strong self-doubt around capabilities to deal with the abuse.

Resilience

- Once the Six understands the way they engage in fear, they can use discernment and slow down reactivity in both directions (that is, either retreat or attack).
- They can engage with courage and bravery.

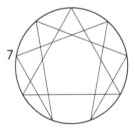

Vulnerability

- Sevens may wrongfully take responsibility believing that because they did not see the signs of abuse, they are responsible.

- Deeper work is needed to examine the pain and process what has occurred.

Resilience

- Sevens seek independence and may simply leave an abusive situation.
- Constantly seeing the positive in any situation, Sevens do not dwell on the past.

An Intervention of the Integration of Movement and Mindfulness

 Sevens are a head type. Their default for handling any trauma is to focus their attention on mentalizing or strategizing. Sevens do this most often by looking for options and alternatives to move away from any perceived pain and discomfort.

Sometimes, Sevens will run from the situation by physically moving away from it. Other times, they will find a way to reframe it by changing their thoughts or their emotional state.

When engaged in a trauma loop, a Seven may feel shut off from these options, but these strategies are still the default.

If, like Avery, you are a Seven, the most appealing path to healing would be to look for options. Having difficulty being present, Avery began her recovery by sensing what was going on in her body in real time. Being aware of the sensations at any given time can help you to remain in the present, as it did for Avery.

From there, you can create a list of appealing alternatives you can employ when trauma is triggered. The list can include ways of physically moving away from the trauma through running (even running in place), taking a pleasurable bath, moving to another room, or going outside where you can walk briskly or take a jog.

You can conclude by creating a list of all your trauma triggers and strategies for ways you can cope when they show up.

Facts About Sexual Abuse

- In the United States, someone is sexually assaulted every sixty-eight seconds.
- One out of every six American women has been the victim of an attempted or completed rape in her lifetime.
- About 3 percent of American men (that is, one in thirty-three men) have attempted or completed a rape in their lifetime.

- Most child victims are between twelve and seventeen years old.
- Almost half of the survivors were sleeping or performing a regular activity at home.
- Close to a third were traveling to and from work or school, or they were traveling to shop or run errands.
- Ages twelve to thirty-four are the highest risk years for rape and sexual abuse or assault.
- There is an increased likelihood that a person would suffer suicidal or depressive thoughts after sexual violence.
- People who have been sexually assaulted are more likely to use drugs than the general public. They are more than three times more likely to use marijuana, six times more likely to use cocaine, and ten times more likely to use other major drugs.[85]

Signs/Symptoms of Sexual Abuse

- As in the case of verbal, emotional, and spiritual abuse, there is a myriad of signs and symptoms of sexual abuse. Physical symptoms include changes in self-care, signs of physical abuse (bruises), sexually transmitted infections (STIs), unhealthy eating patterns and unusual weight gain or weight loss, and self-harming behaviors such as cutting.
- Psychological symptoms include signs of depression, low self-esteem, changes in sleep or appetite, withdrawing from normal activities, and anxiety or worry about situations that did not seem to cause anxiety in the past.
- Other symptoms include falling grades or withdrawing from classes, and an increase in drug or alcohol use.
- For children, signs also include excessive talk about or knowledge of sexual topics, keeping secrets or not talking as much as usual, and regressive behaviors.

85 bit.ly/RAINNOrg

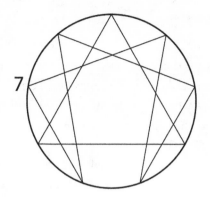

7

CHAPTER FOURTEEN

Mina's Story of Historical and Intergenerational Trauma

M ina, a beautiful, tall woman in her forties, is Lakota Blackfoot Native American from the Great Sioux Nation.[86] Mina has long jet-black hair, a sparkle in her eyes, and a laugh that lights up the room.

Behind that sparkle lies complex historical and intergenerational trauma that goes as far back as 1860. Back then, the U.S. Government created the Bureau of Indian Affairs, an agency responsible for authorizing boarding schools for Native American children. Children as young as four were taken from their families and sent thousands of miles away to be educated in the "white ways of living."

In 1890, during the Battle of Wounded Knee, nearly 300 Lakota men, women, and children were slaughtered by the United States Army. For the Lakota, this became the most well-known and traumatic event in their history.

More than forty years later, when the Lakota medicine man Black Elk was on his deathbed, he could still envision the horror. "When I look back now

---

86 The Great Sioux Nation is the traditional political structure of the Lakota in North America. While the terms *Sioux* and *Lakota* are often used interchangeably, the latter is preferred due to the disrespect attached to the former name, given to them by traders.

from this high hill of my old age," he told writer John G. Neihardt, "I can still see the butchered women and children lying heaped and scattered all along the crooked gulch as plain as when I saw them with eyes still young. And I can see that something else died there in the bloody mud and was buried in the blizzard. A people's dream died there."[87]

Black Elk foreshadowed the emotional and physical repercussions of such a traumatic event on the Lakota generations following Wounded Knee. As a result of the massacre, the Lakota lost their purpose, their land, their people, and their spirit. Those who survived were left disoriented and traumatized trying to rebuild their community.

———•———

It did not help that the government kept taking children from Lakota families and sending them to boarding schools. Late in life, Mina would learn that this had been the fate of her mother and father. First, her mom was put into a sanatorium for tuberculosis when she was just four, and by the time she was of school age, she was taken from her family and sent to boarding school.

Upon arriving at this school, her mother was stripped of her heritage, culture, and language. She was forced to speak English and to dress and act in ways that were contradictory to her roots. For example, the children were commanded to look the teachers in the eyes despite their tradition of *not* looking adults in the eyes as a sign of respect.

What's more, they were shown John Wayne movies and were coached to cheer when the Native Americans were being killed. This forced assimilation into the ways of colonization caused confusion and dissociation for the children.

Years later, Mina's mother would tell of how for the next fourteen years of her childhood, she rarely saw her parents. She was convinced they had abandoned her. She also told Mina stories of how she was beaten, sexually abused, and given alcohol by some of the adults at school.

The years of physical, spiritual, mental, emotional, sexual, and drug abuse the boarding schools put that generation through instigated a cycle of abuse and addiction. By the time Mina's mother returned to her family, she no longer fit into her Lakota culture.

---

87 bit.ly/BlackElkEndOfTheDream

And the years of being away and the unresolved trauma created an emotional disconnect that would eventually also impact her parenting. Though Mina knew she was loved by her mother, her mother's detached and avoidant parenting style—vacillating between being strict, silent, and lenient—confused young Mina. Her father also struggled as he was dealing with PTSD from serving two tours of duty in Vietnam.

To add fuel to the fire, when she was just seven years old, Mina learned that her sister was being sexually abused by their grandfather. This caused Mina to distrust anyone in authority and to steer clear of people who had power over others.

One day after school, Mina came home to find her father had left. Addicted and lacking the tools and support to pursue a healthy and culturally appropriate pursuit to recovery, he simply left. This abandonment left Mina with a deep void in her heart.

The pain of neglect coupled with her sister's abuse drove Mina into escapism, causing her to live a wild life to desperately try and escape the pain in her soul.

———•———

Over the years, Mina watched as one family member after another died from substance abuse or by suicide. Many of her cousins were placed in foster homes by the Department of Human Services. The unresolved grief and loss over the years continued to recycle.

No matter how much fun or distraction she had, though, her ability to reframe her heartache was no longer working.

Resilience in the Face of Intergenerational and Historical Trauma

As Mina turned to counseling to process her unresolved trauma, she discovered she was an Enneagram type Seven who had a strong Eight wing. This discovery helped integrate some of the missing pieces to the puzzle of her life.

Through the lens of being trauma informed, Mina learned about the history of violent trauma against her nation and her family. This helped her develop discernment and empathy. On Mina's path to healing, she leaned heavily into her faith as well as some of the rituals of her Lakota heritage.

Understanding intergenerational trauma was crucial in helping Mina gain empathy for herself and her family. It became clear there were traumas passed down from one generation to the next going back 400 years.

She began to separate what trauma was hers alone and what was carried from her nation's past. Mina moved from her fear and anger to grief for her nation and ancestors.

Learning about her mother's past—including how being taken away from her family and left with no role model for parenting—helped Mina understand why her mother parented the way she did. She recognized why her uncles' return from the boarding schools were so violent and how alcohol, never having been a problem in the long history of her nation, became a problem after the children were sent to boarding schools.

Once Mina began to process her unresolved trauma, it began the process of interrupting the intergenerational trauma cycle for her children. In her pursuit of healing, she intently began to study, listen, and observe her family's history. The stories started to be told. The hidden secrets that carried shame began to lose their stronghold on the family.

> *Mina began her healing by moving into the* **body** *center to slow herself down, then came back into the* **head** *center to understand the trauma, after which she could move into forging meaningful connections with those around her, accessing the* **heart** *center.*

The Nine Types and Historical and Intergenerational Trauma

Body Types and Historical and Intergenerational Trauma

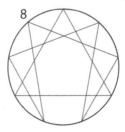

Vulnerability
- When an Eight's family has experienced generations of trauma and it goes unacknowledged, the Eight will move to being an intimidator or a dictator.

- They will push back against all perceived vulnerability.

Resilience

- Eights have strong survival instincts and can be described as nonviolent warriors, seeking justice and fairness. This can help them to break the trauma loop of intergenerational and historical trauma.
- Eights can move into great leadership roles.

Vulnerability

- When dealing with intergenerational trauma, Nines might fall asleep to the facts and become complicit in keeping secrets, therefore ignoring the generational trauma.
- Ignoring the trauma and accepting it as part of the family or community experience inhibits Nines' ability to access the healing process.

Resilience

- When awakened, Nines have the innate capacity to see many ways to move with grace and help their people unite with strength through challenging times.
- Nines respect the past and heal the hatred through harmony.

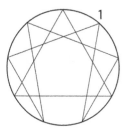

Vulnerability

- Unable to express their powerlessness around the need for reform, Ones might use their energy in a misdirected way to improve other areas of their communities in an effort to avoid the real issues.
- Ones might internalize their oppression and unconsciously act out their frustration toward family members or their community.

Resilience
- Ones who find peaceful solutions for healing will often take on leadership roles in government or social work to assist a community that needs reform.
- Their inner peace engages the power within.

Heart Types and Historical and Intergenerational Trauma

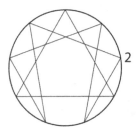

Vulnerability
- Noticing inequities and being drawn to help, Twos might unconsciously enable self-destructive behaviors of people they love.
- While neglecting their own needs, Twos might move into peacekeeping behaviors to maintain the connections, albeit healthy or not.

Resilience
- Twos will move with positivity and a cheerleading energy to gather people together.
- They tend to encourage others in their family and community to look out for each other.

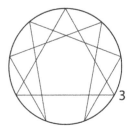

Vulnerability
- Self-deceit and complicit secret keeping allow Threes to look like they are doing well even while they or their families are suffering.
- Threes' constant movement in their daily life does not allow them the space to slow down and feel the emotions that alert them to when systems need to change.

Resilience

- Using the energy of doing what is necessary to move forward while being productive, Threes offer meaningful solutions.
- Threes tend to be authentic with the people around them and desire to share in their story.

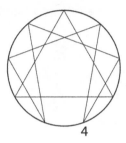

4

Vulnerability

- Without intervention, Fours might remain in the state of enduring emotional dysregulation and parent from that state, thus perpetuating the intergenerational trauma.
- Having a high tolerance for living in sadness and despair, Fours who are stuck in unresolved intergenerational trauma might not have easy access to seeing the need for change.

Resilience

- Fours tend to express the collective sadness and grief of their community creatively and dramatically. This helps both them and their community break the trauma loop.
- Fours often share historical narratives through their artwork and music.

Head Types and Historical and Intergenerational Trauma

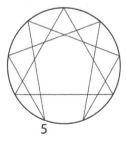

5

Vulnerability

- Fives' engagement in the process of gathering information may cause them not to notice the past and what has happened to them.

- They may be stuck in gathering information and not know when to stop and take action in order to stop the cycle of trauma.

Resilience

- Fives have the capacity to connect the information that cycles down from family systems and communicate the information objectively.
- The wisdom of the Five is easily understood and passed down through generations.

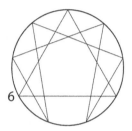

Vulnerability

- Sixes have a push/pull relationship with authority.
- They are more vulnerable to experience historical and intergenerational trauma. This keeps them stuck in the trauma cycle and in a form of denial.

Resilience

- As Sixes establish trust with others over time, they will take responsibility for the cyclical patterns and changes needed to interrupt the intergenerational pattern.
- Despite their drive to remember, Sixes will forgive those who have transgressed them.

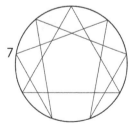

Vulnerability

- Avoiding the pain and living in chaos to distract the Seven from what *is* can keep intergenerational and historical trauma alive and in a continuous loop.

- Sevens might reframe their intergenerational trauma as having relevance and purpose, keeping them from resolving the trauma.

Resilience

- With an optimistic and upbeat attitude, Sevens—with the support of others—can walk through trauma, realizing that pain is part of life's journey and that injustices need not be tolerated.
- They often become spokespeople for social causes. Their charismatic energy will be a pied piper for change within the system.

Interventions for Historical and Intergenerational Trauma

Whether you are suffering from historical or intergenerational trauma, you may feel trapped in the past. To orient you to the present, the practice of focusing on your feet can be helpful. Press your feet firmly into the ground, wiggle your toes, then curl and uncurl your toes several times while you notice the sensations you are experiencing. There are also more in-depth interventions for therapeutic recovery, such as eye-movement desensitization and reprocessing (EMDR), brain spotting, and brain mapping.

Historical Trauma: An Intervention of the Integration of Movement and Meaningful Connections

 These massive group traumas may have occurred as a single episode; however, they tend to be chronic, causing cumulative emotional and psychological pain that significantly alters the person's and group's identity and self-worth. Healing from this type of trauma takes time.

The person's emotions and actions because of these traumatic events over the years are called a historical trauma response (HTR). For many looking for healing, it may be necessary to slow down to connect with their emotions and sensations in the body. For others, movement may be key.

Those who suffer from HTR may benefit from connecting to rhythms and rituals of their ethnic group. For Mina, it was through dancing at powwows. Dancing and the sound of the drums brought her into a stillness internally, making her very present with herself. Every part of her body moved, reconnecting her to internal freedom and power.

Mina also reconnected with the rituals of prayer, the sweat lodge, and the burning of sweetgrass and sage. She also reconnected her children to the reservation where she grew up. They returned every summer to live with their family in a teepee and participate in powwows and other significant Native American rituals.

Intergenerational Trauma: An Intervention of the Integration of Mindfulness and Meaningful Connections

 For those suffering from intergenerational trauma, you might want to start with the practice of a genogram. This connects you to your family's stories and to your family members.

A genogram is a detailed family tree that allows you to chart past generations of your family. With this diagram you can chart data about the relationships in your family, hereditary patterns, and psychological behaviors.[88]

You might want to call your grandma—even your great-uncle and your second or third cousins, to discuss family history and create the genogram.

According to GenoPro, the chart can incorporate "education, occupation, major life events, chronic illnesses, social behaviors, nature of family relationships, emotional relationships, and social relationships. Some genograms also include information on disorders running in the family such as alcoholism, depression, diseases, alliances, and living situations."[89]

Often a genogram will make visible the secrets of the family, the familial patterns, and similarities in repeat traumas. This might help you decide what is yours to own and what is not. You may have been taking ownership of your parents' trauma, for example, and need to release that responsibility.

You may even want to read Mark Wolynn's book, *It Didn't Start with You.*[90]

Facts About Historical and Intergenerational Trauma

Historical and intergenerational trauma are similar, yet different. They often go hand in hand. Both traumas create a legacy effect of unresolved pain, and the symptoms can be passed down vicariously to the survivors' children.

---

88   bit.ly/GenogramVideo
89   bit.ly/IntroToTheGenogram
90   Mark Wolynn, *It Didn't Start with You* (New York: Penguin Life). 2016.
       bit.ly/MarkWolynn-ItDidntStartWithYou

Historical Trauma

Mary Ann Jacobs, PhD, an associate professor and the chair of American Indian studies at the University of North Carolina at Pembroke explains historical trauma:

> [It] is related to a genocide of a people, where some major event is aimed at a particular group because of their status as an oppressed group. It could be a war; it could be cultural, such as when a people's language is banned and they are not allowed to speak or print it. It could be the desecration of monuments, such as graveyards and other sacred sites. Any of those events that have to do with ignoring the humanity of a group and having ... part of social policy, be it formal or informal, where it is not a crime to do [so].[91]

Cultural trauma is a form of historical trauma. It occurs when members of a community—those who share the same skin color, sex, gender, orientation, heritage, or religious background—feel they have been subjected to a horrendous event that leaves indelible marks upon their group consciousness, marking their memories forever and changing their future identity in fundamental and irrevocable ways. It is a collective memory, a form of remembrance that grounds a person in identity formation.

Intergenerational Trauma

Intergenerational trauma is a result of historical trauma or other unresolved traumas. It affects one family, and the trauma within that family is passed down through generations. While each generation of that family may experience its own form of trauma, the first experience can be traced back decades.

In a 2019 article, "The Legacy of Trauma," author Tori DeAngelis pointed to Canadian psychiatrist Vivian M. Rakoff, MD, and her colleagues being the first to write about intergenerational trauma back in 1966 in a paper documenting the "high rates of psychological distress among children of Holocaust survivors."[92]

This type of trauma is part of a legacy that "shares stress." This shared stress is passed down through generations and is seen as hypervigilance, an inability

---

91 bit.ly/HistoricalAndIntergenerationalTrauma
92 bit.ly/LegacyOfTrauma

to express affection and connect, protective parenting, lack of support, and continual survivor coping mechanisms.

Detached parenting, for example, was not seen in the Lakota prior to colonization, the massacre, and mandatory boarding schools. As with many other Native American families, the Lakota held long-established rituals and ways to be with one another emotionally, physically, and spiritually, and to engage in communal living.

Stripped of their rituals, most felt lost. Many Native Americans describe this experience as feeling disoriented. As a result, they focused only on survival. They also lost the intergenerational respect for all family members and their contributions.

Similar to the Indigenous experience, survivors of slavery and the Holocaust experienced trauma which disrupted and annihilated their rhythms of life, rituals, language, customs, and cultural identities.

For many Black slaves in the United States, it was the act of writing and singing spiritual hymns that carried them through the darkest days of racism and slavery. They connected to each other and self through song and being together.

For many Jewish prisoners, what carried them through was their hard work, making sure everyone's basic needs were met. They also stuck together, assisting others to do the same. This deep sense of connection as a group helped many survive the horrific atrocities of the Holocaust.

Signs/Symptoms of Historical and Intergenerational Trauma

- You might feel anger, irritability, internalized aggression, and a lack of trust in others without a clear understanding of why you feel this way.
- Emotional numbing and depersonalization can lead to an inability to connect with others.
- The unresolved and complicated grief might lead to isolation, withdrawal, hyper-vigilance, fearfulness, or fearlessness.
- It may also show up as denial (refusing to acknowledge the trauma happened) and minimization (ignoring the impact of the trauma).
- Memory loss and nightmares might reoccur.
- Generations might struggle with emotions as older generations set the stage for how emotions within the family are dealt with.[93]

---

93 bit.ly/EffectsOfIntergenerationalTrauma

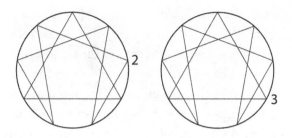

CHAPTER FIFTEEN

Renée and Sharon's Stories of Experiencing a Global Pandemic

We all lived through the COVID-19 pandemic in 2020 and beyond, so there is no need for us to describe the general details around this trauma that was shared at a global scale. Here, we give an account of the events from our perspective as the authors of this book, paying attention to how we as an Enneagram type Two and a Three experienced the pandemic in ways unique to our types.

Renée's Experience

On Thursday, March 5, 2020, my husband and I left for a long weekend to visit our sons in San Diego. Our daughter was leaving the next day for a postponed honeymoon, a cruise around Australia. We had all heard of some problems in China with a virus but did not pay much attention as it seemed to be a localized concern.

Over the next few days, though, the news media expressed a growing concern until they finally reported on the potential of this being a global virus, a pandemic.

While we were in San Diego, we received a call from our daughter and her husband. They had been denied boarding the ship because their flight had connected in Singapore. They had no alternative plans, though. Family got them connected to friends in Melbourne so they could enjoy their honeymoon.

Meanwhile, my husband's fears and mine grew and as we headed back to Phoenix. The flight from San Diego is usually packed, but on that day, it was less than half full. The drop in numbers and the changes in the way the flight staff talked to us was disconcerting.

We were barely home when my daughter called reporting that she was experiencing symptoms of a cold. We all hoped it was just a cold, but it is hard not to worry during a pandemic that a sore throat might be the first signs of the virus.

Not only was I concerned about her wellness; I was also concerned about the fact that she and her husband had to take six flights to get back home at a time when more cases of the virus were being diagnosed, the symptoms were getting worse, and there were warnings about impending travel bans.

We were obviously relieved when my daughter and her husband finally arrived home, a mere ten days after they had left for their three-week honeymoon. However, she was quite sick. Her request to be tested for the virus was denied. She was told that there were "many others in greater need," so she self-quarantined instead.[94]

Despite being much older than my daughter and considered at much higher risk for the virus, all I wanted to do was help her. As an Enneagram type Two, the focus of my attention naturally goes outwards—toward others—wanting to be helpful and to care for them, especially family members and others I love. When someone I care about is in need, my concerns about self-care are difficult to access.

Throughout the pandemic, though, I could neither touch, hold, nor be in the presence of those I love and care about the most. **I missed these types of meaningful connections to the point that my heart literally ached for days.** I felt deprived of connecting deeply with loved ones.

—●—

---

94   Several weeks later, she was tested for both COVID and antibodies, confirming that she did *not* have coronavirus.

At the time I first wrote about my personal experience of the pandemic, I did not know just how much the most meaningful connection in my life would be impacted. In September of 2020, I lost my mother to COVID-19.

She lived in an assisted-living community on the other side of the country from me. The facility where she live had received an award that summer for being one of the safest in their area, having had no reported cases of COVID-19. But in early September, a contract worker who did not know they had COVID-19 infected my mother and six other residents.

To protect the other residents, our family was asked to move my mother out of the assisted-living community. No hospital in the area had beds available, so we relocated her to a family residence. Without the appropriate medical care, my mother continued to decline, losing her appetite and her will to talk or to go on.

A visiting nurse let us know there was no more that could be done to help her, so my mother was transferred to a hospice where she passed away. Due to the pandemic and my mother living on the other side of the country, I was unable to be with her in her last days.

The hospice staff did their best to support my mother and our family. On her final day, the nurse wheeled my mother out onto a lanai where my brothers and sister and all my mother's grandchildren sang to her and said their good-byes. That connection—the face-to-face contact—was more than most families in our situation received.

For me, not being able to be with a loved one as they breathe their last breaths, unable to stroke their hair, kiss them on the forehead, share last words with them, gaze into their eyes or hold their hand is something I think about every day.

But there have also been other losses. Our family has grown in 2021 to include three more precious grandsons. With all my other grandchildren, I had the joy of being present at ultrasound appointments and as they made their way into the world. But with these three—all healthy and full term—it was very difficult not to be able to be in the hospital or have any contact with any of them until it was deemed safe.

It still tears at my heart having to mask up around these little guys, knowing that they cannot see my smile under mask. But for now, this is our world. And for quite some time, we will not yet know how these changes will impact each of these children.

———●———

Under normal circumstances, I work daily to bring my attention inward, asking myself, "What do I need today, and how do I feel? Am I resourced and feeling full enough to help others? If not, what can I do for myself? Perhaps I need to ask others for their help." I typically also scan my reactivity (the ways I have acted in response to events), my feelings, and my thoughts.

It was hard to complete this daily practice without first allowing myself to sit in the sadness of what humanity was experiencing around the globe. From there, I would move into a state of gratitude and appreciation for all the privileges, comforts, and amenities I had. Only after these steps had been completed could I turn my attention inward to do what I normally do.

Sharon's Experience

Not long after midnight on March 3, 2020, an EF3 tornado hit Nashville, Tennessee—my hometown.[95] Around 5 a.m., I made my way to Main Street in East Nashville. The sun was just coming up as I stopped by the counseling center, thankful to find that it had survived the storm.

Next, I drove the five miles away to another one of our businesses. As I made my way through the chaos of Main Street—the destruction reminded me of buildings I had seen in war-torn countries—I was desperately hoping to find our other building unscathed.

Sadly, it was not. Only two walls of our business were left standing. Ironically, one of those walls had a mural of the American flag and bald eagle. It had recently been painted by a Nashville artist.

Two days later, on March 5, I boarded a flight to Tel Aviv. My twelve-year-old son, my sister and her fourteen-year-old son, my elderly parents, and I were heading to Israel. I had mixed feelings around leaving my college-aged daughters and many friends who were all still traumatized by the natural disaster, but I was also over the moon with excitement. We had been planning this trip for two years!

---

95 An EF3 tornado is the third-most intense tornado on the Enhanced Fujita Scale, having wind speeds of up to 165 miles per hour. An EF3 tornado is strong enough to cause significant damage to commercial buildings, let alone homes. It can even turn over trains in their entirety. This particular tornado ended up being the sixth costliest tornado in U.S. history.

Someplace over Europe, my Jewish American seatmate informed me that Israel was closing its borders due to COVID-19. Ours would be the last international flight to be granted permission to land in Tel Aviv.

COVID-19? My mind scrambled to make sense of this news. I had just watched a news conference as I finished packing, and the U.S. government encouraged business as usual. Travelers were simply encouraged not to fly to Asia and a few countries in Europe. Israel was not on that list.

I reminded myself that my father, who often travels to Israel, packed N95 masks for each of us, *just in case.*

Relieved to be allowed access, we joined our group of forty American tourists on a two-week exploration of the Holy Land. The group was a mix of young and old, immunocompromised, and perfectly healthy. We were glad to have a nurse practitioner and an emergency medicine doctor in our group, and we listened and implemented the strategies they shared with us.

As we traveled, the people of Israel continued to provide services, but they added extra measures of caution—requiring social distancing, offering hand sanitizer, and requiring masks and gloves.

We were there when the Israeli government closed down the city of Bethlehem due to three infected persons, and soon afterward, declared a state of emergency and shut down travel throughout the country.

We spent our final days quarantined in the hotel, hoping our return flight would be allowed. As boxed lunches and dinners were passed out, we were issued strict reminders to sit in groups no larger than ten. Access to the hotel amenities were closed, including the gym, pool, nail salon, and the ping pong area—my son and his cousin's favorite place to hang out.

I was amazed at what speed and efficiency this country responded and how everyone cooperated. By the time our flight left, the Israeli army was patrolling the streets, ensuring curfew was enforced.

I was especially grateful for my son's first experience with an event of this magnitude where he witnessed a group come together the way ours did. I was also thankful for our medical team's advice and the Israeli government's response. My "what ifs" were quickly replaced with me writing a chapter for this book. I remember thinking it odd that my thoughts and writing on trauma were easily accessible while the entire world was colliding with trauma.

This experience gave both my son and I a sense of calm within the storm. I did not start to feel anxious until I landed in my own country and saw videos of people hoarding, fighting, and capitalizing on others' pain and suffering.

My college-aged daughter had warned me of the chaos as she tried to buy groceries so we would have food once we got home. I had to see it to believe it, though.

As an Enneagram type Three, my natural tendency is to seek solutions, find the positive in just about anything, and avoid the harder emotions as they might prevent me from getting where I want to go. Driven by efficiency and solutions, I can default to focusing on keeping things moving and on task, focused more on the flow.

As a heart type who has learned to be honest with myself in how I feel, I have found a wealth of feelings I can access and resource. I no longer fear getting stuck in sadness, anger, grief, or disappointment, I know that these feelings will pass.

I do not remember feeling much sadness until I returned to the United States. What triggered the sadness was the shock of what was happening in my country. In Israel, thanks to the efficiency and collaboration of the Israeli government, I had glimpses of hope for the world. I left Israel hopeful.

After being quarantined in Phoenix, Arizona for two weeks with my family, we returned to Nashville. Main Street was still destroyed from the tornado. My city was experiencing concurrent traumas—an EF-3 tornado *and* COVID-19. And the pandemic slowed the recovery efforts for the tornado victims.

My heart grieved deeply for my city. The impact of trauma was everywhere yet was being experienced in isolation. Schools shut down. Meanwhile, Nashville—like countless other cities around the nation—experienced capitol rioting in response to George Floyd's murder.

There definitely were moments when I felt the pull to kick into high gear and make things happen. But then again, what could I do?

As a clinician, I access my personal and professional responses to those in need: my family, my clients, my community, my country, and even globally. Paying attention to all these facets of my life is implicit in answering the call to provide mental health support.

The pandemic emphasized my belief that trauma crosses all boundaries. I was accustomed to assisting in times of trauma. I was on the ground helping with recovery after the tsunami in Sri Lanka, during the 2010 earthquake and coup in Haiti, after Hurricane Katrina, and after the Harvest Festival mass shooting. I have seen first-hand how trauma affects the homeless and the rich, the frontline workers and the victims. It matters not who you are, what you do, or where you live.

Trauma finds you because you are human and because life is fragile.

———•———

As Renée and I wrote this book during a global pandemic, it became more than a book about finding resilience amid trauma. We ourselves were navigating our way through the trauma of the pandemic—not only with our clients, but also with our families and ourselves.

The call to deliver excellent mental health care during a time when our lives were in upheaval motivated me to slow down even more and implement self-compassion and self-care. Writing about trauma and being knee-deep in it offered great accountability for my resilience.

Having suffered tremendous loss and trauma in my past and yet having recovered, I knew where my tendencies would be to slip back into old habits. So, I dug deep with my self-care routine. **Ironically, having to shelter in place became a place of restful solitude for me.** Despite my business suffering great financial losses, I was able to implement coping mechanisms that were helpful.

As a Three, sheltering in place became a respite from internal and external demands, especially as a single parent. Real quick, life became real simple. Faced with the most basic day-to-day priorities, I had two choices: react to the situation, or trust the situation as it unfolded while relaxing my body, heart, and mind.

———•———

From the get-go, I had fully embraced all the necessary protections to prevent getting COVID-19—not out of fear but out of discernment as I have had numerous bouts of pneumonia since I was ten. As a result, my lungs are compromised.

I was in Phoenix visiting family when my mom and daughter came down with COVID. Not long after, I was hit with *extreme* exhaustion. I hoped I was just tired, but then I also tested positive for COVID.

In less than two days of testing positive, I could hardly breathe. By day three, it felt like I was drowning from the inside. I struggled to sleep, worrying that I might die in my sleep. Early the next morning, my daughter took me to the doctor, and she confirmed that I had COVID pneumonia.

I did not want to be admitted to the hospital, convinced that people who went to the hospital for COVID-19 never came out. I made my sister promise to do everything she could so I could remain at my daughter's home. *If I were to die, I wanted to die at home.*

My sister's and daughter's eyes welled up with tears. This was real, not just fear of an unknown virus. My sister began researching, calling friends and doctors for alternative treatments. That day, an off-duty sheriff and a nurse came to our home to administer what would be the first of multiple intravenous treatments packed with vitamins, antibiotics, and steroids.

Meanwhile, I slept for between eighteen to twenty-four hours a day! At times, I would hear my dad, sister, and daughter whispering, but my mind could not comprehend. At one point, my daughter broke down crying due to the weight of making tough medical decisions for both me and our mom. She called my sweet love to help.

He came to Phoenix to support me, sleeping on the floor by my bed at night so he could monitor my oxygen levels and my breathing until I was out of the woods.

In the midst of it all, my daughter took me to my mother's house. I was told it was to say goodbye to her before she would be taken to the hospital. They expected this to be our final goodbye. My mother was not expected to survive COVID—but I did not understand this yet.

By the time I got to see my mom, I was not prepared for the deep grief in the room, nor to witness the state she was in. I could feel tears rolling down my cheeks, yet I could not put together a sentence. It was only then I understood what kind of goodbye this was for.

By God's grace, my mother and I both survived.

It took several weeks before I was well enough to head home. I missed my son, my younger daughter, and our dogs back in Nashville.

My eldest daughter in Phoenix is still recovering from secondary trauma, compassion fatigue, and the grief of almost seeing me die. In so many ways I am glad the ones in Nashville were spared that trauma.

At the time of wrapping up writing this book, I am still processing the trauma of it all. I am careful to pace myself as my body is still recovering, and I allow myself to grieve when sadness wells up in my heart for the many people who died from COVID-19 while not being able to be with loved ones. In those moments of grief, I grab hold of gratitude and tightly hold it, thankful for the life I still get to lead.

As a Three, my biggest growth typically is found around significant challenges or trauma. For whatever reason, the reality of what is going on needs to smack me across the head to stop what I am doing and be present.

The Pandemic: A Collective Trauma

The pandemic is what we would call a collective trauma, an event researcher Gilad Hirschberger describes as "a cataclysmic event that shatters the basic fabric of society. Aside from the horrific loss of life, collective trauma is also a crisis of meaning."[96]

The pandemic destroyed lives. And unless you lived in a village far removed from society, it disrupted the rhythm of life. It uprooted everyone's daily ways of living, created fear of the normal things in life, and disconnected friends and family. What's more, it caused long-term mental and physical health challenges.

Through it all, the healthcare workers worldwide have suffered the greatest toll, working in traumatic situations, spending endless hours caring for critically ill patients.

Case in Point

Nurse Sara's Experience

Compassionate, sharp, and going into her second year of nursing, Sara was working in the cardiac unit at an urban hospital when the pandemic began. She immediately began cross-training in critical and comfort care for patients, something she had no experience in yet.

As the pandemic raged through the summer, Sara realized that for the sake of her friends and family, it was imperative that she self-isolate. After all, she worked night and day treating COVID-19 patients and was not going to risk exposing her loved ones to the virus.

By Christmas 2020, Sara's circle of friends had dwindled to being just her coworkers. Her anxiety was high, and having seen countless patients and even coworkers die, she was suffering from both survivor's guilt and compassion fatigue. Sara watched many coworkers resign from fatigue, something she could understand. She had not seen her immediate family for close to nine months.

---

96   bit.ly/CollectiveTrauma

Complicating the fatigue, loneliness and death was the public's lack of belief that the virus existed. As she struggled to keep giving everything she had to her patients, Sara fought hard against discouragement and disillusionment.

Sara's story is just like that of many healthcare workers who worked tirelessly to keep their communities safe from the illness. The emotional and physical consequences to Sara were monumental.

The emergency response to the pandemic impacted all systems—educational, healthcare, justice, organizational, economic, travel, social, and relational. Due to travel bans and the need for social distancing and self-isolation, the pandemic reduced the workforce and launched us fully into the virtual world.

The impact was staggering for developing countries. The gap of poverty, clean water and necessary resources became wider and wider.

The *Science Advances* journal found staggering income losses after the pandemic emerged in 2020. Across the nine countries they surveyed, an average of 70 percent of households reported financial losses. Just a month into the pandemic, half or more of those surveyed were forced to eat smaller meals or skip meals altogether. That number skyrocketed to almost 90 percent for rural households in the West African country of Sierra Leone.[97]

Children, although originally less likely to get the virus, suffered from the lockdown as their schools and social connections came to a screeching halt. The inability to process the instant change especially caused an increase in behavioral health conditions among children and young people.

Inequities and disparities quickly surfaced too. Many people went into the pandemic already having less wealth, less education, and less access to transportation and healthcare. This put them at a greater risk for contracting and dying from the coronavirus.

For example, as a result of policies that have helped to determine the location, quality, and residential density for people of color, Black and Hispanic people are clustered in the same high-density, urban locations that were most affected in the first months of the pandemic.[98] In addition, Black people and Native American people disproportionately use public transit, which has been associated with higher COVID-19 contraction rates.[99]

---

97 bit.ly/PandemicIncomeLoss
98 bit.ly/COVIDandUS-Economy
99 bit.ly/ContractionRates

The long-term effects of the pandemic will be felt far and wide. Even if you were not struggling with depression or anxiety prior to the pandemic, the pandemic adjustments alone created depression and anxiety for many. If you *were* struggling before the pandemic, those challenges, stressors, or traumas were only amplified moving through the pandemic.

> *The pandemic adjustments created depression and anxiety for many. If you were struggling before the pandemic, those challenges, stressors, or traumas were only amplified moving through the pandemic.*

In all the devastation, it forced countries to come together to implement global solutions for this global trauma. This created a strength and hopefulness that allowed people to see a silver lining.

Some people offered hope by dropping off groceries to the elderly or tutoring children for free. Countless others wore masks to prevent an increase in numbers. Some found hope internally, and though it may have wavered as the pandemic dragged on, this is normal. In one way or another, we all depended on one another, relying on the flicker of hope someone else still had. In fact, it is okay to borrow it until you can find your own. **Trauma is not meant to be carried alone. We must dig deep for hope, and we must give hope freely.**

———●———

With the pandemic being a collective trauma, it is important to understand how much our needs differ, especially as it relates to how we respond differently to being alone.

During the pandemic, *everyone* experienced isolation—whether you were a healthcare worker not being able to be close to or hug your family, a college student not allowed to go home for breaks, or the single person whose rhythm of friendships was built on social experiences outside your home.

Isolation or aloneness is the separation and physical distance from another human being. Loneliness, meanwhile, is the lack of companionship. During the pandemic, many people felt both aloneness and loneliness. With resilience, you can turn loneliness and aloneness into mere solitude—the state of being alone.

For many Enneagram types, moving from isolation to solitude helped them endure the chronic trauma of the pandemic, although they are not hardwired to move into solitude quickly.

But other types have solitude as a resilience trait they can pull from. For many Fives and Sixes, for example, being at home was a welcome encounter to the hustle and bustle of the outside world. They felt safe, certain, and secure. Many had already been preparing for an event such as this.

For Sevens, Eights, Twos, and Threes, their move into solitude may have taken a little longer. Once they did access solitude, they may have found refreshment in the quietness of the mind, rest, and a slower pace of life.

You can access solitude as a gift when you move from isolation to aloneness. It is when you are quiet and still that you might identify your internal resources and can develop your personality and resilience.

Accessing solitude is a conscious decision. It is a portal to reacquainting yourself with who you are. Befriending solitude gives you reprieve from feeling the disconnection from people, experiences, or normal rhythms of life.

The Nine Types and a Pandemic

Body Types and a Pandemic

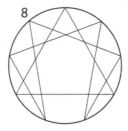

Vulnerability
- Eights' anger toward imposed rules that feel like power and control being exerted over them is typically followed by a strong pushback.
- Believing their bodies are invincible and cannot get sick, Eights in a pandemic might tend to exhibit a lack of self-care.

Resilience
- When Eights engage in their protective instincts, they do what is good for others. They bring energy and passion.
- They are fair, direct, and can motivate and energize others.

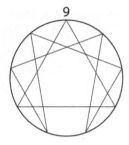

Vulnerability

- When faced with a pandemic, Nines narcotize, procrastinate, become easily distracted, and lose sight of goals.
- They find other ways to stay asleep so they can comfort themselves.

Resilience

- Once awakened, Nines come together with willingness and action plans to address the global needs. In doing this, they are selfless, having the innate ability to clearly hear what the needs of all people are.
- Able to be highly adaptive, Nines not only do what is good for them but what is best for the community.

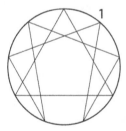

Vulnerability

- Ones see what needs to be corrected. In a global pandemic, there is more than is humanly possible to change. This leaves the One perpetually stuck in the hum of frustration.
- Ones may feel a more intense burden as they tend to feel personally responsible for correcting problems. The combination of the frustration and intensity of the One tends to push people away when the One might need them the most.

Resilience

- Ones truly desire reform and change. They can provide endless solutions for making needed changes.
- A One who is aware of their intensity and frustration can more easily invite others in.

Heart Types and a Pandemic

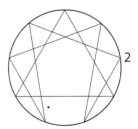

Vulnerability

- Twos might be distracted by the needs of everyone else, leaving them tired and fatigued. Their lack of connectedness to others will create isolation and deep grief.
- They may feel frustrated, unappreciated, and resentful of their inability to give the help they want to give.

Resilience

- Twos' innate resourcefulness in connecting with others gives them the impetus to find solutions to connect to others.
- Loving, caring, nurturing, and generous by nature, Twos help voice the needs of many of those around them, often getting others the help they need.

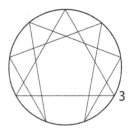

Vulnerability

- Threes tend to be impatient, which makes it harder for them to deal with the magnitude of needs brought on by a pandemic.
- They may jump to creating a strategy to meet the needs of others; however, due to the nature of chaos from a pandemic, the Three will become impatient with the slow process of recovery.

Resilience

- Not allowing their emotions to get in the way, Threes will often jump in and do what is necessary by implementing solutions and persevering. They "just do it."

- Threes bring hope to situations as they can see the end results.

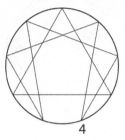

4

Vulnerability
- Fours might collect stories of the tragedy of the pandemic without moving into action.
- Stuck in what is missing, Fours might be more prone to a state of depression.

Resilience
- Fours have an innate capacity to sit with deep tragedy as others recover.
- They will not abandon the emotional healing process of the people they are helping.

Head Types and a Pandemic

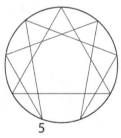

5

Vulnerability
- Fives will find themselves creating charts, collecting data, compiling emergency updates, and doing fact checking.
- Fives' tendency to isolate and do research might keep them unaware of the challenging impact of being alone.

Resilience
- When the accurate information Fives have gathered is shared with others, an opportunity arises to implement the information in helpful and appropriate ways.
- Fives rebound quickly following bouts of isolation and being socially disengaged.

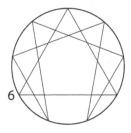

Vulnerability

- Having difficulty with trust, a Six is constantly in self-doubt and attempting to manage fear from a place of suspicion/hesitation or just plunging through. This circumvents any real use of discernment and moving forward in taking action.
- They experience strong self-doubt around capabilities to deal with the situation, keeping them stuck in constant rumination. Second-guessing and self-doubt may keep Sixes from helping, wondering who they can trust.

Resilience

- Many Sixes will say they have been rehearsing for this scenario their entire life and they are ready.
- Sixes' innate skills have them prepared for their own lives, but they are also willing to share resources with those they care for.

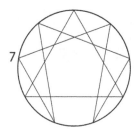

Vulnerability

- Sevens automatically reframe the reality of the events, keeping them from seeing the pandemic from a realistic perspective.
- They may act recklessly toward self and others.

Resilience

- Sevens can learn to tolerate uncomfortable feelings while using discernment, hope, and making their and others lives better.
- They will have many options for solving a problem.

An Intervention of the Integration of Mindfulness and Meaningful Connection

If, like Renée, you are a Two, you may want to allow yourself to sit in the sadness of what others were experiencing around the globe. From there, you can move into a state of gratitude and appreciation for all the privileges, comforts, and amenities you have.

As someone who is naturally outward-focused, you can then work to bring your attention inward, asking, "What do I need today, and how do I feel? Am I resourced and feeling full enough to help others? If not, what can I do for myself? Perhaps I need to ask others for their help." You can scan the ways you have acted in response to events, your feelings, and your thoughts.

An Intervention of the Integration of Movement, Mindfulness, and Meaningful Connections

We had mentioned that accessing solitude is a conscious decision that gives you reprieve from feeling the disconnection from people, experiences, or normal rhythms of life.

Creativity is a practice of solitude. You can express creativity through cooking, journaling, painting, sculpting, writing, listening to music, scrapbooking, gardening, and more. Being creative allows you to move into the inner silence. This, in turn, reminds you of your internal resources, your sense of self, and the courage you have to take on loneliness and transform it into solitude.

You might consider a sketchbook where you can write, draw, or dream. This sketchbook is there to collect all that is within you as you watch the events of the world, your city, and your home.

Sometimes as trauma continues, it is hard to journal or read. If those activities drain you, find a plant to take care of. Military veterans often use nurturing plants to quiet their minds, develop self-care, and remember the potential of life. Taking care of something like a plant can help your mind to slow down. And as a plant grows, you will be reminded that life continues and that time brings change.

Embracing new rhythms of life is crucial. However, it is of equal importance to hold the new rhythms loosely, for it might not always be this way. In your new rhythm, find a space for solitude to develop and grow.

If you are a Three, like Sharon, hiking could also be key to being creative and connected. Sharon hikes with her German Shepherd, making friends along the way as she listens to the river speak and the trees sing. This allows her mind to move into a creative space, affirming her solitude and strength within. In that space, Sharon says, she is not lonely.

Facts About the COVID-19 Pandemic

The novel coronavirus was first detected in Wuhan, China, in December 2019.[100] By the end of January 2020, the World Health Organization declared a public emergency of international concern and by March 11, the WHO declared it to be a pandemic.[101] Symptoms of the virus range from none to life-threatening.

Globally, travel was restricted, countries closed their borders, and businesses and schools were being shut down. There were immediate economic implications around the world, and the educational impact along with social and psychological impact is yet to be seen.

Access to healthcare and global vaccine inequity are just some of the issues highlighted by the pandemic.

At the time of print, the global death toll to COVID-19 has surpassed six million, placing it among the deadliest pandemics in recorded history. Globally, the United States leads with more than eighty million cases and close to a million deaths. Brazil and India follow, each reporting more than half a million deaths.

Meanwhile, the Delta and Omicron variants are raging through communities the world over. [102]

---

100 COVID is short for **co**rona**v**irus **d**isease, and the 19 indicates that it was first identified in 2019.

101 Merriam-Webster defines *pandemic* as an "outbreak of disease occurring over a wide geographic area."

102 bit.ly/COVIDLiveUpdate

Part Three

Practice Interventions

CHAPTER SIXTEEN

The Groundwork for Success

Perhaps you saw some of your story in the stories represented so far. Maybe you could relate to Kim feeling helpless during the derecho windstorm, or to the victims of the Las Vegas Harvest Festival mass shooting event who reacted in such vastly diverse ways. It could be that you connected with Brandon hiding behind drawn curtains years after leaving Chicago and his life in the gangs.

Remember hearing about Pete who got triggered by smells years after 9/11 and Jenni who felt kicked in the gut by a song decades after being freed from trafficking? Remember how victims of the Mendocino Complex Fire who were taken back to the fires when they were stuck in traffic? Maybe their stories helped you realize what still triggers you.

Or perhaps you saw your experiences reflected in Natalia's story of being marginalized and dehumanized. It may be that you could relate to Zoe's story of being trauma bonded to a perpetrator, or to nurse Sara who is still dealing with the emotional and physical consequences of being a frontline worker during the pandemic.

Maybe you saw a bit of yourself in Thomas's inability to connect emotionally except through blowing up in rage, in Amy withdrawing from the world, or Saman working hard to make the world a better place, even at a time when a tsunami devastated his community thousands of miles away from his new home in the United States.

It could also be that you related to Remy's story by not allowing yourself to fully grieve events in your life before moving on to the next thing, or Clint working hard at looking successful so that others will not know how poor a home he came from. Or it may be that Georgette's story of unraveling the ties of colorism and racism struck a chord with you.

Maybe you connected with elements of Carter's story of substance abuse or with elements of Brie overcoming verbal, emotional, and spiritual abuse. Or it might be that Avery's story of sexual assault helped you see events from the past in new light. It may even be that the impact of historical and intergenerational trauma resonated with you.

Even if you could not fully relate to any of those stories, you will have seen some of your story in Renée and Sharon's experiences at the start of the pandemic. And as we had mentioned before, regardless of what has happened to you, the traumatic experience is not your responsibility. What *is* your responsibility is your recovery.

This is empowering news, as trauma robs you of your personal agency.[103] Being in control over your actions, emotions, and thoughts moves you into the driver's seat of your life rather than the passenger seat.

Taking steps toward your recovery is a gift that only you can give yourself. You alone can take the first steps in claiming your power back.

You may need the expertise of a trauma-informed therapist or counselor to partner in your healing—many survivors of traumatic experiences do. While seeking help might feel scary or challenging, it is a good first step. At times, all you might feel able to do is to show up and say, "I'm here. And I need help."

That is a great place to start.

As trauma counselors, we understand that moving through trauma is difficult. We also know how important it is to feel empowered and capable of making and sustaining changes on your own. In this chapter and the next, we will introduce you to interventions that you can try on your own or with the help of a trusted professional.

Whether you are working with a therapist or whether you are trying to reclaim your resilience on your own, we have designed this part as a self-guided approach so you can take some preliminary steps toward your healing.

---

103 Mary C. Lamia, PhD, describes personal agency as "Your ability to take action, be effective, influence your own life, and assume responsibility for your behavior are important elements in what you bring to a relationship." bit.ly/SenseOfAgency

If you notice trauma loops, though, if you struggle to remain in the present, if you experience recurring self-sabotaging behaviors, or if you have continual internal dysregulated emotions, we suggest that you might benefit from professional counseling.[104]

Coping Mechanisms and the Enneagram

Depending on your personality type, you may have developed some coping mechanisms along the way. These may have gotten you this far; however, they will not get you where you want with your trauma recovery. Before you move into understanding how the practices work, look over the list of coping mechanisms below, or identify some coping mechanisms on your own.

1. **Judgment**—Judging yourself or those around you to keep your focus away from the pain
2. **Codependency**—Fixing others' problems while ignoring you and your needs
3. **Workaholism**—Working to fill the void or numb the pain
4. **Nostalgia**—Romanticizing the past while avoiding being present in the moment
5. **Detachment**—Repressing or selectively ignoring information, isolating, or withdrawing
6. **Projection**—Attaching your feelings or motives to someone else
7. **Avoidance**—Avoiding anything negative by self-medicating or focusing only on the positive
8. **Manipulation**—Throwing a fit or become controlling
9. **Stonewalling**—Avoiding confrontation or intimacy altogether, numbing out

You might notice that the coping mechanism you identified coincides with your Enneagram type number. Or, due to trauma, your coping mechanisms

---

104 One of the good things that came from the pandemic is that therapy is available through telemedicine, that is, via phone or video conferencing. Whomever you choose to work with, we recommend that you make sure the therapist has the necessary credentials to be able to call themselves a mental healthcare professional.

Also, while we offer more than thirty practices that you can do on your own, there are many other interventions that you should *only* attempt with the help of a qualified therapist, including somatic experiencing and EMDR.

could align with the number of one of your wings or the other lines you are connected to.

Regardless of the connection to your Enneagram type, this coping mechanism is something you do naturally, something you have found helpful in dealing with the trauma you had gone through. Think of this as a toolbox. It may be that you have always reached for the hammer when you get triggered but today, you realize you have a choice. You can put down the hammer and reach for a sander to finish a job.

What coping mechanisms are no longer helpful to you? You can make a list of those behaviors, thoughts, or emotions that have been holding you back. These must be replaced with healthy responses for you to heal. Pick one reaction—just *one*—to work on.

Moving from Reactivity to Receptivity

Trauma resolution means moving from knee-jerk reactivity to responsiveness and on to receptivity and resilience. This movement requires you to interrupt the trauma loop and coping mechanisms you have acquired to get through your traumatic experience.

> *Trauma resolution means moving from reactivity to responsiveness and on to receptivity and resilience.*

Looking back at your list of coping mechanisms or go-to reactions, what is it that is no longer working for you? Instead of **reacting** to stressors, how would you like to **respond**?

To move from reactivity to responsiveness and on to receptivity, you must interrupt the trauma cycle. This is not a simple or linear process, though. For instance, if you identify as a head type (a Five, Six, or Seven), it may take starting with the body or the heart to access the intervention that works best for you. It may also be that you find success by beginning with a head-based intervention.

The same goes for body types (Eights, Nines, and Ones) and heart types (Twos, Threes, and Fours). You will want to try several interventions. Choose the ones that work for you regardless of your Enneagram type's location in a specific center of intelligence.

Once you have mastered this new practice and you see yourself being more receptive to what is around you, you can work on the next one. In the next chapter, we offer multiple practices you can use to reacting to responding to trauma and in doing so, reclaim your resilience.

CHAPTER SEVENTEEN

The Practices

Trauma interventions are the most helpful if you use an intervention that meets the center (body, heart, or head) where the resistance is most apparent. This is not always obvious. Due to the way your body responds to and hangs on to trauma, resolving the trauma does not necessarily start at your preferred center of intelligence.

Here, we offer the interventions as they relate to the Three-M Triad as a way of moving from reactivity to receptivity and resilience. Listed below are interventions that are categorized according to one of the m's—movement, meaningful connections, and mindfulness—each focusing on one of the centers of intelligence. If you pay attention to the graphics, you will notice that many interventions are associated with more than one center.

But first, a *brief* overview.

Interventions Associated with Movement

These interventions **focus on the body center of intelligence**, utilizing the body and the senses. Of the three m's in the Three-M Triad, we rely here on movement to calm down the nervous system.

Movement encompasses *all* embodied practices—sensations, identifying any discomfort in the body, caring for the body, exercise, taking action, sitting quietly, changing positions, making posture changes, and more.

Regardless of what Enneagram type you are, embodied practices are often the first place you can begin when trying to interrupt the trauma loop.[105]

Interventions Associated with Meaningful Connections

These interventions focus on the **heart center of intelligenc**e, utilizing **connection and relatedness** as intrinsic to the intervention process. These might include other people, places, or objects. Finding community can be part of this process. Language may or may not be included in this process. Quieting interventions are meant to assist the heart types to reengage with themselves. Of the three m's in the Three-M Triad, we rely here on meaningful connections.

Meaningful connections are relationships with people in your life that hold meaning for you, offer you support, allow you to be who you are, and are nurturing and safe. Meaningful connections may be formed with people in your family, or with friends, colleagues, members of your spiritual community, or a self-help group.

Interventions Associated Mindfulness

These interventions focus on the **head center of intelligence**, utilizing **what you think and know** through the gathering of facts or research. It also includes letting go of that information and/or turning your attention to a specific thought or action with focus. Of the three m's in the Three-M Triad, we rely here on mindfulness.

Mindfulness is all about gathering your attention and deliberately placing it somewhere. This may sound simple, but it is not. Being mindful requires that you feel safe enough to gather your attention, so regardless of what Enneagram type you are, when experiencing a trauma feedback loop, executive function often goes off-line, making it difficult to start with mindfulness.

You can begin to reintegrate by accessing your body (using an embodied practice) or your heart center (by working with someone else, thus utilizing a meaningful connection). This will allow you to access your head center where you can then gather attention, use discernment, have clarity, and navigate effectively between thoughts.

---

105 Big names in the trauma field have developed techniques that describe the importance of movement. For more movement techniques, we recommend writings by Bessel van der Kolk, Peter Levine, and Francine Shapiro.

Speaking or writing are common components of these mindfulness interventions, as are mapping things out and mentalizing.

Practices to Access Your Resilience

1. Trauma-Release Exercises (TRE™)

Watch animals long enough—whether in person or on wildlife shows—and you will notice how they "shake it out" after a traumatic encounter. Through his study of how animals release energy, trauma intervention specialist Dr. David Berceli designed trauma-release exercises.

Using a natural shaking response, TRE combines six short exercises to relieve stress, tension, and trauma—especially for anyone who regularly experiences trauma. Starting with your feet and your ankles, you stretch and loosen the muscles all the way from your feet to your psoas muscle, the deepest muscle group within your core, and one that holds onto stress the longest. For the final step, you lay on the floor and pick your pelvis off the floor, stretching your core body muscles until a tremor develops. You can find more information at Dr. Berceli's website.[106]

We were fortunate to partner with Dr. Berceli in his research, and in addition to reporting relief in muscle soreness, TRE participants reported improved quality of sleep, having a general state of calm, experiencing greater patience with clients, feeling more present and engaged with others, and thinking clearer.

2. Tapping

Tapping is based on acupuncture, a therapy developed thousands of years ago. You have acupuncture points on your body that are associated with energy meridians. Simply put, these points on your body are related to various internal organs, thoughts, emotions, and other functions in the body.

Using your index and middle fingers, tap on each of the points listed below for ten seconds before moving to the next point. This helps calm the body and balance it too. Some say affirmations or hum while tapping these points:

- **The eyebrow point:** Where the eyebrows begin, closest to the bridge of the nose

---

106 bit.ly/DavidBerceli

- **On the side of your eyes:** On the bones directly along the outside of either eye
- **Under your eyes:** On the bone directly under either your eyes
- **Under your nose:** The area directly between your nose and your upper lip
- **Above your chin:** The area between your bottom lip and your chin
- **Collarbone:** Starting from where your collar bones meet at the center, go down an inch and out an inch on either side
- **Under your arms:** About four inches beneath the armpit, along the side of your body
- **Side of hands:** The soft, fleshy part of the hand between the pinky finger and the wrist
- **At the top of your head:** Directly on the crown of your head

Tapping is often used in conjunction with other therapies.[107]

3. Planting, Growing, and Gardening

 Putting your hands into soil is grounding. It takes you out of the thinking, thinking, thinking of your head space and brings you back into your body, to a basic place of working with Mother Earth. For those who love working in the garden, it may be helpful to know that you might love this activity so much because it connects you with your body.

But even if you do not have a green thumb, you can try this exercise. It can be as simple as simply repotting a plant. Visit your local plant nursery and choose a plant or an herb that you like. You may want to visit with the salespeople about whether you are considering planting it inside or outside and whether it will need sun or shade to flourish.

If you will simply be repotting a plant you are purchasing, choose a pot you find pleasing and can move if you find it needs more sun, for example. Be sure to find out how often the plant needs water and how much it needs. You may find it calming to attend to your plant's needs and watch it thrive.

---

107 If you want to learn more about tapping, it is also referred to as the "emotional freedom technique" and "thought field therapy."

4. Temperature Change

 The introduction of temperature change can be helpful as a trauma intervention if the sensations arising in your body often feel warm to hot—like when you experience some level of anger.

- With your hands or a washcloth, briefly splash as cold a temperature of water on your face as you can tolerate. If you have access to ice, you may even want to try rubbing ice on your face, or you can drink something ice cold. Notice what changes occur because of this intervention.
- If, however, you are someone for whom the sensations arising in your body feel cold and disconnected, try wiping your face with a piping hot cloth or drinking a hot beverage to help connect you to your senses.
- Whether you benefit from drinking something hot or cold, a change in temperature is often helpful in the interruption of the trauma loop as your attention shifts from the trauma experience to the temperature of the beverage.

5. Reengagement Exercise

 If you notice that you have emotionally checked out or disengaged from the world around you, you can check back in or reengage through deep breathing.

- Take three deep breaths through your nose as you count to four, hold for four, exhale for four, then wait for four before inhaling again.
- As you breathe this way, engage your five senses. Check in with all five senses and identify what it is that you notice. What do you hear? What do you see? What do you feel? What do you taste? What do you smell? (If you are having trouble with this exercise, be more intentional with engaging your five senses by turning on some calming music, holding something warm, cold, or soft, or by lighting a fragrant candle.)
- As you become more aware of the stress while you tune in to your body, allow yourself to continue to breathe through that awareness.

6. Quieting Your Body

 Quieting your body during times of stress can be as simple as addressing the stress that lies right beneath the skin surface of your face, shoulders, and hands.

- Quiet your body by slowing your breathing. Tune in to where you notice the stress in your body.

- Notice your facial expressions. Is your face at rest, or are you frowning? To determine your face's level of rest, scrunch up your face or tighten it, hold for five seconds, and release. You can even blow air into your cheeks and hold for five seconds, then release.
- If you notice tension or tightness in your shoulders, try shoulder shrugs. Raise your shoulders to your ears, hold for five seconds, then relax. Do shoulder shrugs until you feel the release of your shoulders to a resting state.
- The same goes for your hands. Make tight fists, hold for five seconds, then stretch out your fingers as far as you can. Repeat this until your hands are relaxed.

7. Chair Yoga

Gather your attention and place your thoughts on trying these poses. This gets your mind to stop ruminating and focus on the present, on the movement itself. It also allows you to take a brief mental break from your work even while you are at your desk. This benefits your concentration, focus, and energy level.

7.1 Cat/Cow Stretch

- Sit on a chair with your spine long and both feet on the floor. Place your hands on your knees or the tops of your thighs.
- On an inhale, arch your spine and roll your shoulders down and back, bringing your shoulder blades onto your back. This is the "cow" position.
- On an exhale, round your spine and drop your chin to your chest, letting the shoulder and head come forward. This is the "cat" position.
- For five breaths, move between the cow position on inhalation and cat position on exhalations for five breaths.

7.2 Stand Like a Mountain

- Begin by standing like a mountain, that is, stand tall, feeling your feet firmly rooted on the ground, your head reaching toward the sky. You are stable, solid, and dignified.
- Breathe in and out deeply and mindfully, allowing the breath to fill your entire body.
- Upon breathing in, recognize, "I know that I am breathing in."

- Upon breathing out, recognize, "I know that I am breathing out."
- Repeat this as many times as you need to get you rooted in the present.

8. Multi-Sensory Guided Imagery

 Multi-sensory guided imagery includes descriptions related to all five senses. For example, you could imagine smelling and then tasting a warm, gooey chocolate chip cookie while hearing someone you love and trust, gazing into their eyes, and them coming up to you and giving you a gentle and warm embrace.

This guided imagery allows you to feel safe by experiencing and integrating all five senses. This keeps your attention within, not wanting to leave your body. It is meant to evoke a response of relaxation.

Guided imagery usually starts with a breathing exercise to help you bring your attention to your body. After the breathing exercise, read a multi-sensory script or have someone read it to you, whether in person or recorded.

9. Dancing

It is not necessary to have a partner to dance with, nor do you need an audience. Dancing in the privacy of a safe place may allow you to move in ways that are uniquely expressive. For those who enjoy dancing or are willing to try it, dancing can be an effective way to manage energy running through your body.

Rhythmic movements can be soothing. Dancing freestyle—allowing your body to move in any ways you are comfortable—is also very empowering.

10. Recorded Meditations

 Find a guided meditation or some positive affirmations you find appealing. Read them to make sure they feel positive, and good, and safe for you.

- Using the voice-recording function on your smartphone, record the first two or three sentences of the meditation. Play it back to yourself. What does your voice sound like? Do you find yourself believable or do you find it soothing? If not, re-record until you do.
- Then, record the entire meditation. If you continue to have trouble, ask someone you love and trust to record the meditation you have chosen.
- Listen to the meditation as often as you would like but not while you are driving.

11. Imagery for Those with Attachment Concerns

When there have been disrupted attachments early in life, it is difficult to believe that meaningful connections and relationships are possible or consistent and stable. The purpose of this type of guided meditation is to help lay a foundation for believing that others will support and nurture you.

Begin by thinking of all the characteristics of a nurturing connection, whether it is with your mother, father, caregiver, or some other caregiver figure.

Find a meditation that describes this type of relationship or evokes a sense of nurturing from a healthy perspective. Listening to guided imagery about nurturing relationships repeatedly can change the way you think about meaningful connections and relationships. The repeated listening helps to rewire what you believe. It can also inspire a conversation with someone you trust about interrupted or disruptive attachments in their past.

Below is a meditation that you can record and use as a caring and nurturing script. As you move through this guided meditation, if you notice any discomfort, or distracting thoughts, just notice them, then return your attention to your breathing.

11.1 Heart Meditation for Self-Compassion

Sit upright in a chair, adjusting your posture until you find a comfortable position. Place your hands on your lap. Soften your gaze, and when you are ready, close your eyes.

- Breathe comfortably. Take a few breaths and find a comfortable pace of breathing that suits you.
- **Call up an image of a newborn baby.** Notice how small and defenseless this baby is. Imagine the shock and difficulty this baby faced during the birthing process, leaving the safety of the mother's womb.
- As you hold the image of this newborn, place your hand over your heart, and send wishes of goodwill to this small infant. "May you be happy. May you be full of love. May you experience peace. May you be free from suffering. May you live with ease. May you live life to the fullest extent. May you always know that you are perfect with infinite potential."
- Notice any emotions that arise as you share your wishes. Notice any sensations that arise between your heart and body.

- Now call up a picture of yourself at six months old. See your face.
- As you hold the image of yourself as an infant, place your hand over your heart, and send wishes of goodwill to yourself as an infant. "May you be happy. May you be full of love. May you experience peace. May you be free from suffering. May you live with ease. May you live life to the fullest extent. May you always know that you are perfect with infinite potential."
- Notice any emotions that arise as you share your wishes. Notice any sensations that arise between your heart and body.
- **Now call up an image of yourself at five years old.** Notice the expression on your face. Listen to your voice. Notice at five years old where you shined and what you loved.
- As you hold the image of yourself as a young child, place your hand over your heart and send wishes of goodwill to your five-year-old self. "May you be happy. May you be full of love. May you experience peace. May you be free from suffering. May you live with ease. May you live life to the fullest extent. May you always know that you are perfect with infinite potential."
- Notice any emotions that arise as you share your wishes. Notice any sensations that arise between your heart and body.
- **Now pull up an image of yourself as a sixteen-year-old.** Again, notice the expression on your face. Listen to your voice. Notice at sixteen years old where you shined and what you loved.
- As you hold the image of your teenaged self, place your hand over your heart.
- Send wishes of goodwill to your sixteen-year-old self. "May you be happy. May you be full of love. May you experience peace. May you be free from suffering. May you live with ease. May you live life to the fullest extent. May you always know that you are perfect with infinite potential."
- Notice any emotions that arise as you share your wishes. Notice any sensations that arise between your heart and body.
- **Finally, pull up an image of yourself as you are today.** Consider the expression on your face. Listen to your voice. Think about where you shine and what you love.
- As you hold the image of your present self, place your hand over your heart.

- Send wishes of goodwill to yourself. "May you be happy. May you be full of love. May you experience peace. May you be free from suffering. May you live with ease. May you live life to the fullest extent. May you always know that you are perfect with infinite potential."
- Notice any emotions that arise as you share your wishes. Notice any sensations that arise between your heart and body.
- With one hand still on your heart, place the other on your belly. Notice any feelings or thoughts that arise or change.
- Return your attention to your breathing. Place your attention on your body in the chair. When you are ready, open your eyes to a soft gaze.
- Sit quietly for a moment or two.

12. Owning Your Emotions

 Take some time away from others and away from distractions. Turn your attention inward and find a comfortable pace to your breathing.

- Think of a situation that happened recently—not a traumatic one but something that was significant.
- With your attention focused internally, record any bodily sensations that occurred as you considered the situation. Then record any emotions you were aware of about the situation. Finally, record any thoughts you had about the situation.
- Once you have completed writing, review what you wrote, and confirm that these were *your* sensations, emotions, and thoughts, not those of others.

13. Writing Yourself a Love Letter

 When you are in a trauma loop or in fight, flight, freeze, or fawn mode, it might be difficult to access anything positive about yourself or your life. Writing a love letter to yourself at that time might be hard. Here are some guidelines that might help.

When writing yourself a letter, consider using some of these prompts:

- What are you trying to do now with your life? Express compassion for the attempts no matter how many attempts you have made. In fact, consider how courageous you are to keep trying!
- If someone else was going through what you are, what kind words would you have for them?

- What positive attributes have other people noticed about you that you may not have noticed?
- How has your fear or worry protected you and helped you to better understand yourself?
- What emotions would you like to have, and why?
- What will your life look like when you are where you want to be?

When you are done writing this letter, put it in an envelope and mail it to yourself. Just think how it will be to receive this by snail mail!

14. Walking Meditation

 Slowing down to connect with your feelings can help you to de-stress. It connects you to the present by bringing your awareness to quieting stressful thoughts, feelings, or behaviors.

- Begin with walking. As you are walking, focus on your breathing. Inhale deeply through your nose while counting to four, hold for four, exhale for four, then wait for four counts before inhaling again. Repeat this at least three times.
- As your breathing becomes rhythmic, notice your feet as you walk. Do you feel the pressure of each step you take? What does that feel like to you? Can you feel the earth, pavement, or asphalt beneath your feet?
- Continue your breathing as you begin to engage your five senses. What do you hear? What do you see? What do you feel? What do you taste? What do you smell? Simply check in with all five senses and identify what it is that you notice.
- Challenge yourself to walk, breathe and notice all that your five senses are bringing to you.

15. Focusing on the Present

 When facing trauma, your attention tends to move back and forth between the past and future, seeking a way out. It causes you to consider something that happened to you in the past and something that might happen while keeping you from focusing on the present.

Most of the time, your attention is scattered as the head center believes its purpose is to strategize, plan, and organize to mitigate stress and danger. By darting from one thought to another, though, you create more stress and less calm. Through practice, you can notice where your attention is and then move it somewhere else.

Strategies to move the focus of attention to the present are called mindfulness practices. However, this practice includes body sensations, emotions, and thoughts.

- During a repetitive task such as when you are brushing your teeth, practice turning your attention to what is going on in the moment. Focus on picking up your toothbrush, putting toothpaste on it, and placing the toothbrush in your mouth. Notice how you move your hands and what the toothpaste feels like in your mouth, how your teeth feel, and how the toothpaste tastes. Focus on spitting out the excess toothpaste and placing your toothbrush somewhere when you are finished.
- Also pay attention to any emotion you may be experiencing. Whatever the emotion, see if you can gently shift it from what it is to a different emotion. If you are unable to shift the emotion, see if you can stay with that emotion and lower the intensity.

16. Identifying and Expressing Gratitude

 Trauma negatively impacts your ability to identify, access, and experience gratitude. Gratitude can be a positive emotion or a disposition that promotes a sense of appreciation. When feeling grateful—whether for a person, yourself, an event, or for being alive or healthy—you have a warm feeling inside.

Developing a practice for gratitude can be done in many ways. The key to this being effective is to make it a regular practice, hopefully a daily one. A very dear friend gave me (Renée) a gift last year. It is a beautiful large glass jar with *Gratitude* scripted on the outside in beautiful gold lettering. It is a daily reminder to be grateful, and I place a note in it daily for something I am grateful for.

Other gratitude practices you could try:

- Start your own gratitude jar and place a message in it daily.
- Begin each day with expressing your gratitude for being alive.
- Express gratitude to someone whom you speak with daily, such as your spouse or a "gratitude buddy" who can likewise share with you what they are grateful for that day.
- Daily, let someone else know you are grateful for them.
- Scan your body sensations, heartfelt emotions, and discerning thoughts, noticing something in each category you are grateful for.

- Start a gratitude journal.
- As part of your nightly ritual, think of all for which you are grateful that day.
- If all of this is hard, express gratitude for learning these possibilities that you can use once you are ready.

17. Tree Art Exercise

 Making art is a way of expressing yourself. When your words or access to your emotions are blocked, artwork can be helpful to both yourself and anyone working with you to help you discover your resilience.

- Using colored pencils, crayons, or markers, and using the instructions that follow, draw five trees on a piece of paper. If you do not like to draw, collect pictures of trees that best express the five trees.
  - o The first tree represents what feeling grounded (calm in your body), content (feeling happy) and safe (secure) looks like.
  - o The second tree represents what being in the state of **fight** while traumatized looks like.
  - o This third tree represents what being in the state of **flight** while traumatized looks like.
  - o The fourth tree represents what being in the state of **freeze** while traumatized looks like.
  - o The fifth tree represents what being in the state of **fawn** while traumatized looks like.
- Next, look at the first tree again to remind yourself of what your tree of calm looks like.
- As you back away from the exercise, pay attention to how you are revisiting and not re-experiencing the trauma. Acknowledge yourself for that.

18. Carrying an Object

 This exercise is done by selecting one small object that you can always carry with you. The object should be small enough to fit in your pocket or purse. It can be anything but a weapon.

- When choosing the object, it needs to represent a good mood—feeling happy or content, your body being in a state of calm, feeling safe, feeling rooted or grounded, feeling empowered, or any other element that helps to bring you to a felt sense of calm.

- After choosing the object, write down and share with someone the story of why you chose this object and how it helps you regulate your mood. Sharing the story with someone or writing it down makes it more real.
- When triggered, pull out the object and hold it, recalling the sense of calm it represents.

19. Becoming Familiar with Your Patterns and the State of Your Nervous System

You may want to start out by doing this exercise for a short period and then building up to longer periods or even several times throughout the day. You will need a journal or notebook to be able to see the patterns that emerge.

- Begin by recording the date, time of day, and length of time you plan to spend on this exercise.
- Next, record any bodily sensations, emotions, and thoughts you are aware of. Also note any actions you want to take.
- Ask, "Am I in a fight, flight, freeze, or fawn state now? Or am I calm?"
- Take three deep breaths and repeat the questions.
- Record any patterns you notice and consider adjusting your lifestyle to create greater calm.

20. Writing a Story to Examine False Evidence Appearing Real

At first, this exercise should be done when you are with someone with whom you feel safe. It can be a helping professional or a friend. Once you are more comfortable with the exercise, you can do it on your own.

Whether you write this out or tell it to your trusted and safe person, answer these questions:

- When I feel like I want to fight and I do not know why, this is the story I make up about it.
- When I feel like I want to run away from my life, my feelings, and my thoughts, this is the story I make up about it.
- When I feel like I cannot move, this is the story I make up about it.
- When I feel like I want to give in to someone else, this is the story I make up about it.

- Next, considering that the acronym FEAR stands for "false evidence appearing real," write or discuss with your trusted person what pieces of the stories are false evidence appearing real.
- After completion of this exercise, choose another way of looking at FEAR, for example, "fierce, energetic, aware, and resilient." Write down this statement and keep it with you. Whenever you experience yourself moving into a traumatic state of fight, flight, freeze, or fawn, take it out and remind yourself of the truth of the new meaning.

21. Figuring Out the Trigger Point

 If you are someone who manages your fear by gathering information to know as much as you can about a topic, keep track of what you were thinking prior to using or engaging in self-destructive behaviors.

You may even want to keep an inventory of what time thoughts about the self-destructive behaviors first occurred and compare it to when you gave in to the desire.

Next, investigate other thoughts or actions that preceded the first thought of the behavior. This will help you trace back to the triggering event.

22. Safe and Comfortable Environment

 Journal or tell a trusted individual about a place where you feel safe or have felt safe in the past. Where is it? What makes it so special or safe? Recall as many details as you can. Whenever you are worried about being triggered, go to that space in your mind.

If you have no memory of a safe place, create a safe space in your mind. Where is it? What makes it so special or safe? Describe as many details as you can. Then, when you are worried about being triggered, go to that space in your mind.

23. Creating a Trigger List

 Lists or worksheets are helpful in assisting those in the head center to identify, understand, and move forward from a place of fight, flight, freeze, or fawn. If that is you, creating a list of trauma triggers can be quite helpful. This can include triggers in the body or reactions, emotions, and thoughts.

- Examples of body triggers include having trouble breathing or catching your breath, you may be trembling, and you may experience stomach aches.
- Examples of emotional triggers are feeling irritated or agitated, angry, or sad without any reason you can identify. You might also be having emotions that are not aligned with the current situation.
- Examples of thought triggers include not feeling competent or good enough, not being able to make a decision, or not being able to identify what you are thinking. It also includes anticipating danger and having suspicious thoughts with no real justification.

Having such a list of all the body sensations, emotions, and thoughts that are particular to your experience of trauma is both helpful and personal. You can use it to help you identify when danger is immediate or present, or whether you are experiencing fear as part of a trauma loop.

24. Understanding Trauma Reactivity

 This written exercise helps you to make sense of the way you feel trauma in the body and what the sensation is trying to do to guarantee your survival. Knowing that symptoms can appear to keep you alive helps you to relax the judgment you may have about trauma symptoms.

- On one side of a sheet of paper, record all the ways trauma shows up for you, for example through anxiety, isolation, disconnection, headaches, or other ways.
- On the other side, write down what each of the symptoms or reactions is attempting to do to keep you safe. For example, "Anxiety alerts me that I am moving too fast and must take more time for myself."

25. Creating a List of Alternatives

 Head types handle trauma by focusing their attention on mentalizing or strategizing. However, when engaged in a trauma loop, they may feel shut off from these options. You can preempt this by creating a list of appealing alternatives for when trauma is triggered.

The list can include ways of physically moving away from the trauma through running (even running in place), taking a pleasurable bath, moving to another room, or going outside where you can walk briskly or take a jog.

26. Slowing Down

 For all Enneagram types, it is necessary that you slow down during a trauma loop to connect with your bodily sensations, emotions, and thoughts. This process of slowing down can be stressful for some types.

- To slow down while moving, begin with a slow jog. Focus on your breathing. Inhaled through your nose counting to four, hold for four, exhale while counting to four, then wait for four before inhaling again. Repeat this at least three times.
- As your breathing becomes rhythmic, notice your feet making contact with the ground beneath you. What do you notice around you?
- Continue your breathing as you begin to engage each of your five senses. What do you hear? What do you see? What do you feel? What do you taste? What do you smell?
- Check in with all five senses and identify what it is that you notice. Challenge yourself to jog, breathe, and notice all that your five senses are bringing to you.

27. The RAIN Technique

 About twenty years ago, Michelle McDonald coined the term *RAIN* as a method for mindfulness.[108] Using the RAIN technique can help you to move from a state of reactivity to responsiveness or receptivity.

RAIN is an acronym for recognize, allow, investigate, and non-identification. Do these in this order as one leads to the next.

- **Recognize**: Pay attention to or notice what is going on.
- **Allow**: Do not try to change anything. Open a space for whatever is happening to simply be and allow what is.
- **Investigate**: Become kindly curious about what is happening. Explore from a state of kind inquiry and openness.
- **Non-identification**: Know that you are not defined by what is happening. Non-identification paves the way for a natural awareness.

108 bit.ly/RAIN-technique

28. Doing a Butterfly Hug

The butterfly hug is a tool you can use to calm anxiety, when you are experiencing stress in the moment.[109]

• Close your eyes and take a few minutes to simply focus on your breathing.

• Bring awareness to the self. Notice any emotions that are coming up, including any self-judgment. Simply notice.

• Keep breathing.

• Cross your hands over your chest, placing your hands just below your collarbones. You can interlock your thumbs so your hands look like the wings of a butterfly.

• For thirty seconds, slowly tap one hand, then the next, alternating left and right, left and right.

• As you continue to breathe deeply, focus on your awareness, slowing your mind and your body with each breath, simply letting your emotions be.

• When thoughts come up, envision those as clouds floating by. Simply let them pass, avoiding all judgment.

• Keep tapping until the anxiety has passed.

29. Scanning Your Body

Body scanning can be done in a variety of ways. Generally, all body scans require you to gather your attention as best you can and observe your body. You can start to observe from the top down, from the bottom up, or start with any area that is causing you discomfort.

The idea is merely to observe and notice—not to try to change anything. As you scan your body, notice how your body wants to move into fight, flight, freeze, or fawn.

30. Identifying Your Support

Connecting with others is a biological imperative for your survival. However, not all connections are positive and helpful. Developing your social support network is a large

---

109 Developed by Lucina Artigas, MA, MT, and Ignacio Jarero, EdD, PhD, MT, the butterfly hug was used extensively with victims of Hurricane Pauline in Mexico in 1998.

part of developing meaningful connections toward resilience, but trauma interferes with your connection both with yourself and with others.

- Think about the people who currently play a role in your life—family, friends, colleagues, helping professionals, or others.
- As you bring each person to mind, consider if they want the best for you. You could even use the list below to guide you.
- You may be surprised at how you answer these questions. Some of the people may have been helpful in the past but are no longer supportive, while others you have overlooked may be helpful to you now.
  o Do I feel safe with this person?
  o Do they have my back?
  o Do they want the best for me?
  o Can I be honest with them?
  o Do they accept me for who I am and what I am going through right now?
  o If I called on this person, would they be there?
  o Are they part of my social support network?

After this exercise, write down the names of only the ones for whom you could answer yes to without any pause. This is your support network.

- Are there others whose names you would like to add?
- If you do not have many names on your list, ask yourself what you are willing to do to bring more people into your support network.

31. Identifying States of Trauma

 Understanding your triggers is a part of trauma recovery. Identifying when you are in a state of fight, flight, freeze, or fawn may be difficult when you are in that state. However, reviewing past states of trauma response is not as hard.

This exercise is best done when you begin with an agreement with yourself that if you are triggered by recalling memories, you will quit the exercise and find a way to calm your nervous system down.

It can be done through simply thinking, writing down your responses, or verbally sharing them with a helping professional or a trusted friend.

- Think of a time when you felt like you wanted to fight or run away from a situation. Can you identify the triggers that made you want to fight or flee? What were they?

- Think of a time when you wanted to collapse, disappear, or surrender in a traumatic situation. Can you identify the triggers that made you want to collapse, disappear, or surrender? What were they?
- Make a mental or written note of your triggers. Review them often so you become familiar with them so you can avoid or disarm them.

32. Integrated Meditation Practice

 Begin by finding a seat where you can sit upright, and the seat is comfortable and supportive. Uncross your arms and legs and allow your buttocks to feel the full support of the chair.

- Notice where your attention is. Is it on something in your body, on how you are feeling emotionally, or is it on a thought? When you have noticed where it is, gather your attention and turn it to your breathing.
- Place your attention on your breath and follow it as if you were surfing on the wave of your breath. Follow your breath on the inhale—in and down—and on your exhale—up and out. Do it again—in and down, up and out. Continue to breathe this way and find a comfortable pace that works for you.
- Repeat this for at least ten full breaths.
- As you continue to breathe, think of someone you trust (a safe person who has your back) or of a place where you feel safe (or have felt safe in the past).
  - o If it is a person you have chosen, put the person in the room with you. Have them gaze at you, hold your hand, or hold you.
  - o If it is a place you have chosen, picture it in your mind's eye and allow your body to feel all the fullness of that place. Fully bring yourself into that place with all your five senses. Perhaps you sense the way the air feels. Maybe it is the way this place looks. Or perhaps it is the sound of the ocean nearby, or the way it smells or something you can taste.
  - o Merely notice these sensations, nothing more. You need not change anything. Observing them is all you need to do.
- Now place one of your hands on your belly and the other hand on your heart. Continue to breathe at the pace that works best for you to create a sense of calm.

- o See if you can take your sensate experiences and allow them to travel up and fill your chest, the area of your heart, and around your heart. Notice any emotions arising.
  - o Merely to notice your emotions. You need not change anything. Observing them is all you need to do.
  - o Acknowledge that both your sensate feelings and emotions are present and can co-exist.
- Next, move our attention up to the area between your eyes, an area that symbolizes wisdom, clarity, and discernment. Continue your breathing at the pace that works best for you to maintain your calm and relaxed state.
  - o Notice any thoughts that occur to you. You need not change anything. Observing them is all you need to do.
  - o Just as you have acknowledged your sensations and emotions, acknowledge your thoughts. Allow all of them to co-exist.
  - o Your body has offered you information about your senses. Your heart has offered you information about your emotions. And your head has offered you information about your thoughts. What a miraculous being you are with all these portals to knowing yourself. Acknowledge just how amazing and resourceful you are.
- Continue to sit with all of yourself, continuing to breathe in that very calm way.
- As you prepare to return your attention to the room, take an inventory of what you have noticed. Consider what you noticed in each of the three centers and how movement, meaningful connections, and mindfulness may be integrated to bring you a fuller experience of your life while you are calm and safe.
- Gently gather your attention and bring it back to your breathing and to yourself, to your body seated in the chair. When you are ready, open your eyes with a soft gaze.
- Sit quietly, allowing yourself to integrate this experience.

Notice during the exercise whether you were able to sense one or more of your centers and one of the m's in the Three-M Triad:

- any bodily sensations or movement
- any emotions or meaningful connections
- any thoughts or noticing mindfulness

33. Coping with Ongoing Pandemic(s)

During the pandemic, people all over the world changed the way they lived and their daily habits. Gyms closed. Restaurants closed. It was difficult to connect with others.

The typical ways we moved, connected and found peace and calm were not working as easily. And the information we were getting about the virus kept changing. That is why we developed the Three-M Triad of movement, meaningful connections, and mindfulness.

As we examined the common complaints of many, it appeared that anxiety around the lack of freedom of movement and the lack of connection were common. Reminding people of their resourcefulness was helpful. But as the pandemic dragged on quarantining, social distancing, isolation, and restrictions took their toll.

As a reminder, **movement** represents the **body center** types on the Enneagram. These types seek **power and control** to manage their life.

Meaningful connections represent the heart center types on the Enneagram. These types seek recognition, connection, and affirmation.

Mindfulness represents the head center types on the Enneagram. These types seek safety, certainty, and predictability.

You use all three of these strategies, but one may be more prominent. In our counseling work, we used the Three-M Triad daily to check in with ourselves and our clients. Feel free to use these questions to check in with yourself and find ways in which you can discover your resilience amid a pandemic or during other times of overwhelm.

To check in with your body center, ask yourself:
- How does movement address my need for power and control?
- What am I doing to keep my body moving now?
- Are there ways I can move and exercise that I might try?
- What do I have control over?
- What do I have control over that I am not controlling and need to?
- What is out of my control?
- What am I attempting to control that is not helpful or healthy for me?

To check in with your heart center, ask yourself:
- How do meaningful connections address my need for esteem and affirmation?
- Who am I spending time with?

- Are they supportive, nurturing, and accepting?
- Who could I be spending time with that I am not?
- What ways can I connect with others that I am not right now?
- How am I offering support to others important to me?

To check in with your head center, ask yourself:
- How does mindfulness address my need for safety, security, and certainty?
- What is safe in my life now?
- What is predictable in my life now?
- What am I certain about now?
- Am I spending too much time listening to the news?
- If I am in danger, do I have a plan?
- Who can I count on to help me if I have a problem?

Twenty Ways to Improve Your Vagal Tone

 In Chapter Two, we mentioned the potential the vagus nerve—a bundle of cranial nerves that wanders all the way from the brain stem into the stomach—has in stimulating all three centers of intelligence.

Each of the following exercises can work to improve vagal tone, open the centers, and create a sense of relaxation. Vagal tone can be measured through heart-rate variability, a variation in intervals between heartbeats. Hence, many of the practices listed increase heart-rate variability.

1. **Singing, chanting, or humming:** Done in unison, this increases heart-rate variability. It also activates your throat muscles, which stimulates vagal tone.
2. **Sighing:** With a long and deep exhale, sigh out loud.
3. **Laughing:** Laughter increases heart-rate variability.
4. **Gargling:** Hold water in the back of your mouth and agitate it by exhaling.
5. **Saying positive affirmations:** Activate all three centers by saying, "May I be able to move with ease and flexibility, may I enjoy meaningful connection with myself and others, and may I be mindful as I move throughout today."
6. **Exercising:** Even light exercise activates heart-rate variability.
7. **Dancing:** Alone or with others, move your body rhythmically.

8. **Breathing**: Focus on deep and slow breaths, in for five seconds and out for five seconds. That makes for only six deep breaths per minute.

9. **Meditating**: Try various types of meditations, including prayer, sitting quietly, listening to music, reading a guided script, using guided imagery, walking a labyrinth, or reciting a mantra.

10. **Chewing**: Chew your food slowly and well to activate the state of digestion while resting.

11. **Fasting**: Abstaining from food activates heart-rate variability.

12. **Intermittent fasting**: Switch between eating and fasting on a regular basis.

13. **Yoga**: The traditional practice of stretching while also focusing on breathing stimulates vagal tone.

14. **Tai chi**: This ancient Chinese tradition is a graceful form of exercise increasing heart-rate variability and helping release stress.

15. **Qigong**: This is a Chinese technique of meditation, controlled breathing, and guided movement.

16. **Lymphatic massage**: This gentle massage encourages the movement of lymph fluids and toxins from your body.

17. **Getting acupuncture**: Acupuncture of the ear stimulates vagal tone.

18. **Exposing yourself to cold water**: Take a cold shower, swim in icy water, or splash cold water on your face.

19. **Diffusing essential oils**: Certain high-quality, pure essential oils or blends—especially lavender and chamomile—can be used to calm your nervous system through engaging your sense of smell creating a sense of calm. Other oils and blends can assist in rest and digest.

20. **Balancing your microbiome**: Take a quality probiotic to create a healthy environment in your gut where many mood-altering chemicals are created.

CHAPTER EIGHTEEN

Now What?

Where do you go from here? The journey of trauma recovery is long and arduous, but along the way you will find freedom from the more difficult parts of your story. You will reclaim your resilience. Sometimes it is one step forward and two steps back. But as you become better acquainted with your path, you will find the pace of recovery being more familiar territory.

In the first chapter, we talked about what you might be carrying in your trauma suitcase. Your healing journey can be compared to climbing Mount Everest. For such a journey, your luggage would be a backpack—and a heavy one, at that. It would be stuffed with all the physical, emotional, and mental toll of trauma, along with your coping mechanisms and trauma loops.

At first, you might not notice the weight. All you see is how tall Mount Everest is. Even just the sight of it is intimidating. You might even wonder if it is worth the climb.

It may be helpful to sit down for a moment. Take your eyes off the gargantuan mountain and investigate what you are carrying with you. Some of what you have in the backpack may have been with you for a while and is familiar to you, yet those items may no longer be helpful.

There may be some items you need on the climb, while other items you can go without. The items you choose to keep should be essential to you making it to the top of Mount Everest—your recovery. Whatever you choose to pack must offer consistency that your body, heart, and mind can count on.

Along the way and at the summit, especially, there are breathtaking sights to behold. No amount of pain along the way will beat the feelings of empowerment, celebration, and relief you will experience by conquering this mountain.

To make it to the top, you may need to make significant lifestyle changes. For both Renée and I, part of our healing journeys meant focusing on self-care, raising our children, and bringing in a paycheck. For years, those three things were what we focused on.

Having read this book, you have some new items to pack—skills and knowledge about trauma that can help you along the way. But you also know that there are things you need to take out for your load to be lighter.

As you continue on the road to resilience, some of your friendships and life rhythms need to change.

Some people might not understand why you cannot go out every weekend, talk on the phone for hours, or spend money on vacations. Some people might find your new rhythms of life disappointing *to them*. That is okay. You are not here to please them; you are here to heal. As you grow, certain friendships will organically fall away. That is also okay.

A Note About Children

If you have children or adolescents, keep your focus on healing. Remind yourself that their brains are not fully developed until around twenty-five, and trauma changes the brain, biology, and belief system.

Life and growing up is difficult enough for children, let alone facing trauma. Guard their hearts as many will not understand behavior that comes from their trauma.

As my colleague Dr. Karen Purvis likes to say in trainings, "Behavior is the language of children who have lost their voice."

Be patient. Your child is fighting their history and trauma. It is not important that everyone understand this about your child—what is important is that you understand this. **You are your child's advocate at home and whenever they leave the threshold of your home.**

On my road to healing, some questions I often asked myself when I felt pulled to please my friends were, "Are they walking in my shoes? Is their story my story?" Often the answer was no, and it would free me to just keep doing what I needed to do to get well.

So, unpack that backpack, and repack it with what you need to discover your resilience. Then take another look at Mount Everest. It may be a steep climb, but using the insights and the practices, you can use this book as your guide.

Are you at the start of your journey, just getting ready to begin the climb? Are you in the middle of the climb already and you simply paused to reassess? Or if you have made it to the top, are you supporting someone else who is climbing?

Wherever you are on your journey, please know that you are not alone. Everywhere you look is someone who has encountered trauma, is struggling with it, or has overcome it.

No one can make you climb the mountain. The choice to recover lies within your soul—in your body, heart, and mind. But having gotten this far, I am pretty sure you have this. You have the resilience within you to begin this climb. And you have been given tools to know how to pack your backpack, pace yourself, rest when necessary, and fight to climb on!

There will be times you are tired of climbing and tired of trying to find the energy. You might find yourself on the ground, tears streaming down your face. Or you might be limping along, determined to make it through the messy middle.

Either way, be kind to yourself. Extend grace and kindness along this climb. And find people who will cheer you on when you want to give up.

Also, know your limits. You and your body, heart, and mind are a team that must work together to get to where you want to be.

Rest when you need to. Resting will give you the energy to get up the next morning and start your day again. Rest is fuel for your entire being.

Every step you take, every stop you make, every bit of fight in you is benefiting you and those around you.

We need you in this world. We need to learn from you so you can in turn help others. Someone out there is waiting for you to climb, waiting to hear your story, waiting to see that they, too, are not alone.

You might be the voice they hear that tells them, "You've got this. I am right here with you. Do not give up. The hard work will pay off." And best of all, "You matter."

For now, though, keep walking. Keep climbing. Put one foot in front of the other. Breathe. Lean on others. Pay attention to what is happening inside of you. And bit by bit, step by step, you will reclaim your resilience.

POSTSCRIPT

At the time we wrapped up this book for publication, more traumatic events were unfolding around the United States and the world. The Omicron variant of coronavirus is spreading fast just when we thought life might be returning to normal.

Meanwhile, natural disasters seem to be a regular part of life. In the early hours of December 11, 2021, a potent storm system moved through the Eastern United States, resulting in a long-track EF4 tornado that wiped out Mayfield, Kentucky and spawned at least twelve other tornadoes. It is the costliest tornado in US history, plus it occurred in the winter, which is rare.[110]

Five days later, a similar system moved through the Central United States, hammering Nebraska and Iowa with at least twenty-four tornadoes.

And to close out 2021, a "historic wind event" in Colorado led to gusts of greater than 115 miles per hour. It toppled power lines and sparked a fire that destroyed more than a thousand homes in Boulder County.[111]

Just when we thought the world was slowly returning to normal, Russia invaded Ukraine in February 2022. Daily, we were seeing cities be turned to rubble and young and old fleeing for their lives. This war has caused new global supply chain issues, and it has left many dreading that it will turn into World War III.

The pandemic, the devastating weather phenomena, and the threat of a world war underscore the importance of doing what we can to resolve the impact of trauma.

---

110 bit.ly/LongTrackTornado; bit.ly/CostliestTornadoes
111 dpo.st/3HDoMz0

ACKNOWLEDGMENTS

Sharon says...

I am incredibly grateful to my beautiful daughters Shealyn and Sophie Grace for granting me immeasurable grace and love as I navigated single parenting. I am infinitely thankful for you. I am proud of who you are—resilient, strong women. I love you to the moon and back! And Silas, my son: It's just us now, kid. Thank you for being willing to watch *Stranger Things* and patiently waiting for dinner as I worked endlessly writing and editing. :) You bring a kindness to those around you who suffer because it is familiar territory to you, and you always find the silver lining. Thank you for being patient with me and sacrificing our time for this book. I am glad God made me mama to you three!

Mom, your selfless love and involvement with the children created the space for me to heal from trauma so the creative in me could live again. Thank you. Sharmon, my sister, I am grateful for your strength while I struggled to heal from COVID. Thank you for helping nurse my weak body back to wellness.

Grandma Carolyn, I still feel you when I need encouragement and the tears flow, you always told me healing took time. Thank you for pointing me to hope. Fly high, red bird!

Dad, you are always here. Thank you for loving me big and making sure I was seen, heard, and safe. I wish everyone had a dad like you. Oh, and all the free consulting hours—LOL. I'll continue to courage *up*.

To my love: Thank you for sleeping on the floor next to my bed while I struggled to breath and fight. Your energy and knowing that you always have my back kept me going!

Thank you to my circle of friends who are my meaningful connections, those I turn to when seasons get dark or when I need to laugh: Holly Chapman, Angela Parham, Dawn Beatty, Amy Beasley, Pauline Taaffe, and Monica Neubauer. My dear friends, you are the example of people who accepted me where I was at, not where you wanted me to be.

My hiking trail buddies—Abby Peterson, Lee Ann Runyeon, Dana Swaffer, Paige St. John—thank you for keeping it real on the trail, especially during the peak of the pandemic and isolation. And thank you for caring for my family so I could focus on recovering.

Jamie Kyne, my therapist: You faithfully met me where I was at in life. I am a better therapist because of you, and this book was able to be as my trauma resolved. Thank you.

Thank you, Aja, Milton, Robyn, and Seema—my 9Paths team—for all you do and all you did for the business as I recovered. You shouldered the weight so I could spend time writing.

To Jon Shearer, my business coach, for seeing my potential and consistently encouraging me and my ideas. To Lisa Alessi, my Enneagram coach: Thank for reconnecting me to my truest self while I was rebuilding my life and business. To Jacob Thorington, my attorney, and his assistant, Nancy Hagan: You fought tirelessly for me and my kids to have peace and stood firm for me during the toughest season of my life. Thank you for never giving up. Without the peace and order in my life, this book would not have happened. And Clifton Harris: From the day I met you, you have championed my work and have been a true friend and colleague.

Adéle Booysen, you captured our book so eloquently and beautifully; your work will help bring healing to many. Your intellect and editing skills are top-notch, not to mention you're a really cool hang!

Renée, thank you for accepting the challenge to write this book with me. It is beautiful! I am grateful for your resilience through your trauma as you have passed your resilience on to those around you.

Karen Anderson, my friend and publisher, I am grateful for your guidance, creativity, and providing a safe place to land through the years. Thank you, friend.

A very special thanks to Ginger Lapid-Bogda, my friend, mentor, and champion. This book would not be what it is without your involvement and care for me during my family's traumas. You give freely, and you have bestowed jewels of wisdom that have impacted my little family and my future for the better. Thank you for seeing and believing in me—my whole self.

To the One who has caught every tear of mine and will continue to love all of me, thank you.

This book is inspired by trauma survivors: Route 91, 911 First Responders, tsunami and Hurricane Katrina survivors, Sophia's Heart residents, former and active members of the United States Armed Forces, and the many clients who have sought counseling and those who have not. Thank you for allowing me to enter the sacred space of your healing. You inspire me, and my heart is full of gratitude for you.

Renée says…

My husband, children, and their spouses: You believe in me—*always*. You have unconditionally loved and supported me in all the iterations of the work I've been doing with others. And you have grown to acknowledge the importance of an integrative approach to mental health. Nathan: For about twenty years, you have been urging me to write a book to share the work in my clinical practice, telling me, "People out there need to know what you do, Mom." Thank you for the encouragement.

To my mentors: David Daniels was the most approachable mentor I have ever had. He so loved the Enneagram and the promises it offered for resolving and healing so many of the world's maladies. David made anyone who worked with him feel valued and special, and he was a personal cheerleader whenever I wanted to give up. Helen Palmer, Terry Saracino, Peter O'Hanrahan Ginger Lapid-Bogda, I have learned so much from each of you, and you have helped me build a solid foundation for working with the Enneagram.

My Arizona Enneagram Association teachers—Carole Whittaker, Gloria Cuevas-Barnett, Robin Cameron, Erlina Edwards, Jaye Andres, and Andrea Andress—I have been privileged to work with each of you and exchange ideas for how to best bring the Enneagram into the world.

Rick Benson, thank you for introducing me to the Enneagram as something I might consider bringing into my clinical practice. I immediately fell in love with the Enneagram.

To my dear friends and colleagues: Gigi Veasey, we have each supported the other as we've written books recently. Judy Sugg, we have written, presented, and coached one another with a big respect for each other.

With gratitude to all my hospital patients and outpatient clients throughout the years who have placed their trust in me to walk with them in their healing journeys.

To my coauthor Sharon: Thank you for reaching out to me to work with you on writing a book about trauma and the Enneagram. The mutual respect and commitment to work through anything that might have been an obstacle is a testament of the power of using the Enneagram in our personal and professional life.

And to Adéle Booysen, our editor. It has been a delight to work with you. Thank you for working alongside each of us to bring our vision to reality.

ABOUT THE AUTHORS

Sharon K. Ball, MA, is a licensed professional counselor–mental health service provider (LPC-MHSP), national board-certified counselor, and an accredited Enneagram teacher through the International Enneagram Association. Sharon has more than twenty-five years of experience helping people heal from trauma.

As the founder of the 9Paths Center for Well-being, a clinical counseling center, Sharon provides informed trauma care to individuals, couples, and families. She also supervises graduate and post-graduate counselors for Tennessee counseling licensure. Sharon also holds certifications in eye-movement desensitization reprocessing (EMDR), acceptance commitment therapy (ACT), cognitive-processing therapy (CPT). She is also trauma-informed certified (TIC) and certified in dialectical-behavior therapy (DBT) as well as trust-based relational intervention (TBRI).

Because of her background, Sharon has provided trauma-response counseling for victims of mass shootings and hurricanes. She has also been called upon to provide crisis-intervention services during national and international disasters such as the Indian Ocean tsunami and the Haiti earthquake. Some of her work is done years after the traumatic events, such as providing counseling to 9/11 first responders to help them process the trauma of the attacks.

In Tennessee, Sharon is also approved as a family courts' parent coordinator, giving recommendations to the court regarding the best interests of the child. She also works with homeless shelters and works in collaboration the Middle Tennessee Urban League.

Passionate about solving all forms of complex human problems, Sharon also works with businesses and believes that if you are willing to walk down the path toward self-discovery, do the hard work, and grant yourself kindness, you will leverage human connection and align your leadership, organization, and team.

She is a senior member of the Enneagram in Business Network and has completed Yale's School of Management post-graduate program focused on fostering diversity and inclusion.

You can learn more about Sharon's work at www.9Paths.com.

Renée Siegel, MA, a licensed independent substance-abuse counselor (LISAC), master addiction counselor (MAC), and internationally certified coach (ICF-ACC), has been teaching and working with individuals, couples, families, and groups for over forty years. Beginning as a marriage and family therapist and limited licensed psychologist (LLP) in addiction recovery centers in the inner-city of Detroit, Michigan, it was apparent how almost all the families she worked with had trauma in their backgrounds. As a result, Renée pursued additional licenses and certifications in body work (LMT), trauma treatment (EFT), holistic healthcare (HHP), biofeedback (through International Medical University), nutrition (First Line Therapy), and substance abuse and gambling addictions (ICGC-II).

Renée has worked in residential, intensive outpatient programs, and outpatient settings with those impacted by various addictions. She has learned that all addictions have unresolved trauma needing to be addressed in order to move into meaningful long-term recovery. With her background in family therapy, she enjoys working with family members impacted by addictions too.

Through her twenty years of Enneagram study, Renée was impressed by how the Enneagram supported people in making significant changes that are otherwise challenging to sustain. An International Enneagram Association (IEA)-accredited professional, Arizona Enneagram practitioner (AEA), and narrative Enneagram teacher (TNE), Renée leverages the Enneagram as foundational and as a meaningful entrance into personal self-awareness. She believes the Enneagram is both transformative and holistic.

Renée uses a multidimensional approach for sustained wellness and healing by exploring how the body, spirit, and mind help lay the foundation for healing.

Formerly the owner of multiple wellness and healing clinics in Arizona, she is currently in private practice as a counselor and coach. She also currently teaches core curriculum classes for the Arizona Enneagram Association.

Learn more about Renée and her work at www.urpurepotential.com.

The Centers of Intelligence

and Trauma

Each of the nine Enneagram types are a part of one of the three centers of intelligence. Of the three types per center, each expresses the center a little differently. The patterns of that type are also influenced by your DNA, your environment, and the mystery of your origin. Your Enneagram type is often reflected in which center you rely on the most. Although you have access to all three centers, trauma interrupts your ability to fully use each center.

The Body Center Types

For the body center, the trauma response puts your body functions on hyperalert, keeping your heart beating, your lungs breathing, and your basic body functions going while other body functions, like hunger, are being suppressed. The focus is purely on keeping you alive. (This is true even if your Enneagram type is in the heart or head center.)

Resilience	The body offers sensate information, as well as a sense of autonomy, justice, and right action.
Unmet Childhood Needs	The need for autonomy, fair treatment, to be heard, and to feel empowered
Core Motivations	Body types employ autonomy, personal justice, position, power, and attempting to bring life back to the way it should be as a strategy to assure being heard and to minimize discomfort. This can also be referred to as instinctual intelligence. This core motivation is rooted in their unmet childhood need for autonomy, justness, and fairness. The body types respond by seeking to manage life through power and control.
Signs of an Eight as a Body Center Type	• Gut instinct • Physical sensations • Recognize feelings through senses • Clenching of the fists • Rapid heart rate • Lower back issues • Facial scowl
Signs of a Nine as a Body Center Type	• Physical sensations of temperature increase as Nines pull inward • Rapid heart rate • Numbing mentally, emotionally, and/or physically • Mindless activities (narcotization) to remain in the numb body state • A lethargic feeling in the body slowing down their pace in life
Signs of a One as a Body Center Type	• Rigid facial muscles • Clenched jaw • Tightness of shoulders • Tightness of neck • Thin-lipped

The Heart Center Types	
	For the heart center, the trauma response interferes with your relationships with yourself and others, keeping you from fully connecting and engaging by potentially acting frenzied and/or numb.
Resilience	The heart center gives you access to connection, love, empathy, comfort with relationships, positive outlook, and emotional self-regulation.
Unmet Childhood Needs	The need to be seen and for acknowledgment, approval, and validation
Core Motivations	Heart types process life through the lens of how they are receiving–or *not* receiving–affirmation and validation, whether they are liked and seen by others, and the quality of their connections with those around them. This can be referred to as emotional intelligence. The unmet childhood need of heart types is being seen, acknowledged, and validated for who they are, and they respond by seeking esteem and affirmation by using connection and relatedness as their strategy for managing life.
Signs of a Two as a Heart Center Type	• A heightened awareness of the needs and emotions of others • Demonstrate diminished self-care • Unaware of their own emotions • Use giving as a way to stay engaged with others • Experience growing resentment because they are not taking care of self
Signs of a Three as a Heart Center Type	• Set aside their emotions • Their sensitivity is private • Heightened passion for their work replaces emotional expression • Might experience accumulated feelings after ignoring them for too long • Emotions are replaced by the drive for efficiency and productivity
Signs of a Four as a Heart Center Type	• Experience deep and intense emotions • A vast range of emotions • They view all emotions as equally important • Often are stuck in emotions, unable to access discernment • Often being misunderstood

The Head Center Types	
For the head center, the trauma response interferes with your ability to use logic, discernment, and reason by attending to other body functions that are necessary for survival.	
Resilience	The head center allows you access to remaining calm, dispassionate observation, objectivity, situation-specific reasoning and logic. It also offers the capacity to sustain attention, have clarity and focus, and plan for the future.
Unmet Childhood Needs	The need for safety, security, and certainty
Core Motivations	Head types use planning, mapping, and strategizing as a means to manage life. This can be referred to as mental intelligence. Due to their unmet childhood need for consistency and predictability, these types respond by seeking safety, security, and certainty so they can know that life is predictable and that potential danger is being dealt with.
Signs of a Five as a Head Center Type	• Value logic • Gather information • Heightened stubbornness with their opinions • Can physically be with others and yet absorbed in their own thinking • The needs of others are perceived as overwhelming their mental capacity
Signs of a Six as a Head Center Type	• Worse-case scenario thinking increases to prepare for the unknown • Rumination • Second-guess themselves, which paralyzes their ability to take action • Move quickly in fight-flight-freeze-fawn • False evidence appearing real
Signs of a Seven as a Head Center Type	• Using options to strategically avoid pain • Frenzied mental pattern of thinking • Flooding thoughts of possibilities incites impulsive behaviors • Low tolerance for negative thoughts • Compartmentalize recall of situations

Enneagram Types
and Trauma

A Reference Guide

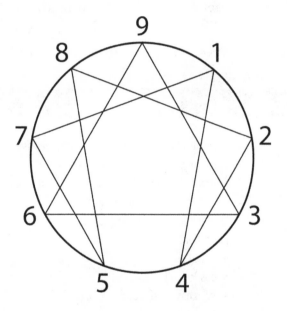

This guide is an overview
of each of the nine types.
It includes each type's vulnerability (▼)
and their resilience (△)
amidst the types of trauma discussed
in Part Two.

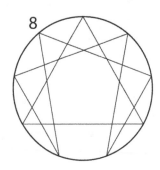

To assure protection and regard in a tough world, Eights believe you must be strong and powerful. Action-oriented, they have a lot of energy and may not be aware of their impact on others. Eights are not afraid to speak their minds and can be direct to the point of being blunt. They see themselves as powerful and protective. Eights seek justice and can be intense. They also can be overly impactful, excessive, and impulsive. They tend to make quick decisions and respect others who do the same.

Type Eight	
Center of Intelligence	**Body** The body offers sensate information as well as a sense of autonomy, justice, and right action.
Core Belief	"The world is filled with injustice. Powerful people take advantage of others' innocence."
Worldview	"The world is filled with injustice, and I am here to offer protection."
Where Attention Is Placed	• Power and control • Justice and injustice • Who has the power • Who is deceiving who • Helping those unable to defend themselves
Performance Under Stress	• Exerting power and/or dominance • Dealing with a situation here and now • Going full-out • Denying fatigue and pain • Intimidation
Avoidance	• Being taken advantage of • Experiencing and expressing vulnerability • Being seen as weak • Not being respected by people they regard

Type Eight	
Eights as Children	Developing Eights may have experienced unjust environments where they felt a need to protect themselves and those around them.
Defense Mechanism	**Denial** • By disavowing its very existence, Eights unconsciously negate what makes them feel fearful. • Denial serves to keep Eights from feeling fatigue, pain, or vulnerability while they live in an intense way and practice excess in much of what they do.
Coping Mechanism	**Manipulation** Throwing a fit or becoming controlling
Gifts Toward Resiliency	Self-confidant, decisive, assertive, direct, self-determined, just, big-hearted, and loyal

Type Eight and Trauma	
PTSD	▼ Because denial is the primary defense mechanism of Eights, it deters them from admitting that there is any problem that they cannot solve. As a result, Eights believe they are invincible. ▼ Eights avoid being vulnerable, seeing it as a weakness. △ What helps is that Eights have an innate ability to push through and persevere when most other types would give up. △ They believe their bodies are invincible, thus they embrace an embodied approach to healing from trauma.
Family Violence	▼ Prone to avoid vulnerability at all costs, Eights will not ask for help, even if they are trapped in intimate-partner abuse. ▼ They move to action quickly, often out of protection for self and others. As a result, family violence can escalate quickly. Due to their innate level of aggression, a type Eight victim may even be mistaken as being the perpetrator. △ Eights are likely to respond to assist others less capable as they have the innate ability to focus on injustice. Stepping up for the sake of someone weaker than them (for example, a child) can help an Eight find a way out of a situation where family violence is prevalent. △ Eights can weather a storm; they have an innate capacity to reset and move on rather than staying trapped in an abusive relationship.

Type Eight and Trauma

Natural Disasters

▼ Eights are either all in or not in at all, so if they choose to disengage, they will take no action. But if they choose to engage, they may overreact and expose themselves to danger. This is due to their power to overcome challenges combined with the adrenaline rush.

▼ Despite a crisis unfolding around them, Eights are unlikely to recognize their limits and may resist asking for help as this can feel vulnerable.

△ Eights' innate leadership qualities can help them weather the storm.

△ They naturally want to protect others and have the capacity to maintain their energy in the long term.

Complicated Grief

▼ Although Eights are typically very present to being with others (through active listening, for example), they are often not present to loss. Much like Threes, they focus on what needs to be done instead.

▼ Eights attend to the details and not the emotional requirements of the experience, which makes them more vulnerable to the impact of complicated grief.

△ When in touch with vulnerability and their personal sadness, Eights can move through the grieving process and access their innocence.

△ Once in touch with the vulnerability of human suffering, Eights can be tender and move toward the grief.

Poverty

▼ Due to the sense of powerlessness that they experience in situations where they lack resources, Eights develop a strategy to find resources. Often these resources are not legal, and they find themselves involved in criminal activity.

▼ By denying the obstacle of poverty and pushing through challenges, Eights develop an even tougher exterior. This prevents them from allowing anyone to see their struggles.

△ As a body-based type, Eights use their strength to push through challenges, gaining strength as they go.

△ They use this strength and anger to find solutions, even when it comes to poverty.

Racism

▼ For Eights, the nervous system often defaults to fight rather than to flee, freeze, or fawn.

▼ When facing systemic racism, Eights can get trapped in a loop of constant reactivity while holding on to the injustice. This can keep the Eight from moving to solutions.

Racism

△ Eights are changemakers, even when fighting systemic racism. They have the capacity to notice racism yet not be held captive by it.

△ Eights' focus tends to be on assisting the underdog rather than focusing on themselves. They have an innate appreciation of the innocence of all living beings, which helps them stand up to racism.

Addiction

▼ Given their lust for energy, Eights tend to see substance abuse and behavioral addictions through a lens of "more is better." This way, their lust for *more* places them at risk of developing an addiction.

▼ Likely addictions include anything where *more* is *better*: alcohol, action gambling, sex, amphetamines, and designer drugs that add energy.

△ Eights can embrace recovery with the same lust they have for their addictions, especially if they find someone or a community that can hold their intense energy.

△ To move into a vulnerable space and be receptive to help, an Eight must embrace the concept of powerlessness and/or a higher power.

Verbal, Emotional, and Spiritual Abuse

▼ Eights rebel against any actions of power over or control toward them, causing them to react rather than pick their battles.

▼ As a result of aversion to vulnerability, if Eights encounter emotional, verbal, and spiritual abuse along with others, a trauma bond can develop quickly and is difficult to break.

△ Instead of being anxious, Eights are more prone to express anger. When they are older and less vulnerable, this can help to protect them from abuse and/or help them break out of the trauma loop of abuse.

△ Their anger continues to help identify the injustices of all forms of abuse early on.

Sexual Abuse

▼ Seeing themselves as invincible, an Eight might verbally or physically engage in the abuse and may deny the experience.

▼ Eights often do not fathom their personal experience of being victimized. Without intervention and insight, Eights may recycle the abuse through intimidating others. This makes it even harder for them to seek help.

△ When Eights do the deeper work in healing, they identify the injustice and unfairness.

△ They embrace their vulnerability and grieve the powerlessness and defenselessness of the experience.

Type Eight and Trauma

Historical and Inter-generational Trauma

▼ When an Eight's family has experienced generations of trauma and it goes unacknowledged, the Eight will move to being an intimidator or a dictator.

▼ They will push back against all perceived vulnerability.

△ Eights have strong survival instincts and can be described as non-violent warriors, seeking justice and fairness. This can help them to break the trauma loop of intergenerational and historical trauma.

△ Eights can move into great leadership roles.

Pandemic

▼ Eights' anger toward imposed rules that feel like power and control being exerted over them is typically followed by a strong pushback.

▼ Believing their bodies are invincible and cannot get sick, Eights in a pandemic might tend to exhibit a lack of self-care.

△ When Eights engage in their protective instincts, they do what is good for others. They bring energy and passion.

△ They are fair, direct, and can motivate and energize others.

Nines believe that to be loved and valued, you must blend in and go with the flow. Consequently, Nines seek harmony and unity, are inclusive, amiable, easygoing, comfortable, and steady. They can also be self-forgetting, conflict avoidant, and stubborn. Nines are easygoing. They go along to get along. They merge easily with the ideas and needs of others, often forgetting their own. Nines often have difficulty identifying a particular idea or opinion they have, and they can easily fall asleep to what is important to them.

Type Nine	
Center of Intelligence	**Body** The body offers sensate information as well as a sense of autonomy, justice, and right action.
Core Belief	"So that life is more comfortable and flows with more ease, I blend in with the beliefs of others."
Worldview	"The world treats people as relatively unimportant for what they are and requires them to blend in to be comfortable. By blending in, I will find a sense of comfort and belonging."
Where Attention Is Placed	• Comfort, peace, and harmony • Other people's agendas
Performance Under Stress	• Passive-aggressive expression of anger and stubbornness • Resistant to others • Some explosive outbursts of anger when they feel pushed too far

Type Nine	
Avoidance	• Conflict • Taking action regarding what is truly essential and supportive of self • Their own ideas and feelings, especially if they perceive it will cause conflict
Nines as Children	Developing Nines may have experienced conflictual environments where they learned to withdraw, become invisible, and/or merge with the concerns of those around them.
Defense Mechanism	**Narcotization** • Nines unconsciously numb themselves to avoid something that feels too large, complex, difficult, or uncomfortable to handle. Examples of numbing might include watching TV, eating, sleeping, drinking or gambling. • They narcotize to avoid conflict and maintain a self-image of being comfortable and/or harmonious.
Coping Mechanism	**Stonewalling** Avoiding confrontation or intimacy altogether
Gifts Toward Resiliency	Receptive, can see many sides of an issue, inclusive, willing to be part of the collective, reassuring, fair, patient, unassuming, diplomatic, gentle, kind, and down to earth

Type Nine and Trauma	
PTSD	▼ In a desperate attempt to calm their nervous system so they can avoid acknowledging the trauma of PTSD, Nines withdraw to a point of disappearing and participating in self-sabotaging behaviors. ▼ While others in their lives may express concern about the effects of PTSD, Nines remain unaware. △ When Nines become aware of repetitive or self-sabotaging behaviors, they can more easily switch to other less self-sabotaging and regulating behaviors. △ Practiced over and over again with an accountability partner, even the most elementary of embodied interventions work well for a Nine.

Type Nine and Trauma

Family Violence

▼ Nines are conflict avoidant and often make excuses for unacceptable behavior.

▼ Due to their motivation to "go along to get along" and not wanting to rock the boat, Nines might be more tolerant of family violence than other types.

△ With an innate capacity to de-escalate, Nines can become aware of their own needs and seek a way out of a relationship marked by intimate-partner abuse.

△ Nines' capacity to defuse a rising conflict allows awareness for better self-care and the need to develop a strategy to attend to their own needs.

Natural Disasters

▼ During a disaster, Nines can lack awareness of the specific impact the event has had on them and others by narcotizing—indulging in activities that are not helpful.

▼ Nines' tendency not to take action can keep them trapped in the crisis of a natural disaster.

△ Once awakened, Nines find power in hearing what their and others' needs are.

△ They have a strong desire to help others and bring the community together, which can unite others in the grip of a natural disaster.

Complicated Grief

▼ Nines may remain asleep to their emotional experience as they encounter grief. In doing so, they function much like Twos by focusing on the needs of those around them.

▼ They can easily get distracted by other issues that need their attention in the moment, especially if there is conflict between others.

△ Nines innately move to a peaceful awareness, allowing for acceptance of loss as a natural part of life. This is an exceptional gift in dealing with grief.

△ The innate virtues of harmony and unity allow Nines to bring together those who are grieving.

Poverty

▼ Nines might see the challenge of poverty as never ending.

▼ They will find ways to escape the pain and discomfort of poverty by overindulging in food and alcohol, and they may lose motivation to make changes.

Type Nine and Trauma	
Poverty	△ When Nines realize that they can work with others to resolve poverty, they will exhibit relentless perseverance and engagement with their community to bring about change. △ Nines will often assist in community-based efforts to eradicate poverty within the community.
Racism	▼ Not being aware of their own needs feeds into Nines being complacent to the powers that be and accepting that living with racism is how life will always be. ▼ To keep harmony, Nines can dismiss racial microaggressions, while their tendency toward passive-aggressive behavior keeps them recycling their suppressed anger. △ Able to see all sides of a situation, Nines have an innate ability to mediate for others, which can help them and others move through racist experiences. △ They also have an innate desire for unity and healing of all. A well-developed Nine will push through the discomfort of conflict to reach a place of unity.
Addiction	▼ Nines naturally seek ways to go with the flow. This makes them susceptible to giving in to peer pressure and thus getting trapped in addiction. Addictions can also develop in response to seeking new and comfortable ways to narcotize to avoid conflict or pain. ▼ Likely addictions include alcohol, marijuana, escape gambling, and overeating. They are also prone to codependency. △ Nines do well in communities of support—almost better than with an individual helping professional. △ Because of their open-mindedness, Nines can take in information from others and integrate it into self and recovery.
Verbal, Emotional, and Spiritual Abuse	▼ When faced with abusive relationships, Nines tend to "go along to get along" and lose any sense of autonomy and opinion. ▼ To avoid conflict in relationships, they might fall for a partner who will always call the shots. △ Because Nines can see all sides of a situation, they may merge with others. But when they awaken to their own needs, they are able to move away from their abuser. △ They also possess the innate ability to hold on to harmony in other areas of their life, which could help them cope and respond to the grip of the abuse.

Type Nine and Trauma	
Sexual Abuse	▼ To numb the pain, a Nine will merge with the perpetrator. ▼ Through the process of merging, the Nine loses their individuality and allows the abuse to go on until there is outside intervention. △ When a Nine awakens to themselves as an individual who disagrees with what is going on, they take action. △ They are even likely to see the good in the other person, making it easier to forgive, yet not forget.
Historical and Inter-generational Trauma	▼ When dealing with intergenerational trauma, Nines might fall asleep to the facts and become complicit in keeping secrets, therefore ignoring the generational trauma. ▼ Ignoring the trauma and accepting it as part of the family or community experience inhibits Nines' ability to access the healing process. △ When awakened, Nines have the innate capacity to see many ways to move with grace and help their people unite with strength through challenging times. △ Nines respect the past and heal the hatred through harmony.
Pandemic	▼ When faced with a pandemic, Nines narcotize, procrastinate, become easily distracted, and lose sight of goals. ▼ They find other ways to stay asleep so they can comfort themselves. △ Once awakened, Nines come together with willingness and action plans to address the global needs. In doing this, they are selfless, having the innate ability to clearly hear what the needs of all people are. △ Able to be highly adaptive, Nines not only do what is good for them but what is best for the community.

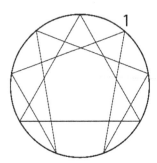

Ones believe they must be good and right to be worthy. Consequently, Ones are conscientious, responsible, improvement-oriented and self-controlled, but also can be critical, resentful and self-judging.

Type One	
Center of Intelligence	**Body** The body offers sensate information as well as a sense of autonomy, justice, and right action.
Core Belief	"You must be good and right to be worthy. I can do this by being conscientious and doing things the right way."
Worldview	"There are so many things in the world that need improvement, and I am here to notice them and improve them."
Where Attention Is Placed	• What can be corrected or improved • What is right or wrong • What *should* be
Performance Under Stress	• Feeling overburdened with changes that need to happen • Being anxious and resentful as my inner critic takes over • Becoming easily frustrated with perceived wrong
Avoidance	• Being wrong • Making mistakes

Type One	
Ones as Children	Developing Ones may have experienced chaotic or disorganized environments where they learned to suppress their anger in response to not being able to create order and a sense of calm.
Defense Mechanism	**Reaction Formation** • Ones try to reduce or eliminate anxiety caused by their behaviors, feelings, or thoughts that they consider unacceptable by responding in a manner that is exactly the opposite of their real responses. • This allows the One to believe they are right regardless of their behavior. For example, a One may have strong ethical beliefs that cheating or stealing is very wrong and yet might cheat or steal.
Coping Mechanism	**Judgment** Judging yourself or those around you to keep your focus away from the pain
Gifts Toward Resiliency	Self-controlled and disciplined, quality-minded, precise, thorough, fair, ethical, upstanding, organized, responsible, and having integrity

Type One and Trauma	
PTSD	▼ Through reaction formation—a disowning of their contradictory thoughts or actions—Ones will identify in those around them the very behavior they do not like about themselves. ▼ For Ones, the focus of attention is more on the need for reform than on what is going on with themselves and others. This keeps them from engaging in compassion for self and others. △ When Ones recognize their powerlessness in regard to their symptoms and own it as a part of the trauma loop, they lighten up on self-judgment and can practice self-compassion. △ Once aware of their self-judgment, Ones can move into more compassion for self and others suffering from PTSD.

Family Violence

▼ With an inner critic stronger in Ones than in any other type, they have a moral dilemma with leaving a primary relationship.

▼ Judging leaving as an incorrect decision, Ones may turn the focus to what they can personally do to improve the relationship.

△ With greater awareness, Ones can turn their focus to the fact that family violence is unacceptable, and they can take a deeper look at what needs to be changed in the relationship.

△ Once their tendency to judge relaxes, it is easier for a One to do the next right thing.

Natural Disasters

▼ When facing a natural disaster, Ones can get stuck in all that needs to be fixed. As a result, they can become inflexible and unable to adapt.

▼ Ones tend to need to do things right, which is often not possible amid a disaster. This can lead to them becoming stuck due to frustration around the chaos and all that is needed for recovery.

△ What can help Ones get through a disaster is their innate attention to getting things back in order. They tend to use proven ways to recover rather than reinvent the wheel, which can speed up recovery.

△ Conscientious and driven to make the situation better for everyone, Ones are naturally drawn to addressing the injustices and disparities that arise in the community after a natural disaster.

Complicated Grief

▼ Ones live with a level of dissatisfaction and a sense of loss. When grief gets complicated, it magnifies the loss already present, causing them to feel that the world and everyone in it could be better.

▼ When they encounter a personal experience with loss, Ones may reach an even deeper low.

△ Daily wanting a better world, Ones innately grieve. Loss is a normal experience for them, something they can grieve daily.

△ Ones will attend to the mores and values of others who are grieving. This can help them move through their own grief.

Poverty

▼ When facing poverty, Ones might become hyper focused on being a good person and on toeing the line.

▼ They want to improve what is within their control but in doing so, Ones may lose sight of the poverty needing to be addressed.

Poverty

△ The attention of a One is placed on improving situations and seeking better outcomes, which can help them break the grip of poverty.

△ Their motivation for a more ideal situation will lead them into career areas like education, healthcare, fitness, nutrition, or government–places where they can make a difference.

Racism

▼ When dealing with systemic racism, Ones are gripped by a constant frustration at not being able to correct the situation, and they repress their simmering reactivity to injustices.

▼ Ones can be rigid regarding what needs to be done to make things right. They can find it difficult to collaborate with others in reaching those goals. As a result, they can get stuck on what needs correction while not getting anything done.

△ Ones who are working on personal growth will check themselves for how they may be contributing to racism.

△ Ones are conscientious around the desire to correct injustices. They persevere to come up with fair and just ways to deal with dilemmas–including racism.

Addiction

▼ Finding it too difficult to deal with more than one flaw or imperfection at a time, Ones rarely have co-occurring addictions. Instead, they tend to have only one active addiction at a time.

▼ Likely addictions include alcohol, eating disorders, all types of gambling, pain medications, benzodiazepines, or marijuana.

△ Ones have an uncanny ability to focus on making amends and righting their wrongs.

△ When it comes to following the steps of a recovery program or the suggestions of a helping professional, Ones can do what is required of them.

Verbal, Emotional, and Spiritual Abuse

▼ Ones might become fierce in choosing a partner whom they can focus on improving to complete what they could not as a young child.

▼ Ones raised in an emotionally, verbally, and spiritually abusive environment may see that as the correct way to live. And with criticism being hardwired in the One's core, noticing rigidity and fundamentalism could be difficult.

△ Naturally focusing on improving the world around them moves Ones to examine their environment and find ways to correct what is within their power to correct.

△ They may more easily accept the responsibility to be a better person.

Type One and Trauma

Sexual Abuse

▼ It is difficult for Ones to ask for help during or after the abuse.

▼ They may see themselves as being bad or wrong, and they may feel they should be punished because they must have done something wrong to deserve the abuse.

△ Once Ones understand they did not deserve the abuse, they will take action and find resources for themselves and others.

△ Seeing the need for reform in certain systems, Ones might be the spokesperson against sexual assault, invest time and energy into a non-profit, or become an educator.

Historical and Inter-generational Trauma

▼ Unable to express their powerlessness around the need for reform, Ones might use their energy in a misdirected way to improve other areas of their communities in an effort to avoid the real issues.

▼ Ones might internalize their oppression and unconsciously act out their frustration toward family members or their community.

△ Ones who find peaceful solutions for healing will often take on leadership roles in government or social work to assist a community that needs reform.

△ Their inner peace engages the power within.

Pandemic

▼ Ones see what needs to be corrected. In a global pandemic, there is more than is humanly possible to change. This leaves the One perpetually stuck in the hum of frustration.

▼ Ones may feel a more intense burden as they tend to feel personally responsible for correcting problems. The combination of the frustration and intensity of the One tends to push people away when the One might need them the most.

△ Ones truly desire reform and change. They can provide endless solutions for making needed changes.

△ A One who is aware of their intensity and frustration can more easily invite others in.

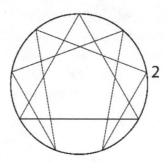

Twos like to help and believe you must give fully to others to be loved. Consequently, Twos are caring, helpful, supportive, generous, and relationship oriented. They also can be prideful, intrusive, and demanding.

Type Two	
Center of Intelligence	**Heart** The heart center offers you emotional intelligence, including being relational, engaged, and connected to others.
Core Belief	"To get what I need in life, I must give. To be loved, I must be needed."
Worldview	"People need my love and support. I am here to give it to them."
Where Attention Is Placed	• On the needs and concerns of others • Supporting and serving others • Giving to get
Performance Under Stress	• Feeling indispensable • Tendency to give too much • Being confused about self-care and attending to their own needs • Upset about having invested too much in relationships that do not work out, leading to becoming resentful
Avoidance	• Knowing and attending to their own needs • Disappointing others

Type Two	
Twos as Children	Young Twos might have experienced an environment where their own needs were unacknowledged and the needs of others took precedence. They learned to suppress their needs, focusing on others to keep them connected to those they loved.
Defense Mechanism	**Repression** • Twos hide information about themselves from themselves that is too difficult to acknowledge consciously. • This allows the Two to continue to give relentlessly believing they are just being helpful although they are repressing feelings of resentment for doing so.
Coping Mechanism	**Codependency** Fixing others' problems while ignoring you and your needs
Gifts Toward Resiliency	Generous, helpful, friendly, caring, supportive, encouraging, optimistic, nurturing, and warm-hearted

Type Two and Trauma	
PTSD	▼ Twos will return to traumatic situations if they think they can be helpful to someone else. By returning, they can easily re-expose themselves to PTSD. △ Twos are hardwired to seek connections, and they avoid being alone. This assists them in finding a person or community to co-regulate with and begin the healing process.
Family Violence	▼ Twos see the potential of who people can become. Combined with their lack of healthy personal boundaries, this makes them especially vulnerable to family violence. ▼ They believe they can help others—often the abuser—even when they cannot. △ As a Two grows in self-awareness, love of self becomes as important as love of others. △ Self-love helps Twos set healthy boundaries and make changes that reflect personal concerns.

Type Two and Trauma

Natural Disasters

▼ Twos' desire to help others can lead to them overextending themselves, which can lead to exhaustion. This can exacerbate the impact of the disaster.

▼ After a disaster, a Two can get stuck in the emotions surrounding the events and not know where to start the cleanup and/or recovery process.

△ Twos have an innate desire to be helpful.

△ They intuitively know where help is needed, are generous with their care, and focused on the needs of others.

Complicated Grief

▼ Focusing on the needs of others, Twos often postpone their grieving process. In fact, Twos may not grieve until they are overwhelmed.

▼ Twos might become resentful of taking care of others.

△ Twos who are in touch with their own sadness become more aware of their own emotions and not just the emotions of others.

△ Once they learn to offer the same love and support to themselves as they offer others, Twos can move through the grief process.

Poverty

▼ Sometimes stuck in appreciation and gratitude, Twos may be unaware of the dire situation they are in.

▼ Twos' innate pride may keep them from asking for help.

△ Their ability to connect with people provides Twos with silver linings, resolving their journey of pain.

△ Rather than being trapped by scarcity, Twos are intuitive people who can find resources, especially if they feel like they are helping others.

Racism

▼ Twos tend to be people-pleasers and in their desire to be liked, they can be inauthentic.

▼ Twos are good at avoiding the concerns at hand as well as the part they play in them.

△ Like Nines, Twos have a strong and authentic desire to heal the differences between people as they want all people to be connected.

△ Seeing the good in all, they easily forgive and move forward.

Addiction

▼ As a means of finding a way to relax, addictions often develop in Twos who have overextended themselves.

▼ Likely addictions include alcohol, pain medications, escape gambling, sleep medications, codependency, abuse of over-the-counter meds, and binge eating.

Type Two and Trauma	
Addiction	△ Twos are optimistic and have a positive outlook. They make easy connections with others, including those in recovery.
	△ Their ease in accessing gratitude and their strong desire to move through problems help them to stay engaged with others in recovery and with recovery communities.
Verbal, Emotional, and Spiritual Abuse	▼ With the focus on the needs of others, Twos are vulnerable to codependent relationships and see it as their mission to stand by, assist, and aid their abuser.
	▼ Twos minimize the effects of the abuse on them.
	△ When Twos realize that they have needs and that having needs is okay, they realize that emotional, verbal, and spiritual abuse is not okay.
	△ They also realize the love and attention they are giving others is, in fact, more authentic when they learn to love, attend, and attune to their own needs first.
Sexual Abuse	▼ Twos often believe that they were the cause of the problem because they did not love the abuser in the right way.
	▼ While they may resent their perpetrator in private, they may also believe that any sexual attention is good.
	△ Always interested in connection, Twos are open to learning about positive and respectful connections.
	△ Twos who learn to spend time alone and develop the connection with themselves will learn to identify their own needs.
Historical and Inter-generational Trauma	▼ Noticing inequities and being drawn to help, Twos might unconsciously enable self-destructive behaviors of people they love.
	▼ While neglecting their own needs, Twos might move into peacekeeping behaviors to maintain the connections, albeit healthy or not.
	△ Twos will move with positivity and a cheerleading energy to gather people together.
	△ They tend to encourage others in their family and community to look out for each other.
Pandemic	▼ Twos might be distracted by the needs of everyone else, leaving them tired and fatigued. Their lack of connectedness to others will create isolation and deep grief.
	▼ They may feel frustrated, unappreciated, and resentful of their inability to give the help they want to give.

Type Two and Trauma

Pandemic

△ Twos' innate resourcefulness in connecting with others gives them the impetus to find solutions to connect to others.

△ Loving, caring, nurturing, and generous by nature, Twos help voice the needs of many of those around them, often getting others the help they need.

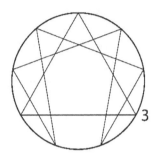

Threes are doers and believe they must perform successfully. They believe you must accomplish and succeed to be loved. Consequently, Threes are industrious, fast-paced, efficient, and goal-oriented. They also can be inattentive to feelings, impatient, and driven based on what others may think and believe about them.

Type Three	
Center of Intelligence	**Heart** The heart center offers you emotional intelligence, including being relational, engaged, and connected to others.
Core Belief	"People are rewarded for what they do and not who they are."
Worldview	"The world is a contest, and I can win if I work hard. Winners are valued."
Where Attention Is Placed	All the things that must be done–tasks, goals, future achievements, efficiency, and being the best
Performance Under Stress	• Wondering if they are doing enough or a good enough job • Being out of touch with their feelings • Working too hard toward the goal of prestige
Avoidance	• Losing face • Failure

Type Three	
Threes as Children	Young Threes might have experienced an environment of support for high achievement and performance, where they learned that being a human-*doer* is seen over a human-*being*.
Defense Mechanism	**Identification** • Threes unconsciously incorporate attributes and characteristics of another person that they deem desirable as a means of bolstering their self-esteem. • It allows the Three to see themselves as successful by imitating successful people or behaviors.
Coping Mechanism	**Workaholism** Working to fill the void or numb the pain
Gifts Toward Resiliency	Adaptable, persevering, self-driven, energetic, dynamic, efficient, pragmatic, ambitious, productive, and they present well

Type Three and Trauma	
PTSD	▼ The fast-paced movement of all that needs to get done is a distraction that keeps Threes in a trauma loop until they are no longer able to complete a task. ▼ Threes often focus on a task with little regard for the impact it has on their health. This keeps them from acknowledging PTSD. △ Once a Three realizes that mental health challenges require slowing down and that doing so does not reflect doing something wrong or inefficiently, they are more likely to embrace the slower pace and will feel successful in accomplishing the task of slowing down. △ When accessing their own sensitivity, it is easier for Threes to reach out and connect with those around them, empowering their journey of healing.
Family Violence	▼ Fear of failure holds a Three captive to not making changes. They tend to stay trapped in a marriage due to their focus on what others would think of them if they left. ▼ Threes are often unaware of their own emotional and physical discomfort, thereby entering a state of numbness that causes them to check out emotionally.

	Type Three and Trauma

Family Violence

△ Once Threes realize that the abuse is not a reflection of them being defective or having done something wrong, they can focus on their own change, needs, and recovery.

△ Once shame has been illuminated, a Three can find a successful path out of shame.

Natural Disasters

▼ The impact of a natural disaster might cause a Three to become frenzied in their behavior, looking for the normal flow of life to return. This frustration over the lack of flow might exacerbate the impact of the disaster and impede recovery efforts.

▼ During disaster recovery, Threes can overextend themselves by working around the clock.

△ With their strong desire for communities to recover and function efficiently and productively, Threes are always ready to work.

△ They tend to have the capacity to develop talent, which can help the community to build and recover.

Complicated Grief

▼ Threes often ignore their internal emotional landscape and may get caught up in the to-dos.

▼ They do not process their emotions in real time. As a result, others may see Threes as cold.

△ When Threes slow down enough to allow the arising emotions, they have access to a wealth of compassion and grace that they can extend to both self and others.

△ Threes are able to attend to details, such as a funeral, setting their feelings aside and showing up for others.

Poverty

▼ Threes feel shame for not having what others have. This might move them into overachieving ways in order to move the spotlight from their lack of food, clothing, or shelter.

▼ Asking for help might expose their poverty, so Threes will mask their vulnerability, even regarding the basic needs of life.

△ Once Threes realize that their overachieving is a result of taking the spotlight off their lack of basic needs, they can begin the journey out of shame.

△ Threes can connect to themselves without a need for success or approval from others, thus freeing them to be who they truly are—separate from their resources.

Racism

▼ Seeking approval and respect, Threes may not be honest in their interactions with others.

▼ The appearance of resolution may be more important to them than the actual work done to achieve resolution.

△ Once Threes have connected with their authentic self, they can have honest, open dialogue about racism.

△ Threes engaged in authenticity will build connections and draw people together, often promoting courageous conversations about racism.

Addiction

▼ To cope with their need to stay in the *doing* mode and to sustain energy to complete tasks, addictions often develop in Threes.

▼ Likely addictions include alcohol, performance-enhancing drugs (such as steroids and amphetamines), and designer drugs (such as ecstasy) which enhance sexual experiences. They may also deal with sexual addictions as well as an addiction to diet pills, appetite suppressants, and action gambling.

△ Threes' competitive desire includes a desire to do recovery right.

△ They may include as many recovery tools as necessary and champion the cause for recovery.

Verbal, Emotional, and Spiritual Abuse

▼ When they are young and encounter an abusive situation that they are powerless to fix, Threes might try to avert the attention placed on the problem and become performers who try to bring approval and a smile to anyone who holds power in their world.

▼ This is the budding root of shame that adult Threes might carry with them, keeping them stuck in abusive relationships.

△ When Threes realize that they can individuate without carrying the shame of the abuse, they might experience real feelings like anger, hurt, or sadness.

△ As they begin to process these feelings, it gives rise to more authentic hope and truth.

Sexual Abuse

▼ After a sexual assault, Threes might move into their *doing* mode, addressing all areas of life except their own heart.

▼ They might also be impatient with the recovery process, expecting more than what is possible.

Type Three and Trauma

Sexual Abuse	△ Moving into their heart and slowing down to feel can help a Three to engage the healing process.
	△ Willing to try new approaches and implement new strategies, Threes will eventually find a way out, and they will not repeat the pattern. They are often emphatic, declaring, "This will *never* happen to me again."
Historical and Inter-generational Trauma	▼ Self-deceit and complicit secret keeping allow Threes to look like they are doing well even while they or their families are suffering.
	▼ Threes' constant movement in their daily life does not allow them the space to slow down and feel the emotions that alert them to when systems need to change.
	△ Using the energy of doing what is necessary to move forward while being productive, Threes offer meaningful solutions.
	△ Threes tend to be authentic with the people around them and desire to share in their story.
Pandemic	▼ Threes tend to be impatient, which makes it harder for them to deal with the magnitude of needs brought on by a pandemic.
	▼ They may jump to creating a strategy to meet the needs of others; however, due to the nature of chaos from a pandemic, the Three will become impatient with the slow process of recovery.
	△ Not allowing their emotions to get in the way, Threes will often jump in and do what is necessary by implementing solutions and persevering. They "just do it."
	△ Threes bring hope to situations as they can see the end results.

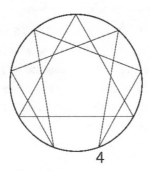

4

Fours are individualistic and romantic. They believe you can regain the lost ideal love or perfect state by finding the love or situation that is unique, special, and fulfilling. Consequently, Fours are idealistic, deeply feeling, empathetic, and authentic. They can also be dramatic, moody, and self-absorbed.

Type Four	
Center of Intelligence	**Heart** The heart center offers you emotional intelligence, including being relational, engaged, and connected to others.
Core Belief	"There is always something missing. I will ultimately be abandoned because of an original loss of connection."
Worldview	"We are all here to be authentic and seek a deeper understanding of life."
Where Attention Is Placed	• What is missing, that others have something that they do not have • What is beautiful and aesthetically pleasing • Finding love, meaning, and fulfillment • In the future *or* in the past
Performance Under Stress	• Problems with emotional regulation • Feeling constantly misunderstood • Deep envy of others
Avoidance	• Being rejected or abandoned • Resisting change for fear of losing themselves • Feeling that they do not measure up or there is something inherently wrong with them

Type Four	
Fours as Children	Young Fours might have experienced an environment where they might not have been seen or acknowledged for their individuality and uniqueness. They learned to express their unique qualities in various forms as a means of being appreciated and understood.
Defense Mechanism	**Introjection** • This is a counter intuitive defense mechanism. Instead of repelling critical information about themselves or an experience, Fours take the information and internalize it, taking it on as their own. • This allows the Four to deal with self-inflicted information rather than respond to criticism or rejection from others.
Coping Mechanism	**Nostalgia** Romanticizing the past while avoiding being present in the moment
Gifts Toward Resiliency	Expressive, creative, sensitive, original, intuitive, perceptive, and unique

Type Four and Trauma	
PTSD	▼ Prone to romanticization, staying in the PTSD trauma loop may be comfortable to Fours. Romanticizing may deter them from seeking help. ▼ The heaviness of the Fours' despair can keep them stuck in the trauma and may make it more difficult to move to resilience. △ Fours have the innate capacity to hold and maintain intense emotion, hence they are not deterred in their recovery journey. △ Fours can be attracted to a community of support for survivors when other types may have some resistance to joining this type of group.
Family Violence	▼ Fours are comfortable with reactivity and can resign themselves to the abusive relationship being familiar territory. ▼ For a Four, returning to the abuser is part of the dramatic experience of life. They may even subconsciously feel like returning makes the abusive relationship more alive.

Family Violence

△ As Fours become receptive to their internal emotional landscape, they can begin to identify that the way some emotions are expressed is not necessarily healthy.

△ They have the ability to access equanimity. This calmness allows them to be present to what is going on in the moment, that it simply is what it is. Having access to equanimity also allows a Four to make an appropriate move out of an abusive situation.

Natural Disasters

▼ When facing a natural disaster, Fours might get stuck in the emotionality of the experience.

▼ Fours are self-focused and lack global awareness. They can also get trapped worrying that they will never recover and that life will always be this way.

△ Fours do not avoid difficult situations, and they have the capacity to sit with others' pain.

△ They can see all the victims are going through, allowing authenticity of the hurt to be seen and heard.

Complicated Grief

▼ Fours romanticize loss and grief to the point of sometimes loving the experience of grief.

▼ Their affinity for grief can lead to an extended grieving process which can keep them from moving forward.

△ Fours do not resist the process of grief.

△ They have the innate capacity to tolerate the intense emotional roller coaster and unpredictability of how and when sadness shows up.

Poverty

▼ Feeling misunderstood, Fours constantly yearn for everything that they believe to be missing from their lives. This makes them susceptible to constantly feeling impoverished.

▼ Fours can accept the tragedy of being raised in poverty. This can prevent them from seeking change.

△ Once Fours can understand the importance and impact of gratitude and appreciation, they organically move out of a poverty mindset.

△ By accessing equanimity, Fours appreciate what is.

Racism

▼ Fours can get stuck in seeing racism as just another frailty of humanity.

▼ While appreciating the dilemmas of those impacted by racism, they might stay in sadness and not do anything to seek change.

Racism

△ When Fours are moved to action, they have the capacity to sustain a conversation about a difficult topic, even engaging in the topic authentically while leaving room for others to do so as well.

△ Fours can use their deeply felt emotion and heartache to bring about transformation.

Addiction

▼ Fours prefer to focus on the past and future. To avoid their current state, they may develop addictions to intensify whatever mood they choose at that time. Because of the deep intensity of emotions, Fours may be ostracized by recovery groups.

▼ Likely addictions include alcohol, love and/or sexual addictions, abuse of sleep medications, heroin and other opiates, marijuana, and hallucinogens. Fours are also prone to a variety of eating disorders.

△ Fours have an innate capacity to not only tolerate but also resolve intense emotional concerns. This helps them to address the underlying causes of addiction.

△ Having a strong desire to be understood, Fours can develop meaningful relationships in recovery and have artistic and creative outlets.

Verbal, Emotional, and Spiritual Abuse

▼ Fours can romanticize the tragedy and normalize the abuse, repeating unhealthy patterns so they can feel more deeply.

▼ Feeling misunderstood, Fours constantly yearn for the perfect relationship that does not exist. This can keep them stuck in any relationship that feels intense.

△ Fours can access a full range of emotions.

△ With support and guidance from others, they can deeply grieve, process, and move forward in their recovery.

Sexual Abuse

▼ Tolerating the symptoms that one encounters in the aftermath of sexual assault, Fours can rationalize the assault as just another part of their difficult life.

▼ Due to how they process shame, it may be difficult for Fours to separate the wrongness and the violence of what happened to them.

Type Four and Trauma

Sexual Abuse	△ When Fours realize how shame has fed into them dealing with the sexual assault, they can access their strong energy fueled by their emotional center. This allows them to follow through with a sound reset, carry on with life, and often not look back. △ Fours' expression of their pain through the arts is often a healing conduit for other victims.
Historical and Inter-generational Trauma	▼ Without intervention, Fours might remain in the state of enduring emotional dysregulation and parent from that state, thus perpetuating the intergenerational trauma. ▼ Having a high tolerance for living in sadness and despair, Fours who are stuck in unresolved intergenerational trauma might not have easy access to see the need for change. △ Fours tend to express the collective sadness and grief of their community creatively and dramatically. This helps both them and their community break the trauma loop. △ Fours often share historical narratives through their artwork and music.
Pandemic	▼ Fours might collect stories of the tragedy of the pandemic without moving into action. ▼ Stuck in what is missing, Fours might be more prone to a state of depression. △ Fours have an innate capacity to sit with deep tragedy as others recover. △ They will not abandon the emotional healing process of the people they are helping.

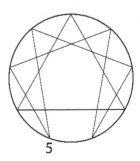

5

Fives like to observe. They believe they must protect themselves from a world that demands too much and gives too little. Consequently, Fives seek self-sufficiency and are non-demanding, analytic, thoughtful, and unobtrusive. They also can be withholding, detached, and overly private.

Type Five	
Center of Intelligence	**Head** The head center allows you to make meaning of the information coming from all the centers, including language, memory, imagination, planning, and more. You mentally map and strategize using this center.
Core Belief	"The world demands too much from people and gives them too little."
Worldview	"Life is imposing and complex, and understanding the complexity gives me a sense of safety."
Where Attention Is Placed	• The intellectual domain • Facts, analyzing, and thinking • Being self-sufficient • Maintaining privacy and boundaries
Performance Under Stress	• Feeling fatigued • Setting firm boundaries • Withdrawing
Avoidance	• Strong feelings, especially fear • Intrusive people • Too many requests • Depletion

Type Five	
Fives as Children	Young Fives might have experienced an environment that placed extreme demands, where they learned to withdraw as a means of protecting themselves.
Defense Mechanism	**Isolation** • Fives withdraw into themselves. This could be by physically removing themselves or mentally withdrawing into their own thoughts. • Isolation helps Fives keep themselves from experiencing emotions and dealing with the demands of others.
Coping Mechanism	**Detachment** Repressing or selectively ignoring information
Gifts Toward Resiliency	Perceptive, innovative, observant, logical, knowledgeable, reasonable, curious, analytical, self-reliant, and dry-witted

Type Five and Trauma	
PTSD	▼ Fives' body center is often shut down and their head center is usually very active. ▼ They can become mentally paralyzed by gathering facts about the problem of PTSD. △ Once Fives find evidence that interventions other than mental ones are the best trauma intervention, they are likely to give them a try–providing that they believe their findings. △ Fives will stay up to date on information about PTSD.
Family Violence	▼ Fives find solace in solitude and in their own thoughts. This makes them vulnerable to staying trapped in abusive relationships. ▼ It is unlike them to trust others or ask for help. Instead, Fives might find themselves trying to research their way out of the abuse. △ Fives could use their ability to research and gain knowledge about family violence. This knowledge can amplify their awareness of the danger they are in and help them to find a safe way to leave. △ Fives value internal resources like solitude. They may benefit from spending time alone practicing self-care and healing. As safety is secured, they will begin to grow emotionally, physically, financially, and spiritually.

Type Five and Trauma

Natural Disasters

▼ During a natural disaster, Fives can be overwhelmed by the chaos. Being overwhelmed, they will retreat inward and quit engaging emotionally.

▼ Fives will turn their focus to the fact that they do not know what is going on. Trying to make sense of the events, they will focus on gathering information instead of taking action.

△ Fives' ability to detach from the emotional impact of events can make them resilient to disasters. It also helps that they are adept at gathering accurate information.

△ Fives can show immense dedication to recovery efforts.

Complicated Grief

▼ Following multiple losses, Fives may be drawn to focusing on the existential nature of loss.

▼ To move through their process of grieving, they may resist support and engagement from others.

△ By compartmentalizing, Fives can handle multiple instances of grief without creating a domino effect.

△ Truly sensitive by nature, Fives want others to reach out to them but not in an intrusive way. They are also innately comfortable with solitude, making it easier to move through grief without being involved in support groups.

Poverty

▼ Fives have a minimalistic view of the world and require very little to begin with. This may keep them from feeling impoverished and can keep them from finding a better way of living.

▼ They may also isolate and compartmentalize their experiences, withholding and living in a world of secrecy.

△ With a true desire to learn and be self-sufficient, a Five might gather information and resources that can help them move out of poverty.

△ They will make changes at a pace that works for them, allowing for sustainability.

Racism

▼ Fives may avoid getting involved in addressing racism due to their concern of the energy they will need to expend.

▼ Thinking they are not ready, they may delay entering the conversation or taking action around racism.

Type Five and Trauma	

| **Racism** | △ Fives will not simply accept what others say as the truth. They will keep gathering information that is current and applicable. |
| | △ Becoming the holders of the history and facts, they do not allow the reality of what is happening to be forgotten. |

Addiction	▼ Addictions develop in Fives as a mechanism to cope with fear— sometimes existential fear. Believing that the world wants too much from them, addicted Fives isolate and withdraw, keeping them from getting the help they need.
	▼ Likely addictions include alcohol, action or escape gambling, sexual addictions, hallucinogens, or other mind-expanding drugs.
	△ Fives research and gather facts about recovery, providing them with resources about addiction and sobriety.
	△ With the support of others, they may be open to implementing evidence-based practices.

Verbal, Emotional, and Spiritual Abuse	▼ Fives retreat into their inner world, which makes them more vulnerable to abuse. They may isolate and compartmentalize their experiences, learning to withhold and live in a world of secrecy.
	▼ Fives might even be drawn to cult-like situations due to the interesting nature of such environments.
	△ With a true desire to learn and be self-sufficient, Fives might gather information and find a confidant they can trust and then make changes at a pace that works for them.
	△ Once a relationship or situation is proven to be abusive in nature, a Five will find a way out.

Sexual Abuse	▼ As victims of sexual assault, Fives become emotionally detached. They might even dissociate as they try to make sense of what is going on.
	▼ Fives have a need for understanding before they can take action. This may allow the cycle of abuse to continue until the Five is armed with enough information to leave.
	△ As Fives work with their ability to compartmentalize, they can slowly begin to integrate various traumatic episodes into their healing process. This allows them to find a comfortable rhythm for healing.
	△ They are generous with their knowledge and are often helpful and sensitive to others recovering from trauma.

Type Five and Trauma

Historical and Inter-generational Trauma

▼ Fives' engagement in the process of gathering information may cause them not to notice the past and what has happened to them.

▼ They may be stuck in gathering information and not know when to stop and take action in order to stop the cycle of trauma.

△ Fives have the capacity to connect the information that cycles down from family systems and communicate the information objectively.

△ The wisdom of the Five is easily understood and passed down through generations.

Pandemic

▼ Fives will find themselves creating charts, collecting data, compiling emergency updates, and doing fact checking.

▼ Fives' tendency to isolate and do research might keep them unaware of the challenging impact of being alone.

△ When the accurate information Fives have gathered is shared with others, an opportunity arises to implement the information in helpful and appropriate ways.

△ Fives rebound quickly following bouts of isolation and being socially disengaged.

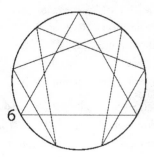

6

Sixes believe you must gain certainty and security in a hazardous world that you simply cannot trust. They often scan their environment for danger. Sixes are intuitive, inquisitive, trustworthy, good friends, and problem-solvers. They can also be doubtful, accusatory, and fearful.

Type Six	
Center of Intelligence	**Head** The head center allows you to make meaning of the information coming from all the centers, including language, memory, imagination, planning, and more. You mentally map and strategize using this center.
Core Belief	"The world is threatening and dangerous, and people simply cannot trust one another. It is essential to be prepared to meet or to avoid the potential hazards of life."
Worldview	"The world is a dangerous place. Truth is hidden. Appearances are suspect. People cannot trust one another."
Where Attention Is Placed	• What could potentially go wrong • Playing devil's advocate • What is dangerous • Difficulties • Hidden meanings
Performance Under Stress	• Balancing the need they have to trust others with the basic mistrust they have • Once the stress or pending danger is real, they tend to push through it well

Type Six	
Avoidance	• Feeling fear directly • Untrustworthiness • Betrayal • Being cornered or controlled
Sixes as Children	Young Sixes might have experienced an unpredictable environment where they learned to prepare for what might go wrong as a means of creating certainty and stability for themselves.
Defense Mechanism	**Projection** • Sixes unconsciously attribute their own unacceptable, unwanted, or disowned thoughts and emotions onto another as if they were the other's. • This functions for Sixes by creating a false sense of making their world more predictable.
Coping Mechanism	**Projection** Attaching your feelings or motives to someone else
Gifts Toward Resiliency	Engaging, responsible, reliable, prepared, dutiful, sensible, loyal, trustworthy, truth-seeking, and faithful

Type Six and Trauma	
PTSD	▼ Constantly scanning for danger, Sixes are most susceptible to engaging in a trauma loop of any sort. ▼ Second-guessing and self-doubt may keep Sixes wondering whom they can trust and keep them from finding help. △ When Sixes determine a situation to be dangerous—regardless of whether it is actually dangerous or not—they can break the trauma loop. △ Finding a trusted source of information is often the first successful intervention for a Six. If they experience success through a suggested process, Sixes are likely to continue to comply with the recommendations.

Family Violence

▼ Sixes' propensity to loyalty and their value of authority cause them to doubt their intuition and question their role in the violent relationship, wondering whether they did something to cause the violence.

▼ They tend to replay what they are experiencing over and over in their head, leading to more doubt and inaction. This is the very essence of being paralyzed or stuck.

△ As Sixes develop, their courage to secure safety and certainty works to their benefit.

△ Once they begin to trust their intuition, Sixes will plan their exit strategy. This strategy is often centered around their safety, wellbeing, and daily routine.

Natural Disasters

▼ Sixes are prone to second-guess which actions to take. This is intensified during a natural disaster.

▼ Their tendency to either move away or plunge through is a fear reaction to the events unfolding around them.

△ With trusted, authoritative information, Sixes will take brave action.

△ They have a dutiful commitment to taking action. Examining strategies and seeing the reality of what is, Sixes will break free from the grip of trauma of a natural disaster.

Complicated Grief

▼ When Sixes feel blindsided by multiple losses, they might spiral into a deeper fear than is typical for their type.

▼ Their fear response might be the freeze response, which could perpetuate the experience of grief.

△ Sixes are often prepared for loss, constantly anticipating what might be—especially if someone is sick or the loss is expected.

△ They innately access the courage they need to move through difficulties associated with complicated grief.

Poverty

▼ Sixes' worry and rumination about the lack of resources is part of who they are, and they may have a hard time breaking free from that cycle.

△ Sixes are realists. When they can see what is, they can implement prudent and pragmatic strategies to get them out of poverty.

Racism

▼ The dance between avoiding fear and plunging into fear head on can get Sixes into lots of trouble.

▼ They may fear taking a stance against racism but then jump into a street fight to deal with the sense of injustice.

	Type Six and Trauma
Racism	△ Sixes are good at strategizing and planning ways to address racism, such as with rallies, demonstrations, or by supporting local agencies. △ They have a global awareness of social justice and will move intentionally into taking action around the injustices.
Addiction	▼ Moving between self-doubt and second-guessing, addictions develop in Sixes to help them cope with anxiety. The addictions will look different when in phobic and counterphobic reactivity to fear. ▼ Likely addictions for a Six in phobic reactivity to fear include alcohol, abuse of benzodiazepines, and escape gambling. For a Six in counterphobic reactivity to fear, alcohol, steroids, action gambling, and amphetamines are likely. △ For Sixes, it is important to know that their sources of recovery options are respected and authoritative. △ Sixes innately comply with treatment protocols offered by authoritative and respected healthcare practitioners.
Verbal, Emotional, and Spiritual Abuse	▼ Having difficulty with trust, Sixes constantly doubt themselves. ▼ When wowed by authoritative figures, Sixes are very susceptible to abusive and cult-like relationships. △ Once Sixes can see the reality of what is, they are able to use discernment and come up with a strategy to move to a healthy place. △ When Sixes move into a counterphobic reactivity to fear, they no longer doubt themselves.
Sexual Abuse	▼ Depending on how a Six is processing fear in the moment, they may retreat as a victim or want to plunge through the fear and retaliate. ▼ They experience strong self-doubt around capabilities to deal with the abuse. △ Once the Six understands the way they engage in fear, they can use discernment and slow down reactivity in both directions (that is, either retreat or attack). △ They can engage with courage and bravery.
Historical and Inter-generational Trauma	▼ Sixes have a push/pull relationship with authority. ▼ They are more vulnerable to experience historical and inter-generational trauma. This keeps them stuck in the trauma cycle and in a form of denial.

Type Six and Trauma

Historical and Inter-generational Trauma	△ As Sixes establish trust with others over time, they will take responsibility for the cyclical patterns and changes needed to interrupt the intergenerational pattern. △ Despite their drive to remember, Sixes will forgive those who have transgressed them.
Pandemic	▼ Having difficulty with trust, a Six is constantly in self-doubt and attempting to manage fear from a place of suspicion/hesitation or just plunging through. This circumvents any real use of discernment and moving forward in taking action. ▼ They experience strong self-doubt around capabilities to deal with the situation, keeping them stuck in constant rumination. Second-guessing and self-doubt may keep Sixes from helping, wondering who they can trust. △ Many Sixes will say they have been rehearsing for this scenario their entire life and they are ready. △ Sixes' innate skills have them prepared for their own lives, but they are also willing to share resources with those they care for.

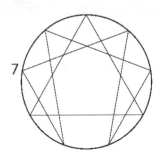

Sevens look for options and opportunities. They believe you must stay upbeat and keep your possibilities open to assure a good life. Consequently, Sevens seek pleasurable options, and are optimistic and adventurous. They also avoid pain and can be uncommitted and self-serving.

Type Seven	
Center of Intelligence	**Head** The head center allows you to make meaning of the information coming from all the centers, including language, memory, imagination, planning, and more. You mentally map and strategize using this center.
Core Belief	"The world limits people, causing them pain and frustration."
Worldview	"To avoid pain, I will explore all the exciting possibilities."
Where Attention Is Placed	• Options • Interesting, fascinating, and pleasurable ideas • New projects • The interrelatedness or interconnectedness of ideas and options
Performance Under Stress	• Anxiety rises as the Seven realizes pain is inevitable • They can also feel anxious when they feel trapped, or when they have overcommitted
Avoidance	• Pain • Frustrations • Feeling trapped or being constrained

Type Seven	
Sevens as Children	Young Sevens might have experienced an overstimulating environment where boredom was avoided at all costs and they learned that this was the strategy in life to avoid pain.
Defense Mechanism	**Rationalization** • Sevens makes excuses for what they do, feel, or think. • This works for Sevens because they can reframe what might be negative or painful into something positive.
Coping Mechanism	**Avoidance** Avoiding anything negative by self-medicating or focusing only on the positive
Gifts Toward Resiliency	Spontaneous, versatile, optimistic, visionary, charming, light-hearted, friendly, innovative, and enthusiastic

Type Seven and Trauma	
PTSD	▼ Sevens look for many other options to participate in, keeping them from addressing symptoms of PTSD. ▼ Despite their focus on avoiding pain, pleasurable activities may incite a trauma loop. △ Sevens place optimistic attention on options and possibilities. This allows them to try new and exciting interventions. △ They have a general hardwired tendency to reframe events, which helps Sevens tolerate many difficult situations.
Family Violence	▼ The positive outlook Sevens have and their avoidance of painful experiences cause them to defend the silver lining in challenging times. This can keep type Sevens in a risky situation, always hoping for and believing the best of their abuser. ▼ A Seven's ability to reframe situations can create an illusion that the violence will go away or that the abuser will change. △ Always hopeful for a positive outcome, Sevens never lose faith in their family members. △ Their ability to reframe is used to Sevens' advantage, allowing them access to forward movement in life and to participate in life with humor and levity.

	Type Seven and Trauma
Natural Disasters	▼ Sevens are experts at avoiding pain in all ways, including when dealing with natural disasters. They anticipate the scenario will improve. ▼ Because they are moving so fast, Sevens might create a safety hazard by not paying attention to what is going on. △ Sevens' positivity provides hope for all, even amid tragedy. △ Naturally prone to strategize and look for options, Sevens come up with innovative ideas for resolution. They genuinely care about everyone getting help.
Complicated Grief	▼ Sevens tend to avoid the experience of anything painful. ▼ As loss is associated with pain, Sevens will go out of their way to find ways to avoid this natural experience of life, often in self-destructive ways. △ Sevens are experts at reframing situations and finding the good or the silver lining. This allows them to move from sadness into a more pleasant experience. △ They are skilled at planning celebrations of life and keeping positive memories alive.
Poverty	▼ Sevens find a silver lining of abundance, even amid extreme poverty. ▼ Often Sevens do not recognize the reality of their circumstances. This might keep them from seeking change. △ Once they face the reality of their situation, Sevens have an innate gift of examining options. △ A realistic reframing to a positive mindset allows a Seven to maintain forward momentum in moving out of poverty.
Racism	▼ Due to their aversion to having difficult conversations, Sevens may ignore racism. ▼ They may even minimize the impact and reality of racism, as if we live in a world where something such as this does not exist. △ Once they grasp the reality of a situation, Sevens will work hard to find solutions and advocate for healing. △ With a cheerleader-like quality, Sevens are hardwired for innate optimism while others might have a sense of hopelessness.

	Type Seven and Trauma
Addiction	▼ Sevens are driven to avoid pain and try new and varied experiences. This makes them prone to addiction, especially when transitioning into adulthood–a life stage when they are at higher risk of being exposed to addictive options and to peer experiences. ▼ Sevens are vulnerable to *all* addictions–alcohol, amphetamines, opiates, hallucinogens, escape and action gambling, sexual addictions, eating disorders, and benzodiazepines. △ Generally, Sevens do well in self-help communities where they can access a variety of people and different ideas and experiences. △ Due to their openness to exploring options, Sevens may be more open to trying out different approaches to recovery, whether conventional or not.
Verbal, Emotional, and Spiritual Abuse	▼ With an innate sense of optimism, Sevens may stay in the loop of chaotic and abusive relationships, believing it will all eventually work out. ▼ Being quite gullible, Sevens can easily be exploited. △ Sevens are skilled when it comes to examining options and opportunities to remove themselves from harm's way. △ Their optimism allows them to reset and find the good in those around them and in their present experiences. It also helps that they are future focused.
Sexual Abuse	▼ Sevens may wrongfully take responsibility believing that because they did not see the signs of abuse, they are responsible. ▼ Deeper work is needed to examine the pain and process what has occurred. △ Sevens seek independence and may simply leave an abusive situation. △ Constantly seeing the positive in any situation, Sevens do not dwell on the past.
Historical and Inter-generational Trauma	▼ Avoiding the pain and living in chaos to distract the Seven from what *is* can keep intergenerational and historical trauma alive and in a continuous loop. ▼ Sevens might reframe their intergenerational trauma as having relevance and purpose, keeping them from resolving the trauma.

Type Seven and Trauma

Historical and Inter-generational Trauma

△ With an optimistic and upbeat attitude, Sevens—with the support of others—can walk through trauma, realizing that pain is part of life's journey and that injustices need not be tolerated.

△ They often become spokespeople for social causes. Their charismatic energy will be a pied piper for change within the system.

Pandemic

▼ Sevens automatically reframe the reality of the events, keeping them from seeing the pandemic from a realistic perspective.

▼ They may act recklessly toward self and others.

△ Sevens can learn to tolerate uncomfortable feelings while using discernment, hope, and making their and others lives better.

△ They will have many options for solving a problem.

A free ebook edition
is available with the
purchase of this book.

To claim your free ebook edition:

1. Visit MorganJamesBOGO.com
2. Sign your name CLEARLY in the space
3. Complete the form and submit a photo of the entire copyright page
4. You or your friend can download the ebook to your preferred device

Morgan James
BOGO™

A **FREE** ebook edition is available for you
or a friend with the purchase of this print book.

CLEARLY SIGN YOUR NAME ABOVE

Instructions to claim your free ebook edition:
1. Visit MorganJamesBOGO.com
2. Sign your name CLEARLY in the space above
3. Complete the form and submit a photo
   of this entire page
4. You or your friend can download the ebook
   to your preferred device

Print & Digital Together Forever.

Snap a photo

Free ebook

Read anywhere

CPSIA information can be obtained
at www.ICGtesting.com
Printed in the USA
JSHW061638140722
28040JS00005B/7